En

Prophetic Ministry is a bi[l] book by David Arns. I guarantee that you will learn new things as you read it. It is completely balanced, theologically accurate and passionately practical, teaching you how to begin moving in the prophetic. Every sentence ministered insight and life to me as I'm sure it will to you also.

David has spent his lifetime examining Scriptures carefully to see exactly what they teach. His presentation is full of Scripture from Genesis to Revelation and his grasp of it is thorough and complete.

I would say this is one of the most balanced and helpful books on the prophetic I have read. I unreservedly recommend it to you.

—*Dr. Mark Virkler, President of Christian Leadership University and*
Communion With God Ministries, Buffalo, NY

In *Prophetic Ministry: A Biblical Look at Seeing,* David Arns succinctly asks, and answers common questions that address much controversy regarding the prophetic today. In clear terms, David speaks to the problem of overly negative aspects of the prophetic movement and offers keen insight into the distinction between prophetic ministry as expressed from the Old Testament paradigm and the character of the same in the New Testament setting. For those that are either new to the prophetic or having years of experience in this dynamic movement, David's book is a worthy treatment that is both enlightening and entertaining.

—*Russell Walden, Prophet and Marketplace Minister,*
www.FathersHeartMinistry.net, Green Valley, AZ

In flight school, aspiring pilots are taught in a flight simulator to take note of what is going on with their bodies in an oxygen-deprived environment. During this time, they are trained to be aware of what is going on with their bodies in the event that something might occur on an actual flight. Similarly, the Lord trains us to be mindful of what is going on in the spiritual realm when He speaks to us prophetically so we can join what He is doing.

In his new book, *Prophetic Ministry: A Biblical Look at Seeing*, David Arns provides a comprehensive study of the wide spectrum of ways God supernaturally speaks to His people. Backed by hundreds of Scriptural examples and actual ministry experiences, David masterfully unpacks what prophetic ministry looks like and how it can be implemented in and through your life.

—*Rob Gross, Pastor, Mountain View Community Church, Kaneohe, HI*

Thank you so much for sharing your book with me, *Prophetic Ministry: A Biblical Look at Seeing*. I found it to be a very good tool for sharing with people who wonder if the prophetic is for today. You used many Scriptures and lots of reference material. I thought your examples using different people were very good. I see that you are a very prolific writer and have taken on writing many books on a variety of somewhat controversial topics. I think you mentioned something like you are writing to help people know why they believe. I think I could easily use your book as a reference for the prophetic.

—*Mary Dorian, Assistant Pastor, Glorybound Ministries Center, Albuquerque, NM*

I think your book is very thorough. It makes for a good textbook that could be used at Bible Colleges—along with someone who is serious about the prophetic.

—*Kyle Miller, Prophet, Teacher, and Musician, ProphetKyle.com, Little Rock, AR*

I just finished looking through David Arns' book, *Prophetic Ministry: A Biblical Look at Seeing*. I was amazed at the depth of research and commented to David, "My first thought was the book could be used as a primary reference tool for a semester-long course on the prophetic." This is one of those books you want to acquire and keep in your study library for future reference.

—*Garris Elkins, Author, Mentor and Teacher at www.PropheticHorizons.com*

I have thoroughly enjoyed reading Dave Arns' latest book, *Prophetic Ministry: A Biblical Look at Seeing.* He rigorously presents Scripture proving that we are all to hear from God. I especially appreciated the emphasis on the instructions of Paul concerning prophecy in I Corinthians 14, where he encourages us all to prophesy. Dave reminds us that these Scriptures are written to the Corinthians who were babes in Christ, lacking spiritual maturity. What an encouragement for all of us, that we can truly *all prophesy!* I believe every Christian should read this book to gain a Scriptural understanding of this powerful gift the Lord has given us to comfort, encourage, and edify the body of Christ.

—*Pastor Carolyn Tracy, Celebration Church, Loveland, Colorado*

Prophetic Ministry:

A Biblical Look at Seeing

THOUGHTS ON. . .

Prophetic Ministry:

A Biblical Look at Seeing

Book 12 in the "THOUGHTS ON" Series
by David M. Arns

First Edition
Copyright © 2017 David M. Arns.
Tenth Printing, September 2023

Paperback ISBN 978-1-97467-556-2
E-book ISBN 978-1-64136-765-3

Books in the "THOUGHTS ON" Series

All the books below are available both in electronic form and in paperback, and are available from the sources mentioned on the website BibleAuthor.DaveArns.com.

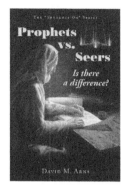

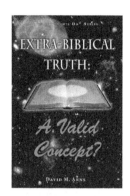

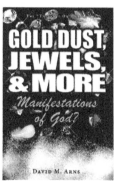

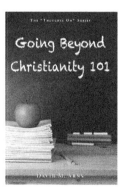

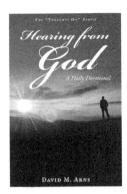
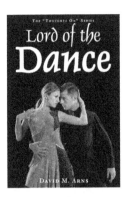
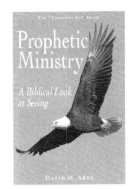

Music in the "Worship On" Series

All the music below is available both as downloadable electronic files and as physical CDs, and are available from the sources mentioned on the website Music.DaveArns.com.

 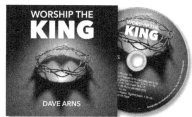

For descriptions and other details of all these books or albums, see the back of this book, or the websites BibleAuthor.DaveArns.com or Music.DaveArns.com, respectively.

Table of Contents

Endorsements 1

Preface 17

Typographical Conventions 21
   Scripture References 22

Chapter 1: Why is there Prophetic Ministry? 25
   Old Testament Prophets 26
      Predicting the Future 30
   New Testament Prophets 33
      Corrective Prophecy 36
      "Flip It, and Flip It Good" 40
         Revelations Without Interpretations 44
      Avoiding "Colored Glasses" 45
      Predicting the Future 52

Chapter 2: Who Can Be Used in Prophetic Ministry? 57
   Prophesying About a Prophecy 57
   Joel's Prophecy 59
   Peter's Confirmation 59
   Paul's Confirmation 61
   The "Prophetic Atmosphere" 63
   False Prophecy and False Prophets 67
      Prophetic "Mistakes" 71
   Co-Laboring With a Prophetic Word 76
      Restoring the Rain 77
      Israel Returning from Babylon 77
      Using Prophetic Words as Weapons 78
   How Often Should We Hear from God? 79
      How Much Will God Tell Us? 81

Chapter 3: How Do You Perceive Prophetic Words? 83
   Does Prophecy Still Happen? 83
      The Sufficiency of Scripture 88
      How to Minister 92

Moving On 93
Seeing. 94
Trances. 98
Peter. 98
Paul 100
Others 101
Ways of Expressing It 103
Translational Bias. 105
Spiritual Interaction 106
Persistence 108
Personal Examples of Seeing. 111
Hearing 115
God's Voice: Audible 116
God's Voice: Internal 119
Hearing From Evil Spirits. 122
Dealing with Antichrist 124
Personal Examples of Hearing 128
Feeling/Touching. 131
Movement/Transportation 137
Traveling in the Spirit. 138
Enoch 138
Elijah 140
Elisha 142
Paul 144
Jesus. 152
The Courts of Heaven 155
Job's Accusations 158
The Fall of Ahab 162
Isaiah's Vision. 166
Daniel 167
Zechariah. 167
David. 169
Bodily Sensations. 170
Personal Examples of Physical Sensation. 173
Impartation of Anointing. 174
What Needs to be Healed. 175
Tasting. 176

Smelling. 177
    Modern Examples 180
Impressions 181
    The "Check in the Spirit". 184
Reading 186
Reading People's Thoughts. 188
Other Ways of Perceiving God's Messages 193

Chapter 4: How Do You Give Prophetic Words? **195**
Speaking. 195
    Ministering Together 197
Writing 198
Prophetic Acts 202
    Getting the Upper Hand in Battle 203
    Trumpets and Shouting 205
    Rent. 207
    Transferring Prophetic Authority 207
    Arrows and Victory in Battle 208
    Jeremiah the Thespian 209
        Smashing the Pot 209
        Wearing the Yoke 210
        Burying the Stones 210
    Ezekiel the Thespian. 211
        A Cartographic Prophecy 211
        A Close Shave. 214
        Healing a Stick. 215
    Unplugging the Ears. 215
    Getting Belted by the Jews 217
    The Symbolism of Prophetic Acts 219
Music. 220

Chapter 5: Where Do We GoFrom Here? **227**
Cultivating Prophetic Gifts in Others. 228
Actually Doing It 230

Appendix A:Bible-Study Strategies. **235**
Multiple Translations 235
Multiple References 236
The Preponderance of Scripture 237

The Plain, Surface Meaning 237
The Bible Itself Defining Its Terms. 238
Reading in Context 240
Now, Onward. 241

About the Author. 243
Books in the "Thoughts On" Series 243
Music in the "Worship On" Series 251

Preface

All Scripture references are from the public-domain King James Version (KJV) of the Bible unless otherwise noted. Other versions of the Bible that may be quoted are as follows:

- AMP: Amplified Bible: Copyright © 1954, 1958, 1962, 1964, 1965, and 1987 by the Lockman Foundation, La Habra, CA, 90631. All rights reserved. www.lockman.org.

- AMPC: Amplified Bible, Classic Edition: Copyright © 1954, 1958, 1962, 1964, 1965, 1987 by The Lockman Foundation.

- ASV: American Standard Version of 1901: Public Domain.

- BBE: Bible in Basic English: This text is in the public domain and has no copyright. The Bible In Basic English was printed in 1965 by Cambridge Press in England. Published without any copyright notice and distributed in America, this work fell immediately and irretrievably into the Public Domain in the United States according to the UCC convention of that time.

- BRG: The BRG Bible: Blue Red and Gold Letter Edition™ Copyright © 2012 BRG Bible Ministries. Used by Permission. All rights reserved. BRG Bible is a Registered Trademark in U.S. Patent and Trademark Office #4145648.

- CEB: Common English Bible: All rights reserved.

- CEV: Contemporary English Version: Copyright © 1995 by American Bible Society. All rights reserved.

- CJB: Complete Jewish Bible, Copyright © 1998 by David H. Stern. All rights reserved.

- DARBY: Darby Translation: Public domain. First published in 1890 by John Nelson Darby, an Anglo-Irish Bible teacher associated with the early years of the Plymouth Brethren.

- DLNT: Disciples' Literal New Testament: Disciples' Literal New Testament: Serving Modern Disciples by More Fully Reflecting the Writing Style of the Ancient Disciples, Copyright © 2011 Michael J. Magill. All Rights Reserved. Published by Reyma Publishing (www.ReymaPublishing.com).

- DOUAY: Douay-Rheims Bible, translated from the Latin Vulgate. Rheims New Testament, 1582; Douay Old Testament, 1610.

- EHV: The Holy Bible, Evangelical Heritage Version®, EHV®, © 2019 Wartburg Project, Inc. All rights reserved.

- ERV: Easy-to-Read Version: Copyright © 2006 by World Bible Translation Center.

- ESV: The Holy Bible, English Standard Version: Copyright © 2001, 2006, 2011 by Crossway Bibles, a division of Good News Publishers. All rights reserved.

- EXB: The Expanded Bible: Scripture taken from The Expanded Bible. Copyright © 2011 by Thomas Nelson, Inc. Used by permission. All rights reserved.

- GNT: Good News Translation: Copyright © 1992 by American Bible Society. All rights reserved.

- GNV: The Geneva Bible (1599), Public Domain.

- GWORD: God's Word Translation: Copyright © 2010 by Baker Publishing Group, © 1995 by God's Words to the Nations. All Rights reserved.

- HCSB: Holman Christian Standard Bible: Copyright © 1999, 2000, 2002, 2003 by Holman Bible Publishers. Holman Christian Standard Bible®, Holman CSB®, and HCSB® are federally registered trademarks of Holman Bible Publishers. Used by permission.

- ICB: International Children's Bible: The Holy Bible, International Children's Bible, Copyright © 2015 Thomas Nelson Inc. All rights reserved.

- ISV: International Standard Version: The Holy Bible: International Standard Version. Release 2.0, Build 2014.07.18. Copyright © 1995–2014 by ISV Foundation. All Rights Reserved Internationally. Used by permission of Davidson Press, LLC.

- JUB: The Jubilee Bible (from the Scriptures of the Reformation), edited by Russell M. Stendal; Copyright © 2000, 2001, 2010.

- LEB: Lexham English Bible: Scripture quotations marked (LEB) are from the Lexham English Bible. Copyright © 2012 Logos Bible Software. Lexham is a registered trademark of Logos Bible Software.

- MSG: The Message: Scripture taken from The Message. Copyright © 1993, 1994, 1995, 1996, 2000, 2001, 2002. Used by permission of NavPress Publishing Group.

- NABRE: New American Bible, Revised Edition © 2010, 1991, 1986, 1970 Confraternity of Christian Doctrine, Inc., Washington, DC. All Rights Reserved.

- NASB: New American Standard Bible: Copyright ©1960, 1962, 1963, 1968, 1971, 1972, 1973, 1975, 1977, 1995 by The Lockman Foundation. All rights reserved.

- NCV: New Century Version: Scripture taken from the New Century Version®. Copyright © 2005 by Thomas Nelson, Inc. Used by permission. All rights reserved.

- NET: New English Translation. The NET Bible®, First Edition (NET); New English Translation, The Translation That Explains Itself™; Copyright © 1996–2005 by Biblical Studies Press, L.L.C. All rights reserved.

- NIV: New International Version: Scripture quoted by permission. Quotations designated (NIV) are from The Holy Bible: New International Version (NIV).

Typographical Conventions

In Scriptural quotes in this book, emphasis (indicated by **boldface** type, and occasionally *italic* **within the boldface**) may be added by the author to draw attention to the portions of the passage that pertain to the topic currently under discussion. This applies throughout, so "emphasis added by author" doesn't need to be stated in every single instance.

In this book, the generic pronouns "he," "him," and "his" are used whenever explicit inclusion of both gender-specific pronouns would result in grammatical cumbersomeness. We know that in Christ, there is no difference between male and female (Galatians 3:28), so the pronouns used in this way should be read as generic, not masculine.

When you see a number prefixed by a "H" or a "G", it represents the word number Hebrew or Greek dictionaries of *Strong's Exhaustive Concordance,* one of the standard tools for Biblical study: *Strong's Hebrew and Chaldee Dictionary of the Old Testament* (Hebrew Strong's) and *Strong's Greek Dictionary of the New Testament* (Greek Strong's), both public domain. So, for example, "G256" indicates that English word being discussed was translated from the word defined in entry 256 in Strong's Greek Dictionary.

In Scripture quotations, the letter case of the English word "Lord" indicates the standard meanings when quoting from the Old Testament. Mixed Case, as in "Lord," indicates the Hebrew name אֲדֹנָי (*Adonay,* H136), while SMALL CAPS, as in "LORD" indicates the Hebrew name יְהֹוָה (*Yahweh,* H3068), also known as the Tetragrammaton, which literally means "four letters." And finally, when the original Hebrew uses the name יְהֹוָה אֱלֹהִים (*Yahweh Elohim,* H3068 H430), it is translated and letter-cased as "Lord GOD."

In order to retain accents and diacritical marks of the original languages—which are very meaningful—Hebrew and Greek words are rendered as small inline images, as in the previous paragraph. This works fine for e-readers such as iBooks and nook, but doesn't work so well on some Kindle e-readers. Because of an inability of some Kindle devices to scale inline images to a size proportional to the currently selected text size, Hebrew and Greek words will likely be larger than the surrounding text. Also, some Kindle devices can't adjust the vertical alignment of images, so the Hebrew and Greek descenders don't actually descend below the text baseline. Although this looks bad on such Kindle devices, no information is lost. If typographical aesthetics are important to you, you may want to get the iBooks version of this book instead.

Scripture References

This book contains a great number of Scriptural references, and the punctuation used within or between them indicates specific things that are helpful to know, in order to gain the most understanding from the passage.

Here are the various punctuation symbols and what they mean:

- Colon (":"): A colon separates the chapter being specified from the verse being specified, as in "John 3:16" referring to "the book of John, chapter three, verse sixteen." There are two situations in which a colon is not present in a reference:

  - When *all* the verses in a particular chapter are being included, as in "I Corinthians 13 is known as 'The Love Chapter.'"

  - When the Bible book being referenced has only one chapter, in which case there is no need to specify *which* chapter, as in "But you, dear friends, build yourselves up in your most holy faith and pray in the Holy Spirit (Jude 20)."

- Comma (","): Separates non-contiguous references in a list, or non-contiguous verses in a single chapter, as in "God's glory, which was demonstrated in raising Lazarus from the dead, is mentioned in John 11:4, 40." That is, chapter 11, verses 4 and 40, but not the intervening verses.

- En-dash ("–"): An en-dash indicates a range of chapters or verses, inclusive of both endpoints. For example, "The story of Gideon is found in Judges 6–8" (the book of Judges, starting in chapter 6 and going through chapter 8) or "The story of Jesus healing Bartimaeus of blindness is found in Mark 10:46–52" (the book of Mark, chapter 10, starting in verse 46 and going through verse 52).

- Lowercase letters: These indicate a specific phrase or thought in a particular verse, and it is usually used when the idea under discussion is not the first thing the verse mentions. For example, "Greater is He that is in us than he that is in the world (I John 4:4b)." In this case, the "b" is used to indicate that the given phrase is the *second*, not the first, important point in that verse.

- Lowercase "f": The single lowercase F indicates "and the single verse following," as in "During Jesus' temptation in the wilderness, he hung around with wild animals and angels (Mark 1:12f)." Note that "1:12f" means the same as "1:12–13."

- Lowercase "ff": The two lowercase Fs indicate "and (an unspecified number of) verses following;" for example, "Jesus' command to wait for the power of the Holy Spirit is shown in Acts 1:4ff." Note that "1:4ff" could mean the same as "1:4–5" or "1:4–6" or "1:4–7" or "1:4–8" and so forth, so the end of the passage referenced should be clear from the context. If the ending point is not clear, the en-dash (see above) will be used to avoid confusion.

- Greater-thans and less-thans (">" and "<", respectively): These symbols indicate a reference in the Old Testament being quoted in the New Testament. For example, "Peter quoted Joel in his Pentecost sermon (Acts 2:17<Joel 2:28)." Or, "Joel's prophecy of the outpouring of the Holy Spirit was fulfilled at Pentecost (Joel 2:28>Acts 2:17)." Which one you use depends on whether the Old Testament passage or the New Testament passage is the main point of the sentence.

- Parallel lines or "pipes" ("||"): These parallel lines indicate parallel verses; i.e., multiple accounts of the same story. For example, "All four gospels quote John the Baptist stating one of Jesus' main purposes on earth, that of baptizing people in the Holy Spirit (Matthew 3:11 || Mark 1:8 || Luke 3:16 || John 1:33)." The parallel lines can also indicate synonymous phrases, as in,

"When the 120 disciples in the upper room were 'filled with the Spirit' || 'baptized in the Spirit,' they spoke in tongues."

Chapter 1:

Why is there Prophetic Ministry?

This book is written with the understanding that "prophet," "seer," and "man of God" are all synonymous terms. There is substantial Scriptural support for this idea, and it is presented in detail in Book 1: *Prophets vs. Seers: Is There a Difference?* so it will not be repeated here. If you are interested in examining the pertinent passages yourself, please refer to that book.

So, proceeding with the view that the Biblical definitions of "prophet," "seer," and "man of God" are all pretty much interchangeable terms, we need to investigate what such people do. What *is* the nature, Scripturally speaking, of the prophetic ministry? As usual, in order to arrive at a reliable conclusion, we must get our answers from the Bible, rather than from what we may have heard somewhere, our denominational persuasions, and so forth.

But first, let me reiterate a statement I made in the Preface of the book: To avoid grammatical cumbersomeness in the text, when I am using male pronouns, I am usually using their generic forms, not their gender-specific forms, unless the context clearly indicates maleness. Ladies, the Bible acknowledges the existence and validity of prophetesses, so statements about "prophets" and "seers" could apply to either men or women. The same goes for the Biblical phrase "man of God."

Obviously, this would include "women of God"—prophetesses—who have the same calling in the body of Christ as their male counterparts.

For those readers who have been taught that prophecy as a whole has ceased (one aspect of the larger doctrine of cessationism), and thus have unwittingly been part of a movement to turn the church into a non-prophet organization, it might be startling to note that I'm casually talking as if prophetic ministry still occurs today. And indeed I am, and indeed it does. And so does everything else that the doctrine of cessationism claims to have ceased.

If you want to investigate why cessationism is unscriptural, there is thoroughgoing coverage of it, and why its conclusions are completely contrary to the whole of the Bible, in the chapter "But Didn't God Stop Doing This Stuff Centuries Ago?" in Book 7: *Be Filled with the Spirit*. Because it is covered there in detail, it will be covered in this book only briefly; refer to that book for a lengthy discussion of numerous flaws in the "logic" of cessationism. Then return to this book for details on the topic of prophetic ministry.

Old Testament Prophets

What was the purpose of the prophetic ministry in the Old Testament? To answer this question, one approach would be to gather examples from all the prophetic utterances by all the prophetic people in the Old Testament (and there are a lot), and analyze them, categorize them, and come to a conclusion based on the frequency and types of messages.

Or, we could read what God says is the purpose of prophetic ministry. Fortunately, there is a place in the Bible where God specifically states what prophets are supposed to do. Reading this will save us much time over the previous approach (although the previous approach would still be very instructive).

Take a look at what God says to Jeremiah in the following passage. Even though this particular passage is a rebuke to false prophets, God clearly reveals, by comparing the actions of false prophets to those of true prophets, what the purpose of true prophetic ministry is:

> Jeremiah 23:21–22: I have not sent these prophets, yet they ran: I have not spoken to them, yet they prophesied. [22]But **if they had stood in my counsel, and had caused my people to hear my words, then they should have turned them from their evil way, and from the evil of their doings.**
>
> > v. 22, NIV: But if they had stood in my council, they would have proclaimed my words to my people and **would have turned them from their evil ways and from their evil deeds.**
> >
> > CEV: If they had been in a meeting of my council in heaven, **they would have told you people of Judah to give up your sins and come back to me.**
> >
> > NIRV: Suppose they had stood in my courts. Then they would have announced my message to my people. **They would have turned my people from their evil ways. They would have turned them away from their sins.**
> >
> > NLV: But if they had listened to Me, then they would have made My words known to My people. **And they would have turned them back from their sinful way and from the sinful things they did.**

This is very enlightening: the main purpose—or at least *one* of the main purposes—of prophetic ministry is to turn people away from their sin and turn them toward God. This should not be surprising; there are numerous examples of this in the Old Testament:

> II Kings 17:13, 22–23 (NASB): Yet **the Lord warned Israel and Judah, through** *all* **His prophets and every seer, saying, "Turn from your evil ways and keep My commandments,** My statutes according to all the law which I commanded your fathers, and which I sent to you through My servants the prophets." . . . [22]And the sons of Israel walked in all the sins of Jeroboam which he did; they did not depart from them, [23]until the Lord removed Israel from His sight, **as He spoke through** *all* **His servants the prophets.** So Israel was carried away into exile from their own land to Assyria until this day.
>
> II Kings 21:10 (NIV): The **Lord said through his servants the prophets:** [11]"Manasseh king of Judah has committed these detestable sins. He has done more evil than the Amorites who preceded him and has led Judah into sin with his idols. [12]Therefore this is what the Lord, the

God of Israel, says: I am going to bring such disaster on Jerusalem and Judah that the ears of everyone who hears of it will tingle."

II Kings 24:2 (NET): The Lord sent against him Babylonian, Syrian, Moabite, and Ammonite raiding bands; he sent them to destroy Judah, **as he had warned he would do through his servants the prophets.**

II Chronicles 24:18 (GWORD): They abandoned the temple of the Lord God of their ancestors and worshiped idols and the poles dedicated to the goddess Asherah. This offense of theirs brought God's anger upon Judah and Jerusalem. [19]**The Lord sent them prophets to bring them back to himself. The prophets warned them, but they wouldn't listen.**

II Chronicles 36:15 (ESV): **The Lord, the God of their fathers, sent *persistently* to them by his messengers,** because he had compassion on his people and on his dwelling place. [16]But **they kept mocking the messengers of God, despising his words and scoffing at his prophets,** until the wrath of the Lord rose against his people, until there was no remedy.

Ezra 9:11 (NLT): **Your servants the prophets warned us** when they said, "The land you are entering to possess is totally defiled by the detestable practices of the people living there. From one end to the other, the land is filled with corruption."

Nehemiah 9:26, 30 (TEV): "But your people rebelled and disobeyed you; they turned their backs on your Law. **They killed the prophets who warned them, who told them to turn back to you.** They insulted you time after time, [27]so you let their enemies conquer and rule them. In their trouble they called to you for help, and you answered them from heaven. In your great mercy you sent them leaders who rescued them from their foes." . . . *Year after year* **you patiently warned them. You inspired your prophets to speak,** but your people were deaf, so you let them be conquered by other nations.

Isaiah 30:9–11 (HCSB): They are a rebellious people, deceptive children, children **who do not want to obey the Lord's instruction.** [10]**They say to the seers, "Do not see," and to the prophets, "Do not prophesy the truth to us.** Tell us flattering things. Prophesy illusions. [11] Get out of the way! Leave the pathway. Rid us of the Holy One of Israel."

Jeremiah 7:25 (AMP): Since the day that your fathers came forth out of the land of Egypt to this day, **I have *persistently* sent to you all My servants the prophets, sending them *daily*, early and late.** [26]Yet the people

28

would not listen to and obey Me or bend their ears [to Me], but stiffened their necks and behaved worse than their fathers.

Jeremiah 25:4–5 (NIV): And though **the Lord has sent *all* his servants the prophets to you *again and again,*** you have not listened or paid any attention. [5]**They said, "Turn now, each of you, from your evil ways and your evil practices,** and you can stay in the land the Lord gave to you and your fathers for ever and ever."

Jeremiah 26:5 (AMP): . . .and to **hear and obey the words of My servants the prophets, whom I have sent to you *urgently and persistently*—** though you have not listened and obeyed. . .

Jeremiah 35:15 (TEV): **I have *continued* to send you *all* my servants the prophets, and they have told you to give up your evil ways and to do what is right. They warned you not to worship and serve other gods,** so that you could go on living in the land that I gave you and your ancestors. But you would not listen to me or pay any attention to me.

. . .and so forth. Many more examples were omitted for the sake of brevity, but the ones above are more than sufficient to show that the main purpose of the prophetic ministry is to turn people away from sin, and toward God. Why did God do that over and over and over again? It states His motivation clearly in II Chronicles 36:15, above: *because He had compassion* on them. When people turn away from God (the only source of life), there is no alternative but death. In other words, sin kills people (Romans 6:23). And God, in His love, doesn't want us to die, so He persistently pleads with us to turn toward Him (Ezekiel 18:31, 33:11).

As is clear throughout the Bible, our choices have consequences. In the passages above, the prophets' messages often included a warning or reminder that continued sin would result in very unpleasant consequences. In keeping with His love and compassion, God often responds to our rebellion with actions that we consider unpleasant. This is often interpreted by unbelievers as God being spiteful and petty, and just throwing around His power as He gleefully presses the proverbial "Smite" button and smacks us around for our disobedience.

Nothing could be further from the truth. In response to our rebellion, God usually lets us reap what we have sown—which is painful enough—and sometimes even resorts to actively chastising us so we will be more likely to come to our senses, repent, and turn to Him while we still have the opportunity to do so (see Hebrews 12:5–11 and also the section entitled "When God Does 'Bad' Things" in Book 6: *Free to Choose?*). If we are still rebelling against Him when we physically die, there is no more opportunity to repent, and there is an unavoidable eternal torment ahead of us (see Hebrews 10:26–27, 12:25 and also the "Eternal Judgment" chapter of Book 8: *Going Beyond Christianity 101*). *That* is what God is trying to steer us away from when He warns us to repent.

Predicting the Future

Another function of prophets in the Old Testament is to predict the future. God has many plans to accomplish certain things, and He will get them done whether we resist Him or cooperate with Him. There are, of course, consequences for us either way, but we will not stop God from getting done anything He wants to get done.

Part of the prediction process that prophets did was in an attempt to persuade people to abandon their sinful lives and turn to God. These warnings often included very detailed and accurate statements of what would happen to them if they didn't repent. See the stories around the passages above for more detail on that topic.

But warnings about judgment for rebellion were certainly not the only topic about which the prophets foretold things. An enormous number of their prophecies were foretelling things about the coming Messiah, Jesus Christ. Below is a *very* abbreviated list of just a few dozen prophecies about Jesus—there are literally hundreds of them.

- He would be born of a woman (Genesis 3:15 > Matthew 1:20, Galatians 4:4)

- He would be born in Bethlehem (Micah 5:2 > Matthew 2:1, Luke 2:4–6)

- He would be born of a virgin (Isaiah 7:14 > Matthew 1:22–23, Luke 1:26–31)

- He would be in the lineage of Abraham (Genesis 12:3, 22:18 > Matthew 1:1)

- He would come from the tribe of Judah (Genesis 49:10 > Luke 3:33, Hebrews 7:14)
- He would be heir to King David's throne (II Samuel 7:12–13, Isaiah 9:7 > Luke 1:32–33, Romans 1:3)
- His throne will be eternal (Psalm 45:6–7, Daniel 2:44 > Luke 1:33, Hebrews 1:8–12)
- He would be called Immanuel (Isaiah 7:14 > Matthew 1:23)
- He would spend a season in Egypt (Hosea 11:1 > Matthew 2:14–15)
- A massacre of children would happen at His birthplace (Jeremiah 31:15 > Matthew 2:16–18)
- A messenger would prepare the way for Him (Isaiah 40:3–5 > Luke 3:3–6)
- He would be rejected by his own people (Psalm 69:8, Isaiah 53:3 > John 1:11, 7:5)
- He would be a prophet (Deuteronomy 18:15 > Acts 3:20–22)
- He would be preceded by Elijah (Malachi 4:5–6 > Matthew 11:13–14)
- He would be declared the Son of God (Psalm 2:7 > Matthew 3:16–17)
- He would bring light to Galilee (Isaiah 9:1–2 > Matthew 4:13–16)
- He would speak in parables (Psalm 78:2–4, Isaiah 6:9–10 > Matthew 13:10–15, 34–35)
- He would be sent to heal the brokenhearted (Isaiah 61:1–2 > Luke 4:18–19)
- He would be a priest after the order of Melchizedek (Psalm 110:4 > Hebrews 5:5–6)
- He would be called King (Psalm 2:6, Zechariah 9:9 > Matthew 27:37, Mark 11:7–11)
- He would be praised by little children (Psalm 8:2 > Matthew 21:16)
- He would be betrayed (Psalm 41:9 > Luke 22:47–48)

- His betrayal price would be 30 pieces of silver (Zechariah 11:12–13 > Matthew 26:14–16)
- His price money would be used to buy a potter's field (Zechariah 11:12–13 > Matthew 27:9–10)
- He would be falsely accused (Psalm 35:11 > Mark 14:57–58)
- He would be silent before his accusers (Isaiah 53:7 > Mark 15:4–5)
- He would be spat upon and struck (Isaiah 50:6 > Matthew 26:67)
- He would be hated without cause (Psalm 35:19, Psalm 69:4 > John 15:24–25)
- He would be crucified with criminals (Isaiah 53:12 > Matthew 27:38 Mark 15:27–28
- He would be given vinegar to drink. (Psalm 69:21 > Matthew 27:34, John 19:28–30)
- His hands and feet would be pierced (Psalm 22:16, Zechariah 12:10 > John 20:25–27)
- He would be mocked and ridiculed (Psalm 22:7–8 > Luke 23:35)
- Soldiers would gamble for His garments (Psalm 22:18 > Luke 23:34, Matthew 27:35–36)
- His bones would not be broken (Exodus 12:46, Psalm 34:20 > John 19:33–36)
- He would pray for his enemies (Psalm 109:4 > Luke 23:34)
- Soldiers would pierce His side (Zechariah 12:10 > John 19:34)
- He would be buried with the rich (Isaiah 53:9 > Matthew 27:57–60)
- He would resurrect from the dead (Psalm 16:10, Psalm 49:15 > Matthew 28:2–7, Acts 2:22–32)
- He would ascend to heaven (Psalm 24:7–10 > Mark 16:19, Luke 24:51)
- He would be seated at God's right hand (Psalm 68:18, Psalm 110:1 > Mark 16:19, Matthew 22:44)

- He would be a sacrifice for sin (Isaiah 53:5–12 > Romans 5:6–8)

In fact, God bluntly states that He tells people about things before they happen:

Isaiah 42:8–9 (NIV): "I am the Lord; that is my name! I will not give my glory to another or my praise to idols. ⁹See, the former things have taken place, and **new things I declare; before they spring into being I announce them to you.**"

Isaiah 48:3 (NIV): "**I foretold the former things long ago,** my mouth announced them and I made them known; **then suddenly I acted, and they came to pass.**"

If the prophet receiving such information were not to tell others, it would have little benefit beyond that of the prophet interceding. While intercession is no small matter, prophetic revelation can be a blessing to *so* many more people if the people actually hear about what God is saying. And we can see from myriad places in the Bible, God does indeed expect prophetic revelation to be shared with others in the lion's share of the cases.

There are also many prophecies about the end times—the close of history when God makes all things new—and other topics. Those two topics—turning people back to God and predicting the future—seem to be the two main functions of Old Testament prophetic ministry. So now let's compare those functions to the functions of New Testament prophetic ministry.

New Testament Prophets

The above was a short recap of the ministry of prophets in the Old Testament. Do New Testament prophets have the same purpose and function? Let's examine some Scriptures and see.

Perhaps the most commonly quoted verse that describes New Testament prophetic function is this one:

I Corinthians 14:3: But he that prophesieth speaketh unto men to **edification, and exhortation, and comfort.**

> AMP: But [on the other hand], the one who prophesies [who interprets the divine will and purpose in inspired preaching and teaching] speaks to men for their **upbuilding and constructive spiritual progress and encouragement and consolation.**

> NIV: But everyone who prophesies speaks to men for their **strengthening, encouragement and comfort.**

> ESV: On the other hand, the one who prophesies speaks to people for their **upbuilding and encouragement and consolation.**

The first word used in the KJV above is "edification." What does that mean? As shown by the other translations, it means to "build up" and "strengthen." "Exhortation" means to encourage, and "comfort" means consolation. Note that all three of these things are positive, and indeed, prophetic ministry, Old Testament or New, is intended for the people's benefit. In presenting a message that is purportedly from God, it should be delivered with a strong indication of God's love, because if it is not, the hearer has good reason (and probably also motivation) to discount it.

This is true even for the Old Testament prophets who were announcing judgment upon sinful and rebellious people. The prophecies were presented with grief, compassion, and/or tears for the seriousness of the consequences, should the recipients of the prophetic words fail to heed God's warnings (or because they already *had* failed to heed them):

> Isaiah 16:9 (AMP): Therefore **I [Isaiah] will weep** with the weeping of Jazer for the vines of Sibmah. **I will drench you with my tears,** O Heshbon and Elealeh; for upon your summer fruits and your harvest the shout [of alarm and the cry of the enemy] has fallen.

> Jeremiah 8:21–9:1 (NIV): Since my people are crushed, **I am crushed; I mourn, and horror grips me.** 22Is there no balm in Gilead? Is there no physician there? Why then is there no healing for the wound of my people? 9:1Oh, that my head were a spring of water and my eyes a fountain of tears! **I would weep day and night for the slain of my people.**

> Jeremiah 13:16–17 (NET): Show the Lord your God the respect that is due him. Do it before he brings the darkness of disaster. Do it before you stumble into distress like a traveler on the mountains at twilight. Do it before he turns the light of deliverance you hope for into the

darkness and gloom of exile. [17]But if you will not pay attention to this warning, **I will weep alone because of your arrogant pride. I will weep bitterly and my eyes will overflow with tears** because you, the Lord's flock, will be carried into exile.

Lamentations 2:11 (NLT): **I have cried until the tears no longer come; my heart is broken. My spirit is poured out in agony** as I see the desperate plight of my people. Little children and tiny babies are fainting and dying in the streets.

Daniel 4:19 (NLT): Upon hearing this, Daniel (also known as Belteshazzar) was overcome for a time, frightened by the meaning of the dream. Then the king said to him, 'Belteshazzar, don't be alarmed by the dream and what it means.' Belteshazzar replied, '**I wish the events foreshadowed in this dream would happen to your enemies, my lord, and not to you!**'

In these, and many more omitted for the sake of brevity, the godly prophets were grieved and heartbroken with compassion by the seriousness of the messages God was having them deliver. They were exemplifying what Paul said many years later:

I Corinthians 13:2 (BBE): And **if I have a prophet's power,** and have knowledge of all secret things; and if I have all faith, by which mountains may be moved from their place, **but have not love, I am nothing.**

But because the word "comfort" is used in I Corinthians 14:3, some have taken this to mean that all prophetic words given today should be "comfortable"—that is, warm and fuzzy, pleasant, and agreeable. If we take it to that extreme, though, we find ourselves unable to obey another Scripture, namely:

Ephesians 4:15 (CEV): **Love should always make us tell the truth.** Then we will grow in every way and be more like Christ, the head. . .

Is it possible to tell the truth—even uncomfortable truth—*and* do it in love at the same time?

Yes. In *all* our speech—which, of course, includes prophetic words—we are exhorted to:

> Ephesians 4:29 (NKJV): Let no corrupt word proceed out of your mouth, but what is good for necessary edification, **that it may impart grace to the hearers.**

One very under-utilized aspect of the grace mentioned above—of which the Greek root word is χάρις (*charis*, G5485)—is that it enables us to avoid sinning:

> Titus 2:11–12 (NIV): For **the grace of God** that brings salvation has appeared to all men. [12]It **teaches us to say "No" to ungodliness and worldly passions, and to live self-controlled, upright and godly lives in this present age. . .**

(For much more discussion on this topic, see Book 2: *Is It Possible to Stop Sinning?*) So, yes, most definitely, our words—*especially* our prophetic words—should impart grace.

Corrective Prophecy

There are cases where God will cause modern-day prophetic words to contain corrective exhortation, which might easily be considered "uncomfortable," at least in the short term. But like any good parent, God sometimes disciplines us (even at the risk of making us momentarily uncomfortable) so that we don't suffer more severe and eternal consequences later:

> Hebrews 12:5–11 (NLT): And have you forgotten the encouraging words God spoke to you as his children? He said, "My child, don't make light of the Lord's discipline, and don't give up when he corrects you. [6]For the Lord disciplines those he loves, and he punishes each one he accepts as his child." [7]As you endure this divine discipline, remember that God is treating you as his own children. Who ever heard of a child who is never disciplined by its father? [8]If God doesn't discipline you as he does all of his children, it means that you are illegitimate and are not really his children at all. [9]Since we respected our earthly fathers who disciplined us, shouldn't we submit even more to the discipline of the Father of our spirits, **and live forever?** [10]For our earthly fathers disciplined us for a few years, doing the best they knew how. But God's discipline is always good for us, **so that we might share in his holiness.** [11]No dis-

cipline is enjoyable while it is happening—it's painful! But **afterward there will be a peaceful harvest of right living** for those who are trained in this way.

So the question we're trying to answer is this: Is it a valid New Testament concept to have "corrective" prophetic ministry? After all, since prophetic ministry is for "edification, exhortation, and comfort," and corrective prophecies would almost certainly be *un*comfortable, wouldn't corrective prophetic ministry be off the table, even if it *was* done in love?

If we take I Corinthians 14:3 away from its context, we could come to that conclusion. However, as any student of the Bible knows, removing a snippet of Scripture from its surrounding context allows unwarranted, and oftentimes downright unscriptural, meaning to be ostensibly derived "from" it.

So let's look at a couple verses from later in that same chapter:

> I Corinthians 14:24–25 (AMP): But if all prophesy [giving inspired testimony and interpreting the divine will and purpose] and an unbeliever or untaught outsider comes in, **he is told of his sin and reproved and convicted and convinced by all, and his defects and needs are examined (estimated, determined) and he is called to account by all,** [25]**The secrets of his heart are laid bare; and so, falling on [his] face, he will worship God,** declaring that God is among you in very truth.

> NET: But if all prophesy, and an unbeliever or uninformed person enters, **he will be convicted by all, he will be called to account by all.** [25]**The secrets of his heart are disclosed,** and in this way **he will fall down with his face to the ground and worship God,** declaring, "God is really among you."

> NLT: But if all of you are prophesying, and unbelievers or people who don't understand these things come into your meeting, **they will be convicted of sin and judged by what you say.** [25]As they listen, **their secret thoughts will be exposed, and they will fall to their knees and worship God,** declaring, "God is truly here among you."

Notice the two kinds of people who are recipients of this kind of corrective prophetic ministry: "unbelievers" and "people who don't understand these things," as the NLT phrases it. The meaning of the word "unbelievers" is clear: those who do not yet believe in Jesus as their Savior and Lord. But the other phrase—those "people who don't understand these things"—what does that mean? Is it people who don't understand the Gospel of the Kingdom? No, since Paul already included such people in the previous phrase; he described them as "unbelievers."

To understand this verse better, it helps to think about what "these things" means. What has Paul been talking about? He's been talking about moving in the supernaturally empowered spiritual gifts.

So Paul is talking about prophetic ministry to people who don't understand that spiritual gifts—for example, prophetic ministry—are real. But what good would that do, since they don't believe in it? It would do a lot of good, because when the secrets of their hearts are revealed, they realize that the gifts of the Holy Spirit, prophecy and all the rest, are indeed real. It only takes one undeniable encounter with the supernatural to overturn decades of wrong teaching. There's nothing like an authentic encounter with prophetic ministry to show people that such things really do exist.

And notice Paul's description of what happens in such prophetic ministry: *the secrets of their hearts are brought to light.* That's hard to argue with.

But still someone might say that it isn't edifying to expose the secrets of someone's heart. Isn't it? As long as it is done in love (as I Corinthians 13 directs), it can be extremely edifying. In addition to v. 25 above, where the recipient falls on his face in worship and acknowledges that God is indeed among you, let's look also at the verse immediately following the two listed above:

> I Corinthians 14:26 (CEB): **What is the outcome of this,** brothers and sisters? When you meet together, each one has a psalm, a teaching, a revelation, a tongue, or an interpretation. **All these things must be done to build up the church.**

To what is Paul referring when he says "what is the outcome of this?" Specifically, what does "this" refer to? It refers to what he was just talking about in the previous verses, which includes prophetic ministry revealing the secrets of people's hearts. So yes, it can be edifying and up-building if it is done with an honest love for the person receiving the prophetic messages. Remember, I Corinthians 13 (the love chapter) is smack in the middle of I Corinthians 12 and I Corinthians 14 (the gifts chapters).

I've heard it said that corrective prophecy is exclusively the bailiwick of those called to the *office* of a prophet. Is that true? Based on the Scripture above, it doesn't look like it. Let's read it again:

> I Corinthians 14:24–25 (NET): But if *all* prophesy, and an unbeliever or uninformed person enters, **he will be convicted by *all*, he will be called to account by *all*.** [25]**The secrets of his heart are disclosed,** and in this way **he will fall down with his face to the ground and worship God,** declaring, "God is really among you."

Notice: *all* are prophesying when the unbeliever or uninformed person enters, and he is convicted by *all*, he will be called to account by *all*. But not all people are prophets, as Paul said a bit earlier in the same letter:

> I Corinthians 12:29 (NIV): Are all apostles? **Are all prophets?** Are all teachers? Do all work miracles?

It is important to reiterate that although not all people are prophets, *all can prophesy*, as shown not only by the passage above, but by v. 31 of the same chapter:

> I Corinthians 14:31 (RSV): For **you can all prophesy** one by one, so that all may learn and all be encouraged. . .

It is sometimes thought that God's discipline always comes as hardship or disaster—as if "pruning" is unavoidably a violent and agonizing amputation—but that is not true. Indeed, that *can* be the case, but it is usually because we haven't listened to His wisdom when He speaks to us. In other words, we can learn the easy way or the hard way. But He prefers to prune unhelpful things out of our lives by simply speaking to us:

> John 15:3 (AMP): You are cleansed and pruned already, **because of the word which I have given you** [the teachings I have discussed with you].

However, if we don't listen to His still, small voice, God will probably resort to more public (read: "less comfortable") modes of exhortation, as in Matthew 18:15–17, in an effort to steer us out of danger.

The point is that even very serious corrective words can be given with love and compassion, and when given this way, will promote edification (strengthening), exhortation (to return to God), and comfort (in the long term).

"Flip It, and Flip It Good"

The phrase used as the title of this section, "Flip it, and flip it good," was coined by Doug Addison, a highly prophetic speaker and founder of InLight Connection (dougaddison.com). If you are familiar with his teachings, you've probably heard him say that phrase. But what does it mean?

Simply put, it is an encouragement to speak prophetic words in an encouraging way, especially those that contain an element of correction or rebuke. Here's an example. Suppose Joe Regularperson gets a prophetic insight in which he realizes that a man in his church is actively involved in an adulterous affair with another woman, and is planning on seeing her again right after the church service. Now keep in mind, this is an actual word from God, not just suspicion and judgmentalism run amok. How should Joe deliver this word? After all, it would have to be in a way that is compatible with these Scriptures:

> Ephesians 4:29 (NIV): Do not let any unwholesome talk come out of your mouths, but **only what is helpful for building others up according to their needs,** that it may benefit those who listen.

> Colossians 4:6 (NASB): **Let your speech always be with grace,** as though seasoned with salt, so that you will know how you should respond to each person.

If you've been into prophetic ministry for any length of time, it is very likely that you've heard that every prophetic word necessarily includes one or more of the following: the *revelation*, the *interpretation*, the *communication*, and the *application*. Note that the first three pertain to the person receiving the message from God and delivering it to the intended hearer, and the final one pertains to the hearer's response to the delivered word. Here's the point of this group of concepts:

1. **Revelation:** This is the actual content of what God reveals to the prophetic person. Revelation from God can be perceived in any of a number of ways; these will be discussed below, in the chapter "How Do You Perceive Prophetic Words?".

2. **Interpretation:** This is how the prophetic person arrives at the meaning of what was delivered to him by the Holy Spirit. The interpretation is sometimes also given by the Lord, and sometimes it is not. If it is not, the person receiving the word must be very careful, loving, and Biblical in seeking the interpretation, so no ungodly bias or Scriptural ignorance creeps in and causes error and damage.

3. **Communication:** Once the prophetic person has received and interpreted a revelation which is for someone other than himself, he must convey the meaning of it (communicate it) to the recipient in a Godly, loving way that follows the guidelines of the two Scriptures quoted above.

4. **Application:** Once the word has been delivered to the recipient, it is his responsibility to pray about it for confirmation, and then obey whatever the Lord has brought to his attention.

Item #3 is where the "Flip it, and flip it good" comes in. A word can be received faithfully and interpreted accurately, but then delivered in a judgmental, condescending, cruel way. Communication happens through a variety of modes, and an effective prophetic person must master them all to avoid hurting people and doing more harm than good.

For example, facial expressions are *very* communicative. If God shows you sin in someone's life (or he confides in you about some sin he is trying to overcome), and your response includes a facial expression of disgust and revulsion, that can be absolutely devastating. The same goes for body language. And, of course, word choice and attitude are extremely important as well.

So, back to Joe Regularperson. He accurately gets a prophetic word about someone's secret sin, and interprets it accurately. An immature prophet might announce "Thus saith the Lord. . ." and publically blast the person, exposing his sin to the whole church, basically ruining his life and driving him away from the church, and very possibly from God, permanently. Obviously, this is not a godly way to communicate a prophetic word—it violates the two Scriptures above, as well as this one:

Proverbs 10:12 (JUB): Hatred stirs up strifes, but **love covers all sins.**

Joe, being experienced in prophetic ministry, takes Doug Addison's advice, and "flips it." And he does it *good.* Such a prophetic word about the upcoming illicit tryst, but delivered in an edifying, encouraging, and reconciling way might come out like this: "I believe the Lord showed me something for you. I feel like you will soon be tempted toward sin, but God assures you He will provide a way out of the temptation. He will give you all the strength you need to be victorious, and then you will be able to strengthen others facing the same temptation. God loves you very much and is so pleased when you choose His ways!"

Note that Joe didn't exalt himself, even subtly, by saying something to the effect of "Thus saith the Lord!" It's always better to say something like "I believe God is saying. . ." or "I think the Lord has told me something. . ." or even "It seems to me. . ."

Why is it better to say it in one of these latter ways? Because it is always possible that your prophetic word is wrong, and if the word is accompanied by "Thus saith the Lord!", you will seriously damage your own credibility, as well as give the hearer reason to disregard prophetic ministry altogether. Since we are commanded *not* to despise prophesying (I Thessalonians 5:20–21), a wrong prophecy that contains "Thus saith the Lord!" encourages people to sin in this way.

And even if your prophetic word is correct, adding "Thus saith the Lord!" to it communicates a subtle message of "If you disregard me, you're disregarding God!" That comes across as very arrogant and distasteful to the hearer.

To build someone up, even when delivering a corrective word, make every effort to deliver it in such a way that, as much as possible, the recipient can retain his dignity. In the following passage, Jesus makes it clear that dignity is to be preserved whenever possible:

> Matthew 18:15–17 (NLT): If another believer sins against you, *[Plan A]* go privately and point out the offense. If the other person listens and confesses it, you have won that person back. [16]But if you are unsuccessful, *[Plan B]* take one or two others with you and go back again, so that everything you say may be confirmed by two or three witnesses. [17]If the person still refuses to listen, *[Plan C]* take your case to the church. Then if he or she won't accept the church's decision, *[Plan D]* treat that person as a pagan or a corrupt tax collector.

And by the way, even if a situation gets all the way to "Plan D," that doesn't mean that we despise, abhor, loathe, or scorn the person who wouldn't listen to correction; we are simply to treat him as a "pagan or a corrupt tax collector"—as an unsaved person. How should we treat unsaved people? We should love them, so they will see the character of Christ in us, and want to participate.

So as we are communicating God's words to those around us, we should keep in mind Jesus' approach to speaking God's words:

> John 12:49 (CJB): For I have not spoken on my own initiative, but **the Father who sent me has given me a command, namely, what to say and** *how to say it.*
>
> GWORD: I have not spoken on my own. Instead, **the Father who sent me told me what I should say and** *how I should say it.*
>
> MSG: I'm not making any of this up on my own. The **Father who sent me gave me orders, told me what to say and** *how to say it.*
>
> NLT: I don't speak on my own authority. The **Father who sent me has commanded me what to say and** *how to say it.*

So again, we should not shame or despise people who are unwilling to do life as they should. Shame is not a good motivator; it is counterproductive and very destructive. So, in *all* cases, prophetic words should be given in a way that is as loving, encouraging, and dignity-preserving as possible, even when a word is corrective in nature.

Revelations Without Interpretations

Is it possible for God to give you a revelation and then not give you the interpretation of it? Is it likely to happen, at least sometimes? Yes, and this is actually not all that uncommon. There are at least a couple reasons why this situation would arise.

First, when multiple prophetic people are ministering simultaneously, the Lord might give the revelation to one person, and the interpretation to another person, so together, they reinforce the validity and agreement of the message (as in, "out of the mouth of two or three witnesses let every word be established. . ."), which makes it more credible and reliable in the eyes of the recipient.

Second, there may be no need for an interpretation because the meaning of the words and/or symbolism presented in the revelation is so glaringly obvious to the recipient (even though it may be completely obscure to the speaker), that an interpretation wouldn't add anything significant.

So if you have a revelation that you feel like you're supposed to speak, but you don't have the interpretation, don't feel like you have somehow failed. Simply speak what you've been given, and any of the following three things (and probably more) could be the result:

- You may get the interpretation after you are faithful in speaking what you were already given, as in:

  Luke 19:17 (NLT): "'Well done!' the king exclaimed. 'You are a good servant. **You have been faithful with the little I entrusted to you,** so you will be governor of ten cities as your reward.'"

  It's very plausible that God might have the viewpoint of "Why should I give you something else? You haven't done anything with what I've already given you!"

- Somebody else may receive the interpretation, as in:

  I Corinthians 14:30–31 (GWORD): **If God reveals something to another person who is seated, the first speaker should be silent.** [31]All of you can take your turns speaking what God has revealed. In that way, everyone will learn and be encouraged.

As members of the body of Christ, we all grow when we learn to appreciate and trust the Holy Spirit in one another.

- The interpretation wouldn't be needed at all, because the meaning is already clear to the hearers, as in:

  Genesis 37:7–8 (NIV): "We *[Joseph and his brothers]* were binding sheaves of grain out in the field when suddenly my sheaf rose and stood upright, while your sheaves gathered around mine and bowed down to it." **⁸His brothers said to him, "Do you intend to reign over us? Will you actually rule us?"** And they hated him all the more because of his dream and what he had said.

Only God knows how He's been dealing with the intended recipient of each prophetic word, and He knows best whether an interpretation is necessary at all, and if so, who should give it. That said, *usually* an interpretation is given along with the revelation, and *usually* it is given to the same person that received the revelation. But God is not constrained in this area.

One more thing: it is possible to get a get a word from God about a situation, and it is not to *ever* be shared with anyone. These cases are probably a small minority, since the purpose of prophetic words is edification of the body, but it is possible. If you get a prophetic word about some situation, it is possible that God intends for you to intercede in prayer, but not share the content with any other person. Such intercession can be powerful, and indeed edifying to the body, though invisible. Since this is a possibility, always check with the Lord to see if a word should be shared, especially if you get the word when no one is requesting prophetic ministry.

Avoiding "Colored Glasses"

This concept pertains primarily to the Interpretation and Communication aspects of delivering a prophetic word.

In the physical world, colored glasses are optical filters that let some colors through unimpeded, but dramatically attenuate or even completely stop other colors. As a result, the original balance of colors that would have been seen is altered. Therefore, the image seen by the person wearing the colored classes can be very different from what would be seen without the colored glasses. This, of course, can cause confusion and misinterpretation, and the wearer of such glasses can completely miss important parts of the information that would otherwise be clearly visible.

In the prophetic world, "colored glasses" are internal biases, on the part of the prophetic person, that influence how a prophetic word is interpreted and/or communicated to the recipient. The result of such bias invariably dilutes or even taints the prophetic word so it is—at least—less powerful than God originally intended. Or, the prophetic word could be made ineffectual, or even harmful if the influence of the bias is large enough.

The influence of these "colored glasses" could show up in prophetic words when they touch on any one of a number of areas that fit into the category of "disputable matters" in the Romans 14:1 sense:

- Behavior: hobbies, topics of conversation, diet, physical contact, music styles, spanking, vaccinations, home schooling, etc.
- Appearance: clothing, hair style or color, tattoos, piercings, etc.
- Associations: friends, music groups, political parties, church denominations, etc.

Of course, other topics could fit into the "disputable" category as well. What someone from one country, ethnic group, region, church, organization, or family might consider perfectly normal and acceptable behavior, might be terribly offensive to the convictions of someone else, in spite of the fact that the Bible doesn't explicitly say whether that behavior is sinful or not (hence its "disputability"). What should the offended person do?

Take, for example, a person who has suffered physical or sexual abuse earlier in life. Even if that person has been emotionally healed to the point that there is no more PTSD, bad dreams, night terrors, or the like, that person may still be hypersensitized to all forms of physical contact, simply because of how it *could* be done maliciously. Even if there's no evidence or reason to believe that someone else is being malicious in any way, or has any ungodly intentions, a person who has suffered such abuse may be very gun-shy about physical contact, no matter how innocuous. The laying on of hands, a hug, or even sitting next to someone might feel unacceptable, even if it's someone else receiving it.

This is usually not an issue in prophetic ministry (or life in general) if such a person is *aware* that he is hypersensitized because of his own experiences. And if that person feels a preference, or even a God-given conviction, to abstain from any particular behavior, or to implement tight constraints on how it may be done, that is perfectly fine. The problem of "colored glasses" arises when that person doesn't take into account, or even realize, his own hypersensitization, and attempts to impose his own opinions, preferences, and/or convictions on others.

Now again, this discussion is not in reference to things that are un-ambiguously identified in the Bible as sins; it is in reference to those things Paul refers to as "disputable matters." Here's what Paul says about them:

> Romans 14:1 (NIV): Accept him whose faith is weak, **without passing judgment on disputable matters.**
>
> AMP: As for the man who is a weak believer, welcome him [into your fellowship], but **not to criticize his opinions or pass judgment on his scruples** or perplex him with discussions.
>
> CEV: Welcome all the Lord's followers, even those whose faith is weak. **Don't criticize them for having beliefs that are different from yours.**
>
> TLB: Give a warm welcome to any brother who wants to join you, even though his faith is weak. **Don't criticize him for having differ-ent ideas from yours about what is right and wrong.**
>
> TEV: Welcome those who are weak in faith, but **do not argue with them about their personal opinions.**

Notice the wording above: Paul is talking about people who are in-deed "believers," "the Lord's followers," and "brothers." But these peo-ple still have different opinions, scruples, beliefs, and ideas than the believers, Lord's followers, and brothers that Paul is addressing. Both groups of people—the ones Paul is talking *to*, and the ones Paul is talk-ing *about*—are saved, but still may have different opinions on some things. To put it in modern terms, they agree on the essentials of the faith (the "majors"), but may disagree on the secondary items (the "mi-nors"). One of the main dangers of having "colored glasses"—the internal biases—is that secondary items are given "essential" status, which causes no end of strife and conflict.

Now of course, no one wants to be considered "weak in faith," so there is a tendency to apply that descriptor to the *other* person, as in, "Surely that couldn't refer to *me*." But even then, it's not necessarily a matter of "strength of faith" or "weakness of faith," but simply how God has given to Person A a conviction about some disputable matter, which happens to be different than the conviction God gave Person B about that same disputable matter.

Convictions about disputable matters can be very strong indeed, and even strong enough that a person who holds such a conviction cannot imagine that everybody else wouldn't have the same conviction he does. In stronger cases, it can lead to thinking (or saying), "How can you even claim to be a Christian if you believe like that?" In prophetic ministry, this can easily lead to the biasing of a prophetic message, simply because it touches upon a personal conviction about a disputable matter which, by its very definition, is *not* universal, but which may nevertheless be very strong in some people.

If a conviction about a disputable matter is not recognized as simply an opinion or personal conviction, and *not* a universal truth, it may not even occur to such a person that any different conviction could ever be valid. And here's where a particularly subtle form of manipulation can occur. This kind of manipulation is usually inadvertent, but it is manipulation nonetheless.

Suppose Joe Regularperson has an intense personal conviction (read: "strong opinion") about some disputable matter. Upon seeing Fred behaving in a manner inconsistent with the personal conviction Joe feels so strongly, Joe subconsciously realizes that Fred will not likely be swayed by Joe simply stating that he has a different opinion. At this point, Joe could feel a temptation to intensify his exhortation and describe Fred's behavior as "inappropriate." Why? Because the word "inappropriate" implies an undeniability of truthfulness and a universality of application.

In essence, Joe's characterization of Fred's behavior as "inappropriate" implies "Everybody else agrees with me, so you are clearly the one in the wrong." After all, this carries much more weight than "I have a different opinion than you." With a strong opinion about something, it is so easy to slip into a mindset of "Everybody ought to have the same opinion I do."

Many times, when one person declares another person's disputable actions or attitudes to be "inappropriate," what really should have been expressed is "I wouldn't do that myself" or "I am personally not comfortable with that." True, a statement of this form exerts less control over the other person, but it leaves open the possibility that someone else may indeed be comfortable with it, and that it's between him and God. It also leaves open the possibility that someone might have an opinion that's different than mine, and still not be wrong. In other words, we leave the Holy Spirit's job to the Holy Spirit. After all, He's pretty good at it. . .

Again, this form of subtle manipulation is usually not intentional, but especially in prophetic ministry, in which guidance is often a major factor, we must be especially aware of this possibility in order to keep our motives—and our prophetic words—true to what God actually said, rather than what we think God "surely" must have meant.

When one person states that another person "should" take some action regarding a disputable matter—usually to stop it, whether or not the word "inappropriate" was actually used—there are some unavoidable, but usually unintentional, implications/presumptions that the speaker makes in order for him to consider his directive valid:

- The speaker is setting himself up as the standard against which everyone else's behavior is measured.

- The speaker is presenting himself as one who knows enough about the other person's life to make valid determinations.

- The speaker is presenting himself as one having the authority to evaluate, define, and enforce his preferred behavior in others.

- The speaker is, by his very statement, declaring the other person to be in the wrong, because the other person is not conforming to the speaker's statement of "proper" behavior.

So, how should we handle disputable matters? Each person should act according to what He feels is right before God, realizing that other people may disagree, act differently than we'd like, and still be right with God:

Romans 14:5b: Let every man **be fully persuaded in his own mind.**

CEV: But each of you should **make up your own mind.**

CEB: Each person must **have their own convictions.**

GWORD: Every person must **make his own decision.**

TLB: On questions of this kind **everyone must decide for himself.**

MSG: So, each person is free to **follow the convictions of conscience.**

TEV: We each should firmly **make up our own minds.**

This is a restatement of something that Paul said to the Corinthian church, in a similar discussion:

I Corinthians 10:29b: . . .for why is my liberty judged of another man's conscience?

AMP: For why should another man's scruples apply to me and my liberty of action be determined by his conscience?

CEB: Why should my freedom be judged by someone else's conscience?

ERV: My own freedom should not be judged by what another person thinks.

TLB: But why, you may ask, must I be guided and limited by what someone else thinks?

MSG: . . .I'm not going to walk around on eggshells worrying about what small-minded people might say; I'm going to stride free and easy, knowing what our large-minded Master has already said.

So if we take Paul's exhortation to heart, how will we behave toward each other? Paul continues:

Romans 14:13a: Let us not therefore judge one another any more. . .

AMP: Then let us no more criticize and blame and pass judgment on one another. . .

CEB: So stop judging each other.

GWORD: So let's stop criticizing each other.

MSG: Forget about deciding what's right for each other.

NLT: So let's stop condemning each other.

Then in both discussions, Paul adds that, in any area where we have freedom (our convictions allow something) but someone else does not (their convictions prohibit that same thing), we shouldn't *flaunt* our freedom in an area for the purpose of embarrassing or humiliating that person—that would not be a loving thing to do.

But we also know from other places in the Bible (e.g., Proverbs 29:25) that neither should we determine our behavior based on what other people think. This would be fear of man, which is a trap. Paul says it like this:

> Romans 14:14: I know, and **am persuaded by the Lord Jesus,** that there is nothing unclean of itself: but **to him that esteemeth any thing to be unclean,** *to him* **it is unclean.**
>
> AMP: I know and **am convinced (persuaded) as one in the Lord Jesus,** that nothing is [forbidden as] essentially unclean (defiled and unholy in itself). But [none the less] **it is unclean (defiled and unholy)** *to anyone who thinks it is unclean.*
>
> CSB: I know and **am persuaded in the Lord Jesus** that nothing is unclean in itself. Still, **to someone who considers a thing to be unclean,** *to that one* it is unclean.
>
> MSG: I'm convinced—**Jesus convinced me!**—that everything as it is in itself is holy. **We, of course, by the way we treat it or talk about it, can contaminate it.**

So how do we know if a disputable matter is a sin for someone or not? Actually, you only know whether or not it's a sin for yourself; you *don't* know if it's a sin for someone else, because you don't know how the Lord has been dealing with that other person.

Paul addresses this idea as well. One of the examples Paul uses is whether it is, or is not, a sin to eat meat that has been offered to an idol. At the end of his teaching, Paul says this:

> Romans 14:23b: . . .whatsoever is not of faith is sin.

AMP: For whatever does not originate and proceed from faith is sin [whatever is done without a conviction of its approval by God is sinful].

CEV: . . .anything you do against your beliefs is sin.

ERV: And if you do anything that you believe is not right, it is sin.

TLB: Anything that is done apart from what he feels is right is sin.

MSG: If the way you live isn't consistent with what you believe, then it's wrong.

NLT: If you do anything you believe is not right, you are sinning.

The problem (or perhaps I should say *one of* the problems) with colored glasses, both the physical kind and the internal-bias kind, is that after a while, the abnormally colored world starts to seem normal. And because that's the way the world looks to you, it's so easy to assume that, surely, the world looks like that to everybody. *But it doesn't.*

All of this is to emphasize that, during prophetic ministry, it is *very* important that prophetic people be diligent not let their own opinions, preferences, and convictions concerning disputable matters come across as universal truths that apply (or even *ought to* apply) to everyone.

Predicting the Future

As we saw above, one of the functions of Old Testament prophets was to predict the future. Is this still one of the functions of prophets, now that we're in the New Testament? I have heard people say that the future-predicting function is no longer a part of New Testament prophetic ministry; is that a Scripturally sound conclusion? Let's take a look.

Jesus did much prophecy that was future-predicting in nature. For example:

Matthew 24:1–2 (NIV): Jesus left the temple and was walking away when his disciples came up to him to call his attention to its buildings. ²"Do you see all these things?" he asked. "I tell you the truth, **not one stone here will be left on another; every one will be thrown down.**"

Matthew 24:3–44 (NIV): As Jesus was sitting on the Mount of Olives, the disciples came to him privately. "Tell us," they said, "when will this happen, and what will be the sign of your coming and of the end of the age?" [4]Jesus answered: "Watch out that no one deceives you. [5]**For many will come in my name, claiming, 'I am the Christ,' and will deceive many. [6]You will hear of wars and rumors of wars,** but see to it that you are not alarmed. Such things must happen, but the end is still to come. . . . [44]So you also must be ready, because **the Son of Man will come at an hour when you do not expect him.**"

. . .and many, many more. Some people still discount the New Testament future-predicting function of prophets, even after seeing the above passages and others like them, because when Jesus made these prophecies (according to this line of thought), it was not "really" the New Testament times yet because Jesus had not been crucified and resurrected yet.

Okay, so are there prophecies that are future-predicting in nature, that were made *after* Jesus' death and resurrection? After all, one cannot deny that after Jesus' resurrection, it was "really" New Testament times. And there are indeed examples of future-predicting prophecies in New Testament times:

Acts 11:27–28 (GWORD): At that time **some prophets came from Jerusalem** to the city of Antioch. [28]One of them was named Agabus. **Through the Spirit Agabus predicted that a severe famine would affect the entire world.** This happened while Claudius was emperor.

Acts 21:10–11 (BBE): And while we were waiting there for some days, **a certain prophet, named Agabus,** came down from Judaea. [11]And he came to us, and took the band of Paul's clothing, and putting it round his feet and hands, said, **The Holy Spirit says these words, So will the Jews do to the man who is the owner of this band, and they will give him up into the hands of the Gentiles.**

II Timothy 3:1–5 (TEV): Remember that **there will be difficult times in the last days.** [2]People will be selfish, greedy, boastful, and conceited; they will be insulting, disobedient to their parents, ungrateful, and irreligious; [3]they will be unkind, merciless, slanderers, violent, and fierce; they will hate the good; [4]they will be treacherous, reckless, and swollen with pride; they will love pleasure rather than God; [5]**they will hold to the outward form of our religion, but reject its real power.** Keep away from such people.

II Peter 3:3–4 (RSV): First of all you must understand this, that **scoffers will come in the last days** with scoffing, following their own passions

⁴and saying, "Where is the promise of his coming? For ever since the fathers fell asleep, all things have continued as they were from the beginning of creation."

So here we have Agabus, Paul, and Peter—all unquestionably *after* Jesus' resurrection—prophesying about future events. Could anyone still really hold onto the idea that future-predicting prophecy is a thing of the past? And then there's this one:

> Revelation 4:1 (AMP): After this I looked, and behold, a door standing open in heaven! And the first voice which I had heard addressing me like [the calling of] a war trumpet said, Come up here, and **I will show you what must take place in the future.**

> [To hear this passage set to music, listen to the song *Holy is the Lord* on the album *Go Into All the World*, or scan the QR code at right.]

> PHILLIPS: Later I looked again, and before my eyes a door stood open in Heaven, and in my ears was the voice with the ring of a trumpet, which I had heard at first, speaking to me and saying, "Come up here, and **I will show you what must happen in the future.**"

> TLB: Then as I looked, I saw a door standing open in heaven, and the same voice I had heard before, which sounded like a mighty trumpet blast, spoke to me and said, "Come up here and **I will show you what must happen in the future!**"

Almost the whole book of Revelation, written by John, is a prophecy about future events! So not only do we see that future-telling prophecy is a real thing in the New Testament, but we also must realize Jesus plainly said that that would be the case:

> John 16:13 (AMP): But **when He, the Spirit of Truth (the Truth-giving Spirit) comes,** He will guide you into all the Truth (the whole, full Truth). For He will not speak His own message [on His own authority]; but He will tell whatever He hears [from the Father; He will give the message that has been given to Him], and **He will announce and declare to you the things that are to come [that will happen in the future].**

> CJB: However, **when the Spirit of Truth comes,** he will guide you into all the truth; for he will not speak on his own initiative but will say

only what he hears. **He will also announce to you the events of the future.**

ERV: But **when the Spirit of truth comes, he** will lead you into all truth. He will not speak his own words. He will speak only what he hears and **will tell you what will happen in the future.**

TLB: **When the Holy Spirit, who is truth, comes,** he shall guide you into all truth, for he will not be presenting his own ideas, but will be passing on to you what he has heard. **He will tell you about the future.**

In this context, the Spirit of Truth "came" at Pentecost. So it is unquestionable that future-predicting prophecy is a real and valid operation in New Testament times.

In the above passages we have seen that there are at least these four purposes of the prophetic ministry, be that in the Old Testament or the New. These four (and there certainly may be more), in no particular order, are:

- Edifying, building up, and strengthening people;
- Exhorting, encouraging, and motivating people to turn to (or *back* to) God;
- Comforting, consoling, reassuring people that God is loving and good, and He has their best interests in mind; and
- Instructing, warning, notifying, and/or preparing people for future events or eventualities.

Now that we've seen what prophecy can be used for, let's examine who can be used in this type of ministry.

Chapter 2:

Who Can Be Used in Prophetic Ministry?

This is a very good question, because there are large chunks of Christendom who believe that prophecy as a whole has ceased—that it doesn't happen to anybody anymore, and whoever claims to prophesy must necessarily be a false prophet. Such a claim is often accompanied by the snippet of Scripture from I Corinthians 13:8 that says, "Prophecy will cease." True, it will, but it certainly hasn't yet. This topic of whether God still does prophecy and other supernatural things will not be covered here, because it is already covered in great detail in Book 7: *Be Filled with the Spirit;* refer to that book for further information.

So, proceeding with the assurance that prophecy, as well as other miraculous manifestations of the Holy Spirit, are still happening and will continue to happen until the Lord comes back, we now address the question of who can be used in this way.

Prophesying About a Prophecy

The prophet Moses was rather intimately familiar with the ways of God, since he regularly talked *face to face* with God (Exodus 33:11, Numbers 12:7–8, Deuteronomy 5:4, 34:10), and spent eighty days—

yes, *eighty* full days (Exodus 24:18, 34:28)—in the tangible, visible, glory cloud of God (see Book 4: *Gold Dust, Jewels, and More: Manifestations of God?* for an in-depth examination of this topic).

At one point, while in the wilderness, when the Israelites were complaining and complaining, Moses went to God and told Him he couldn't handle them all by himself anymore; he needed help. So God took of the spirit on Moses and put it on the seventy elders of Israel and they all prophesied. Then shortly after that, it was discovered that two of the elders who were not in that particular gathering prophesied also. Joshua was upset with them—of all the *gall!* Those two missed the meeting! They weren't even part of the "in" crowd!

> Numbers 11:26–29 (NLT): Two men, Eldad and Medad, had stayed behind in the camp. They were listed among the elders, but they had not gone out to the Tabernacle. Yet the Spirit rested upon them as well, so they prophesied there in the camp. [27]A young man ran and reported to Moses, "Eldad and Medad are prophesying in the camp!" [28]Joshua son of Nun, who had been Moses' assistant since his youth, protested, "Moses, my master, make them stop!" [29]But Moses replied, "Are you jealous for my sake? **I wish that *all* the LORD's people were prophets and that the LORD would put his Spirit upon them *all!*"**
>
> v. 29, CEB: Moses said to him, "Are you jealous for my sake? **If only *all* the Lord's people were prophets with the Lord placing his spirit on them!"**
>
> JUB: And Moses said unto him, Art thou jealous for my sake? **It would be good that *all* the Lord's people were prophets** and that the Lord would put his spirit upon them!

Here is Moses, a man who well knew God's ways (Psalm 103:7), saying that it would be good if all God's people were prophets. Was he right? Or was he just engaging in a bit of wistful sentiment?

The particular wording of the CEB above, and some other translations, could be construed nowadays as meaning, "If only this would happen! But it never will. . ." That little addendum "but it never will" is especially easy to assume if we've been brought up under cessationist teaching, which says that God doesn't work supernaturally anymore. But we also know that that assumption is inappropriate (read: "wrong") because of what Joel (and Jesus and Paul and Peter, etc.) said later. The prophet Moses essentially prophesied about what the prophet Joel would later prophesy about.

Joel's Prophecy

So what *did* Joel say in his prophecy?

Joel 2:28–30 (GWORD): "After this, **I will pour my Spirit on** *everyone.* Your **sons** and **daughters** will prophesy. Your **old** men will dream dreams. Your **young** men will see visions. [29]In those days I will pour my Spirit on **servants,** on both men and women. [30]I will work miracles in the sky and on the earth: blood, fire, and clouds of smoke."

Note that it explicitly says *everyone.* Or, as other translations render it, "all flesh," "all mankind," "all humanity," "all kinds of people," "every person," or "all of you." Wow. You'd need help to try to misinterpret that! Sons *and* daughters—no gender-related differences when it comes to receiving the Holy Spirit or engaging in prophetic ministry. Old *and* young—no age-related differences either. Even servants—the lowest people on the social totem pole, be they male or female—are able to receive the Spirit. That pretty much covers it: *all* mankind.

And notice one of the things these people upon whom the Spirit is poured out will do: they'll prophesy. This outpouring of the Holy Spirit, that comes upon *all* mankind, enables people to prophesy.

So yes, Moses was right.

Peter's Confirmation

Students of the Word will also be aware that the prophecy of Joel, quoted above, was fulfilled on the day of Pentecost. There was the sound of a rushing mighty wind, tongues of fire appeared above each of the 120 people gathered to pray, they were all filled with the Holy Spirit and began to speak in tongues.

Soon a crowd gathered to see what was going on, and Peter tells them:

> Acts 2:14–18 (NLT): Then Peter stepped forward with the eleven other apostles and shouted to the crowd, "Listen carefully, all of you, fellow Jews and residents of Jerusalem! Make no mistake about this. [15]These people are not drunk, as some of you are assuming. Nine o'clock in the morning is much too early for that. [16]No, **what you see was predicted long ago by the prophet Joel:** [17]'In the last days,' **God says, 'I will pour out my Spirit upon** *all* **people.** Your **sons** and **daughters** will prophesy. Your **young** men will see visions, and your **old** men will dream dreams. [18]In those days I will pour out my Spirit even on my **servants—men and women alike**—and they will prophesy.'"

So Peter, quoting Joel, makes it sound like prophetic utterances, far from being the purview of only ultra-mature "elite" Christians, should be a normal part of every Christian's life. Note v. 18 above: "My servants," God says, "will prophesy." If you consider yourself a servant of God, you are authorized, privileged, and commanded to prophesy. How cool is that! The God and Creator of the universe, speaking directly to *me!* After all, what is prophecy, except hearing God's Spirit speak directly to your spirit? And if you look at the lifestyles of godly people throughout the Bible, you will see that prophecy indeed was a normal part of life. And that hasn't changed.

But someone might object to Peter's Pentecostal interpretation of Joel's prophecy by saying, "But Joel said people would *prophesy!* At Pentecost, they only spoke in tongues." Paul addresses this in I Corinthians 14, where he says:

> I Corinthians 14:5 (NASB): Now I wish that you all spoke in tongues, but even more that you would prophesy; and **greater is one who prophesies than one who speaks in tongues,** *unless he interprets,* **so that the church may receive edifying.**

The whole purpose of prophetic utterances is to edify the hearers, but they are unlikely to be edified if they don't know what is said. But when a manifestation of tongues is understood by the listeners, in essence it is the same as prophecy. There are two Scriptural ways for a message in tongues to be understood, and therefore be edifying, to its hearers. The first way is by the interpretation of tongues that Paul mentions above, and the second way is through the hearers already knowing and understanding the language being spoken, like what happened at Pentecost, in Acts 2. So it looks like Peter's correlation of Joel's prophecy and the events of Pentecost was warranted after all.

Hearing God on behalf of another is what most people think of when they think about prophetic words, but hearing God's wisdom and direction for your own specific situation is no less prophetic. And prophetic input from God—hearing God and obeying Him—is absolutely essential to living a Godly life.

Paul's Confirmation

Unsurprisingly, the apostle Paul agrees with Peter. In his extended teaching on how to use the gifts of the Spirit, Paul includes these exhortations:

I Corinthians 14:1 (NIV): Follow the way of love and **eagerly desire spiritual gifts,** *especially the gift of prophecy.*

I Corinthians 14:5 (NET): **I wish you all spoke in tongues, but** *even more that you would prophesy.* The one who prophesies is greater than the one who speaks in tongues, unless he interprets so that the church may be strengthened.

I Corinthians 14:31 (NASB): For **you can** *all* **prophesy one by one,** so that all may learn and all may be exhorted. . .

I Corinthians 14:39 (BBE): So then, my brothers, **let it be your** *chief desire* **to be prophets;** but let no one be stopped from using tongues.

Paul is really stressing this idea of prophetic ministry coming through everyone in the body of Christ, and that we should all seek it passionately. But why? What's so good about being a prophet, or about prophesying? As we saw in the previous chapter of this book, the purpose of prophetic ministry is for edification, exhortation, comfort, and foretelling future events. And as we see here, to edify other believers—to build up and strengthen others in the church—is really good:

I Corinthians 14:4 (NET): The one who speaks in a tongue builds himself up, but **the one who prophesies builds up the church.**

> I Corinthians 14:12 (TEV): Since you are eager to have the gifts of the Spirit, you **must try above everything else to make greater use of those which help to build up the church.**
>
> I Corinthians 14:26 (NASB): What is the outcome then, brethren? When you assemble, **each one has** a psalm, has a teaching, has **a revelation,** has a tongue, has an interpretation. **Let all things be done for edification.**

As we can see, the purpose of prophetic revelation is to edify, to build up, the church. But that's what *all* the spiritual gifts are for, so why is prophecy singled out as being the best? Why are we, as the above Scriptures enjoin us to do, to eagerly desire "especially" the gift of prophecy? Why should it be our "chief" desire? Probably because receiving God's wisdom on *any* situation can make it better. Prophecy, being basically a communication mechanism from God to us, allows His wisdom (if we're listening) to come to bear on any and all situations in our lives.

Other gifts of the Spirit seem to be more special-purpose. Extremely valuable when needed, yes, but not applicable in every situation. For example, if everyone in a particular group is healthy, the gifts of healing would not be needed at the moment. Or, if no one has just given a message in tongues, interpretation would be unnecessary at the moment. But God's wisdom is *always* welcome and beneficial. Thus, prophecy is able to edify yourself and/or others more often, and that is desirable.

One more interesting tidbit. Some Christians think (and I thought it myself for quite a while) the moving in the miraculous gifts of the Holy Spirit—prophecy or otherwise—was the domain of the few elite extra-mature people in the Body of Christ. But Paul says otherwise. We've seen numerous examples of Paul's commandments *to* use, exhortations of *why* to use, and explanations of *how* to use the spiritual gifts in his first epistle to the Corinthians. Can we therefore assume that they were examples of the elite extra-mature believers postulated above?

In a word, no. Let's read how Paul describes the believers in Corinth:

> I Corinthians 3:1 (AMP): However, brethren, I could not talk to you as to spiritual [men], but as to **nonspiritual [men of the flesh, in whom the carnal nature predominates]**, as to **mere infants** [in the new life] in Christ [unable to talk yet!] ²**I fed you with milk, not solid food, for you were not yet strong enough [to be ready for it]; but even yet you are not strong enough [to be ready for it].** . .

> NLT: Dear brothers and sisters, when I was with you I couldn't talk to you as I would to spiritual people. **I had to talk as though you belonged to this world or as though you were infants in Christ. ²I had to feed you with milk, not with solid food, because you weren't ready for anything stronger. And you still aren't ready.** . .

That's quite a revelation! Paul says that the believers in the Corinthian church were not only not mature, but were "mere infants" who had to be fed with milk, because they weren't ready for solid food yet. *But he still taught them how to move in the miraculous gifts of the Holy Spirit!* This clearly shows that the gifts of the Spirit, prophecy or otherwise, are for everyone, even the newest baby Christian. Indeed, how could we ever expect to grow if we don't let His Holy Spirit move through us? If we don't let the Holy Spirit move through us—for *whatever* reason—that would deprive us of the very thing we need in order to mature in the Lord.

The "Prophetic Atmosphere"

What is an "atmosphere?" It is a rather modern phrase to describe something that's been happening throughout Biblical history. An "atmosphere" is a heavy anointing or a manifest presence of God in which certain blessings are more freely accessible than usual, and in some cases, the blessings happen whether people specifically asked for them or not.

Because of the subject matter of this book, we will talk here about "prophetic atmospheres," but there are also cases of an atmosphere of healing (Luke 5:17, Acts 5:15), of tongues (Acts 2:4), of conviction (Acts 2:37), and so forth; it depends on what God is pouring out at the moment.

While this particular usage of the word "atmosphere" to describe the ambient spiritual condition is somewhat new, the concept is very Biblical, both in the Old Testament and the New. Does the Bible actually describe situations like this? Are there actual prophetic "atmospheres" in which prophetic activity happens freely, and sometimes overwhelmingly? Yes; let's look at some. The Scriptures below show some of these situations in which there was a prophetic atmosphere, and people just started prophesying whether they were specifically seeking the Lord for it or not.

First, let's look at when Moses and the seventy elders of Israel gathered around the tabernacle to meet God. We saw this passage earlier, but let's look at another aspect of it:

> Numbers 11:25: And the Lord came down in a cloud, and spake unto him, and took of the spirit that was upon him, and gave it unto the seventy elders: and it came to pass, that, **when the spirit rested upon them, they prophesied, and did not cease.**

Two of the elders in this group, for whatever reason, didn't make it to that particular meeting. But the Holy Spirit fell on them as well, and then what happened? *They prophesied:*

> Numbers 11:26–29: But there remained two of the men in the camp, the name of the one was Eldad, and the name of the other Medad: and **the spirit rested upon them; and they were of them that were written, but went not out unto the tabernacle: and they prophesied in the camp.** 27And there ran a young man, and told Moses, and said, Eldad and Medad do prophesy in the camp. 28And Joshua the son of Nun, the servant of Moses, one of his young men, answered and said, My lord Moses, forbid them. 29And Moses said unto him, Enviest thou for my sake? **would God that all the LORD's people were prophets, and that the LORD would put his spirit upon them!**

Then there's King Saul: Samuel anointed him as king, and then prophesied over him. Included in that prophecy was this:

> I Samuel 10:5–6 (RSV): After that you shall come to Gibe-ath-elohim, where there is a garrison of the Philistines; and there, as you come to the city, **you will meet a band of prophets** coming down from the high place with harp, tambourine, flute, and lyre before them, **prophesying.**

⁶Then the spirit of the LORD will come mightily upon you, and you shall prophesy with them and be turned into another man.

Interesting: Samuel says very matter-of-factly: "You will prophesy."

I Samuel 10:10–11 (RSV): When they came to Gibe-ah, behold, a band of prophets met him; and the **spirit of God came mightily upon him, and he prophesied among them.** ¹¹And when all who knew him before saw how **he prophesied with the prophets,** the people said to one another, "What has come over the son of Kish? Is Saul also among the prophets?"

Fast-forward a few years. Saul gets into the unfortunate habit of disobeying God and then making excuses. So God decides to give the kingdom to David, a man after His own heart. But Saul, consumed with jealousy over what David had, and what Saul himself no longer had, tries to kill David. Perhaps Saul was thinking that if he just murdered God's anointed, God would bless him again. Ya think? As one of my pastor friends says, "Sin makes you stupid."

So King Saul was trying to capture and kill David before he can take the throne. Saul sends a garrison of men to capture David, while David was hanging around the prophet Samuel. God "takes them out of commission," so to speak, as well and the next two garrisons of men that Saul sends:

I Samuel 19:19–24 (NIV): Word came to Saul: "David is in Naioth at Ramah"; ²⁰so he sent men to capture him. But when they saw a group of prophets prophesying, with Samuel standing there as their leader, the **Spirit of God came upon Saul's men and they also prophesied.** ²¹Saul was told about it, and **he sent more men, and they prophesied too.** Saul sent men a third time, and **they also prophesied.**

So these three detachments of soldiers couldn't perform their duty for Saul—capturing David—because they were so busy prophesying! Talk about a powerful prophetic atmosphere! So finally Saul, apparently thinking, "If you want something done right, do it yourself. . .", goes there himself to capture David:

²²Finally, he himself left for Ramah and went to the great cistern at Secu. And he asked, "Where are Samuel and David?" "Over in Naioth

at Ramah," they said. ²³So Saul went to Naioth at Ramah. But **the Spirit of God came even upon him, and he walked along prophesying** until he came to Naioth. ²⁴He **stripped off his robes and also prophesied in Samuel's presence.** He lay that way all that day and night. This is why people say, "Is Saul also among the prophets?"

So the same thing happens to Saul himself. Again, that must have been a seriously prophetic atmosphere!

Amos apparently had some experience with prophetic atmospheres; listen to what he wrote:

Amos 3:8: The lion hath roared, who will not fear? **the Lord GOD hath spoken, who can but prophesy?**

CEV: Everyone is terrified when a lion roars—and **ordinary people become prophets when the LORD God speaks.**

CJB: The lion has roared. Who will not fear? ADONAI, **God, has spoken. Who will not prophesy?**

GWORD: The lion has roared. Who isn't afraid? **The Almighty LORD has spoken. Who can keep from prophesying?**

NET: A lion has roared! Who is not afraid? **The sovereign LORD has spoken! Who can refuse to prophesy?**

NIRV: A lion has roared. Who isn't afraid? **The LORD and King has spoken. Who can do anything but prophesy?**

Isn't *that* interesting! Far from the idea of "prophecy doesn't happen anymore," the Bible says that when you actually hear God speak, you can't help it!

And this one is particularly fascinating. Remember Caiaphas? He was the high priest of Israel during the latter part of Jesus' earthly ministry. Caiaphas was the ringleader and organizer (the mob boss) in the plot to arrest and crucify Jesus (Matthew 26:3, 57, John 18:28).

But unbeknownst to Caiaphas, he was an example of what Amos stated above. Check this out:

John 11:48–52 (RSV): "If we *[the chief priests and Pharisees]* let him *[Jesus]* go on thus, every one will believe in him, and the Romans will come and destroy both our holy place and our nation." ⁴⁹But one of them,

Caiaphas, who was high priest that year, said to them, "You know nothing at all; [50]you do not understand that it is expedient for you that one man should die for the people, and that the whole nation should not perish." [51]**He did not say this of his own accord, but being high priest that year** *he prophesied* **that Jesus should die for the nation,** [52]**and not for the nation only, but to gather into one the children of God who are scattered abroad.**

Here is Caiaphas proclaiming basically that same thing that John the Baptist preached: "Behold the Lamb of God Who takes away the sin of the world!" Surely Caiaphas would have been horrified if he had understood what he was saying. But the Lord has spoken; who can but prophesy?

So it's clear that all believers can be used in prophetic ministry. Now let's examine a concept that makes a lot of potential prophets nervous, sometimes even to the point of avoiding prophetic ministry altogether.

False Prophecy and False Prophets

Because the purpose of prophetic ministry is to communicate God's words, wisdom, direction, and character to the listeners, it is a serious thing indeed for someone to impersonate God—to claim "This is what the Lord says"—when God didn't say that at all. Impersonating God, or trying to pass oneself off as God, is basically what Lucifer did when he rebelled against God and attempted to stage a coup (Isaiah 14:12–17). I'm sure you remember that that attempt was a spectacular failure.

In the Old Testament, when relatively few people had the Holy Spirit residing inside them, people were more susceptible to deception from those claiming to be prophets, but really weren't. Since the Spirit of Truth was not inside most people, a slick false prophet could lead them astray rather easily. Therefore, there were severe consequences for people who took it upon themselves to speak their own words but claim their authority was from God.

Here's an example of those severe consequences:

Deuteronomy 18:20 (TEV): But if any prophet dares to speak a message in my name when I did not command him to do so, **he must die for it,** and so must any prophet who speaks in the name of other gods.

Such severe consequences have made many a modern-day believer more than a little nervous about stepping out into a prophetic ministry, even when they feel a distinct call to it. Is the death penalty still in effect for modern-day prophets who don't do it right?

Actually, it is not, and here is why. As we saw in the earlier sections of this chapter, the Holy Spirit has been poured out on *all* mankind: men and women, young and old, all the way down to the lowest social strata. Because of that, the responsibility to ascertain the truthfulness or validity of a prophetic utterance now falls on the hearer.

Paul states it this way:

I Corinthians 14:29 (NIV): Two or three prophets should speak, and **the others should weigh carefully what is said.**

BBE: And let the prophets give their words, but not more than two or three, and **let the others be judges of what they say.**

GWORD: Two or three people should speak what God has revealed. **Everyone else should decide whether what each person said is right or wrong.**

Wait: can that be right? In the BBE translation above, it says that the others (those who are not prophesying at the moment) should be judges of what the prophets said. But we're not supposed to judge, are we? Doesn't the Bible say, "Judge not, and you won't be judged?"

This is a very common misunderstanding, which is caused by that fact that two very different concepts are expressed by the same English word "judge." The first concept that "judge" can mean is "condemn," and indeed we are not to condemn each other. God has forgiven us, so we have no right to condemn one another.

The second concept expressed by the English word "judge" is "make a determination," and this is absolutely essential to live a godly life on earth. In fact, Jesus *commands* us to judge in this way:

> John 7:24 (AMP): Be honest in your judgment and do not decide at a glance (superficially and by appearances); but **judge fairly and right-eously.**
>
> TEV: Stop judging by external standards, and **judge by true standards.**

This kind of judging, the *right* kind, is nothing more than testing and evaluating something by comparing it to God's character and His Word, to determine whether or not the thing being judged is good. Paul says it this way:

> I Thessalonians 5:20–21 (AMP): Do not spurn the gifts and utterances of the prophets [do not depreciate prophetic revelations nor despise inspired instruction or exhortation or warning]. ²¹But **test all things carefully [so you can recognize what is good].** Hold firmly to that which is good.
>
> CEB: Don't brush off Spirit-inspired messages, ²¹but **examine everything carefully** and hang on to what is good.
>
> PHILLIPS: . . .never despise what is spoken in the name of the Lord. ²¹**By all means use your judgement,** and hold on to whatever is really good.
>
> MSG: . . .don't stifle those who have a word from the Master. On the other hand, don't be gullible. ²¹**Check out everything,** and keep only what's good.
>
> TLB: Do not scoff at those who prophesy, ²¹but **test everything that is said to be sure it is true,** and if it is, then accept it.
>
> VOICE: Don't downplay prophecies. ²¹**Take a close look at everything, test it,** then cling to what is good.

So judging—in an evaluative, non-condemning way—is indeed required in order to avoid being gullible and easily deceived. This is true not only in the context of evaluating prophecies as shown above, but in *all* of the Christian life.

As a person is learning to move in the gifts of the Spirit and to operate in the ways of the Kingdom, he will likely make some mistakes in the process. Note that this is referring to making honest mistakes in the process of learning something new; this is *not* addressing deliberate, malicious attempts to lead people astray.

As we learn, it is a guided trial-and-error process, whereby we learn ever better how to recognize when it is the Holy Spirit speaking to us, when it is our own thoughts, and when it is the enemy's ideas. The following passage describes this learning process:

> Hebrews 5:12–14 (AMP): For even though by this time you ought to be teaching others, you actually need someone to teach you over again the very first principles of God's Word. You have come to need milk, not solid food. [13]For everyone who continues to feed on milk is obviously inexperienced and unskilled in the doctrine of righteousness (of conformity to the divine will in purpose, thought, and action), for he is a mere infant [not able to talk yet]! [14]But solid food is for full-grown men, for those **whose senses and mental faculties are trained by practice** to discriminate and distinguish between what is morally good and noble and what is evil and contrary either to divine or human law.

Look at v. 14! That is very encouraging: we can get trained by practicing! And also notice the phrase "discriminate and distinguish"—that perfectly describes the non-condemning kind of judging we are commanded to do.

Let's look at a few more translations of v. 14 so we can get a better feel for what it's saying:

> ASV: But solid food is for fullgrown men, even those who **by reason of use have their senses exercised** to discern good and evil.
>
> CJB: But solid food is for the mature, for those **whose faculties have been trained by continuous exercise** to distinguish good from evil.
>
> DLNT: But the solid food is for the mature—the ones **because of habit having their faculties trained** for discernment of both good and evil.
>
> PHILLIPS: "Solid food" is only for the adult, that is, for the man **who has developed by experience** his power to discriminate between what is good and bad for him.

NIRV: Solid food is for those who are grown up. **They have trained themselves** to tell the difference between good and evil. That shows they have grown up.

The reason this verse is so encouraging is that it shows we can all get to the point of maturity by exercising our senses, by continuously training our faculties by diligent exercise, by developing from experience our power to discriminate, and training ourselves to tell the difference between what is of God and what is not. Of course, it will take some diligence, but *maturity is attainable,* and the above verse tells us how to do it. Now *that* is exciting!

Prophetic "Mistakes"

A concept that can appear superficially similar to "false prophecy" but is actually very different, is when a prophetic prediction or promise is given, and reality turns out differently, but the prophecy was still not in error.

Say *what?* How can that be? If a prediction is made but doesn't come true, how can that be anything but a false prophecy? Let's take a look at some passages and see this in action.

Does Isaiah strike you as a false prophet? Let's read one of his prophetic pronouncements:

II Kings 20:1 (NIV): In those days Hezekiah became ill and was at the point of death. The prophet Isaiah son of Amoz went to him and said, "This is what the Lord says: Put your house in order, because **you are going to die; you will not recover.**"

Okay, so Hezekiah is going to die of the illness he was suffering. Then a couple verses later, we read this:

II Kings 20:4–5 (NIV): Before Isaiah had left the middle court, the word of the Lord came to him: [5]"Go back and tell Hezekiah, the leader of my people, 'This is what the Lord, the God of your father David, says: I have heard your prayer and seen your tears; **I will heal you.** On the third day from now you will go up to the temple of the Lord.'"

So Isaiah gave a prophetic word, and then shortly afterwards, gave a prophetic word that said the opposite. Is that allowed? Was Isaiah a false prophet? Hold that thought, and let's look at another example:

> Jonah 3:4 (NLT): On the day Jonah entered the city, he shouted to the crowds: **"Forty days from now Nineveh will be destroyed!"**

But you know the story: Nineveh was *not* destroyed in forty days. What gives? Was Jonah a false prophet too?

The answer is no: Isaiah was not a false prophet, nor was Jonah a false prophet. But how do we explain the fact that they gave prophetic words that were not fulfilled as prophesied? The apparent incongruity evaporates when we realize that God loves us, and the fact that love, by its very nature, is necessarily an act of free will.

In Isaiah's case, the two verses between the passages shown above talk about Hezekiah humbling himself before God and praying intensely. And God answered his prayer. In Jonah's case, the reason that Nineveh was not destroyed is because the people repented of their sin, and turned to God for mercy. And God answered their prayer.

This idea of prophecies turning out differently than prophesied, but still *not* being false prophecies, sticks in the craw of many people: how could such a contradiction be resolved? Similarly, there are many Christians who cannot reconcile God's sovereignty with man's ability to disobey Him. In both cases, it is not a lack of power on God's part, it's just that raw power is not the only factor. Both situations—prophetic utterances that don't come to pass but are still not false prophecies, and reconciling God's sovereignty with man's disobedience—are resolved by taking into consideration man's free will. (For great detail on the topics of God's sovereignty and man's free will, see Book 6: *Free to Choose?*.)

Further clarification of the apparent self-contradiction of non-false prophecy that still didn't turn out as prophesied comes from I Samuel, Jeremiah, and Ezekiel. Let's look at I Samuel first. In this part of the story, David and his men are in a town called Keilah, and Saul wants to go there and capture him:

> I Samuel 23:7–13 (NIV): Saul was told that David had gone to Keilah, and he said, "God has handed him over to me, for David has impris-

oned himself by entering a town with gates and bars." [8]And Saul called up all his forces for battle, to go down to Keilah to besiege David and his men. [9]When David learned that Saul was plotting against him, he said to Abiathar the priest, "Bring the ephod." [10]David said, "O LORD, God of Israel, your servant has heard definitely that Saul plans to come to Keilah and destroy the town on account of me. [11]Will the citizens of Keilah surrender me to him? **Will Saul come down, as your servant has heard?** O LORD, God of Israel, tell your servant." **And the LORD said, "He will."** [12]Again David asked, **"Will the citizens of Keilah surrender me and my men to Saul?" And the LORD said, "They will."** [13]**So David** and his men, about six hundred in number, **left Keilah** and kept moving from place to place. When **Saul** was told that David had escaped from Keilah, **he did not go there.**

Did you see that? When David asked God if Saul would come to Keilah, the Lord said, "He will." *But Saul didn't.* And when David asked God if the men of Keilah would turn him over to Saul, the Lord said, "They will." *But they didn't.* What is going on? Was God wrong? Is God a false prophet? Of course not.

Given the situation as it was when David asked his questions, the Lord's answers were completely correct and accurate. So why didn't things turn out the way God said they would? *Because David used his free will to choose to leave Keilah.* Therefore, the situation changed, and the answers that were applicable to the situation *before* David left were no longer applicable to the situation *after* David left. But God's answers were not wrong when He gave them, because He was answering based on the current circumstances.

And notice the domino effect: Because David chose to leave Keilah, Saul did not go there (but he would have otherwise). And because Saul did not go there, the men of Keilah did not turn David over to him (which they would have otherwise).[1]

---

[1] This realization has enormous implications in other areas of Biblical understanding also: specifically, that God's foreknowledge does *not* imply predestination (in the Calvinistic sense of fated inevitability). See Book 6: *Free to Choose?* for much more discussion on this and related topics.

Now take a look at something God spoke to Jeremiah:

Jeremiah 18:7–10 (ESV): If at any time **I declare** concerning a nation or a kingdom, that **I will pluck up and break down and destroy it,** [8]and if that nation, concerning which I have spoken, turns from its evil, **I will relent** of the disaster that I intended to do to it. [9]And if at any time **I declare** concerning a nation or a kingdom that **I will build and plant it,** [10]and if it does evil in my sight, not listening to my voice, then **I will relent** of the good that I had intended to do to it.

TEV: If at any time **I say that I am going to uproot, break down, or destroy any nation or kingdom,** [8]but then that nation turns from its evil, **I will not do what I said I would.** [9]On the other hand, if **I say that I am going to plant or build up any nation or kingdom,** [10]but then that nation disobeys me and does evil, **I will not do what I said I would.**

Very interesting. This is not simply a human prophet saying this, but God Himself declaring that something will happen, and then it doesn't! Again, was God a false prophet when He gave this warning? Of course not. But even though such messages as Jeremiah is describing come *from* God, they almost certainly come *through* human prophets—rarely is it a deep bass voice rumbling out of the heavens.

The apparent disconnect evaporates when you take into account the free-will acts of the people. In vv. 7–8, the reason God changes His mind, *even though He had already pronounced judgment,* is that the people repented of their sin and turned to God. In vv. 9–10, the reason God changes His mind, *even though He had already pronounced blessing,* is that the people rebelled against God and turned to sin. This is a classic case of "you reap what you sow," in either direction.

Now let's check out Ezekiel's take on this concept:

Ezekiel 33:13–16 (ESV): **Though I say to the righteous that he shall surely live,** yet if he trusts in his righteousness and does injustice, none of his righteous deeds shall be remembered, but in his injustice that he has done **he shall die.** [14]Again, **though I say to the wicked, 'You shall surely die,'** yet if he turns from his sin and does what is just and right, [15]if the wicked restores the pledge, gives back what he has taken by robbery, and walks in the statutes of life, not doing injustice, **he shall surely live;** he shall not die. [16]None of the sins that he has committed shall be remembered against him. He has done what is just and right; he shall surely live.

Again, God pronounces life, and the man dies. Or God pronounces death, and the man lives. Yet God is not a false prophet, nor is He a liar. So how can we resolve the apparent contradiction? By realizing that people made free-will choices after the pronouncements, and those choices changed the situation. In other words, *the prophetic word was correct at the time it was given,* but the man's free-will decision altered the circumstances that warranted the original prophetic word.

Here's another example:

Amos 7:1–6 (HCSB): The Lord God showed me this: **He was forming a swarm of locusts** at the time the spring crop first began to sprout— after the cutting of the king's hay. ²**When the locusts finished eating the vegetation of the land, I said, "Lord God, please forgive!** How will Jacob survive since he is so small?" ³**The Lord relented concerning this.** "It will not happen," He said. ⁴The Lord God showed me this: **The Lord God was calling for a judgment by fire. It consumed the great deep and devoured the land.** ⁵**Then I said, "Lord God, please stop!** How will Jacob survive since he is so small?" ⁶**The Lord relented concerning this.** "This will not happen either," said the Lord God.

Notice that in both of these cases, a judgment God was planning and had already announced to one of His prophets, was aborted when that prophet interceded for the people. This shows us that prophecies about judgments are not necessarily set in stone, but are warnings to God's people of what is threatened (if the enemy is behind it) or justly planned (if God is behind it) *unless prayer and intercession are made to avoid it.* This should be very encouraging to the body of Christ, because prayer really can change God's intentions.

These are simply examples of God acting toward us like we act toward Him. And that, in itself, is simply the law of sowing and reaping:

Psalm 18:25–26 (AMP): With the **kind and merciful** You will show Yourself **kind and merciful,** with an **upright** man You will show Yourself **upright,** ²⁶With the **pure** You will show Yourself **pure,** and with the **perverse** You will show Yourself **contrary.**

Romans 2:9–11 (NIV): There will be **trouble and distress for every human being who does evil:** first for the Jew, then for the Gentile; [10]but **glory, honor and peace for everyone who does good:** first for the Jew, then for the Gentile. [11]For God does not show favoritism.

Galatians 6:7–8 (NASB): Do not be deceived, God is not mocked; for **whatever a man sows, this he will also reap.** [8]For the one who sows to his own **flesh** will from the flesh reap **corruption,** but the one who sows to the **Spirit** will from the Spirit reap **eternal life.**

How this applies to prophetic ministry is obvious. Suppose you prophesy to someone, and after that prophetic pronouncement, the recipient changes his ways (either direction). That is a *new factor* that alters the situation, and may well render the already-given prophecy null and void, *without it having been a false prophecy.* If we disallow this possibility, we are forced to conclude that Isaiah, Jeremiah, Ezekiel, Jonah, Amos, and even God Himself are false prophets.

This is why, whenever we receive a prophetic word, we need to go to God ourselves and pray about whether it applies to us, and then proceed according to what God says. Hence the I Corinthians 14:29 and I Thessalonians 5:20–21, discussed earlier.

Co-Laboring With a Prophetic Word

What does it mean to "co-labor" with a prophetic word? Basically, it means to do our part to cooperate with what God has promised. This is not being presumptuous; it is being obedient. In any two-party convenant, both parties must participate.

Perhaps the most obvious example of this is the taking of the Promised Land. God had promised the land to Israel but they had to go in and actually possess it:

Deuteronomy 6:3 (ESV): Hear therefore, O Israel, and be careful to do them *[God's commands]*, that it may go well with you, and that you may multiply greatly, as the Lord, **the God of your fathers, has promised you, in a land flowing with milk and honey.**

Deuteronomy 10:11 (ESV): "And the Lord said to me *[Moses]*, 'Arise, go on your journey at the head of the people, **so that they may go in and possess the land,** which I swore to their fathers to give them.'"

But there are numerous other examples as well.

Restoring the Rain

After the three and a half years of drought prophesied by Elijah because of the sins of Ahab and Jezebel, Elijah heard the voice of God:

> I Kings 18:1 (NIV): After a long time, in the third year, the word of the Lord came to Elijah: "Go and present yourself to Ahab, and **I will send rain on the land.**"

That sounds rather open-and-shut, doesn't it? God bluntly states, "I will send rain on the land." But notice that God gave Elijah a part to play as well: to "go and present yourself to Ahab."

But even more than that, Elijah felt the need to cooperate with God's promise of rain by intense intercession for that very thing God had promised:

> I Kings 18:42–45 (NIV): So Ahab went off to eat and drink, but **Elijah climbed to the top of Carmel, bent down to the ground and put his face between his knees.** 43"Go and look toward the sea," he told his servant. And he went up and looked. "There is nothing there," he said. **Seven times Elijah said, "Go back."** 44The seventh time the servant reported, "A cloud as small as a man's hand is rising from the sea." So Elijah said, "Go and tell Ahab, 'Hitch up your chariot and go down before the rain stops you.'" 45Meanwhile, the sky grew black with clouds, the wind rose, a heavy rain came on and Ahab rode off to Jezreel.

Why did the prophet pray? After all, God said He would send rain. In modern terminology, Elijah was "leaning into" the word from the Lord—he was co-laboring with the words God had spoken.

Israel Returning from Babylon

Jeremiah saw the nation of Israel (as well as its neighbors) getting more and more corrupt, and he prophetically warned them numerous times that they would reap severe consequences if they didn't repent of their rebellion and idol worship. They didn't (repent) and they did (reap severe consequences): Judah and Jerusalem were conquered, their soldiers were killed, their cities were destroyed, and their civilians were hauled off to Babylon as slaves.

But there was another part to Jeremiah's prophecy:

Jeremiah 25:11 (NIV): This whole country will become a desolate waste-land, and **these nations will serve the king of Babylon seventy years.**

Okay, so that's a done deal, right? After seventy years, Israel would be released to return home; after all, God had said it. But at the end of those seventy years, the prophet Daniel felt the need to co-labor with God and he interceded that God's word come to pass:

Daniel 9:2–3 (NIV): . . .in the first year of his *[Darius's]* reign, I, Daniel, understood from the Scriptures, **according to the word of the Lord given to Jeremiah the prophet, that the desolation of Jerusalem would last seventy years.** ³**So I turned to the Lord God and pleaded with him in prayer and petition,** in fasting, and in sackcloth and ashes.

When the seventy years were up, Daniel didn't just sit back and wait for God's words to come to pass; he actively prayed and interceded for them to be fulfilled. Daniel, too, was "leaning into" the prophetic word.

Using Prophetic Words as Weapons

Paul urged Timothy to take the prophecies that were given to him and use them as weapons to "fight the good fight" of faith:

I Timothy 1:18–19a (NIV): Timothy, my son, I give you this instruction in keeping with the **prophecies once made about you, so that by fol-lowing them you may fight the good fight,** ¹⁹**holding on to faith and a good conscience.**

v. 18, GWORD: Timothy, my child, I'm giving you this order **about the prophecies that are still coming to you: Use these prophecies in faith and with a clear conscience to fight this noble war.**

NLT: Timothy, my son, here are **my instructions for you, based on the prophetic words spoken about you earlier.** May they help you fight well in the Lord's battles.

TEV: Timothy, my child, I entrust to you **this command, which is in accordance with the words of prophecy spoken in the past about you. Use those words as weapons** in order to fight well. . .

So even though Timothy had had prophetic words spoken over him, it was up to him to obey those words and use them to cooperate with God. Timothy was "leaning into" those prophetic words and co-laboring with God in what was spoken over him.

How Often Should We Hear from God?

The idea that God wants to speak to us is exciting, and the realization that we can practice to get better at hearing and recognizing Him is encouraging, but how often can we expect it to happen? Is it realistic to assume that there will be large periods of time—weeks, months, years, decades—between one communication from God and the next?

Actually, no. God has much to say, and He wants to speak to people through those who are listening to Him. Look at how often God spoke to Isaiah:

Isaiah 50:4 (AMP): [The Servant of God says] The Lord God has given Me the tongue of a disciple and of one who is taught, that I should know how to speak a word in season to him who is weary. **He wakens Me** *morning by morning,* **He wakens My ear to hear as a disciple [as one who is taught].**

CSB: The Lord God has given me the tongue of those who are instructed to know how to sustain the weary with a word. **He awakens me** *each morning;* **he awakens my ear to listen like those being instructed.**

ERV: The Lord God gave me the ability to teach, so now I teach these sad people. *Every morning* **he wakes me and teaches me like a student.**

EXB: The Lord God gave me the ability to teach [tongue of a student/learned one] so that I know what to say to make the weak [weary] strong. *Every morning* **he wakes me. He teaches me [awakens my ear] to listen like a student. . .**

GWORD: The Almighty Lord will teach me what to say, so I will know how to encourage weary people. *Morning after morning* **he will wake me to listen like a student.**

Is there a New Testament confirmation on this? Yes:

> I Corinthians 14:26 (CEB): What is the outcome of this, brothers and sisters? ***When you meet together,* each one has a psalm, a teaching, a revelation, a tongue, or an interpretation.** All these things must be done to build up the church.

So this tells us two very important points: *who* may be used in supernatural ministry ("each one"), and *when* it happens ("when you meet together"). So an important question is this: how often did they meet together? We need to know the answer to this in order to know how often we can expect to hear God speaking.

> Acts 2:46–47 (GWORD): The believers had a single purpose and went to the temple **every day.** They were joyful and humble as they ate at each other's homes and shared their food. ⁴⁷At the same time, they praised God and had the good will of all the people. **Every day** the Lord saved people, and they were added to the group.

> Acts 5:42 (GWORD): **Every day** in the temple courtyard and from house to house, they refused to stop teaching and telling the Good News that Jesus is the Messiah.

> Acts 16:5 (GWORD): So the churches were strengthened in the faith and grew in numbers **every day.**

> Acts 17:17 (GWORD): He held discussions in the synagogue with Jews and converts to Judaism. He also held discussions **every day** in the public square with anyone who happened to be there.

> Acts 19:9 (GWORD): But when some people became stubborn, refused to believe, and had nothing good to say in front of the crowd about the way of Christ, he left them. He took his disciples and **held daily discussions** in the lecture hall of Tyrannus.

> Hebrews 3:13 (GWORD): Encourage each other **every day** while you have the opportunity. If you do this, none of you will be deceived by sin and become stubborn.

So we are supposed to hear from God every time we get together with other believers, and the Biblical model is to get together with other believers every day. This doesn't have to be in a formal, institutional church service, but is simply the fellowship of the saints—just doing life together.

How Much Will God Tell Us?

Well, how much should we expect God to tell us? Is He hesitant to tell us things? Actually, He *likes* to tell us things:

Amos 3:7: Surely the Lord God will do **nothing,** but he revealeth his secret unto his servants the prophets.

CEV: **Whatever** the Lord God plans to do, he tells his servants, the prophets.

GWORD: Certainly, the Almighty Lord **doesn't do anything** unless he first reveals his secret to his servants the prophets.

NLT: Indeed, the Sovereign Lord **never does anything** until he reveals his plans to his servants the prophets.

The above Scripture is both thrilling and a bit convicting. It's thrilling because God wants to tells us everything. And then we may realize, "But He's not telling *me* very much. . ." Notice the small but very important phrase above: He tells *His servants* the prophets. Until we submit our lives to Him in the deeper things, we won't be able to handle—bear up under, endure—the weight of glory that would be manifested if He told us all He wants to. We have to submit to His instruction and training just to *survive* the knowledge and understanding He wants to give us.

Like Jesus told the disciples:

John 16:12 (TEV): I have much more to tell you, but **now it would be too much for you to bear.**

So God wants to tell His servants the prophets everything, and as we saw earlier, Moses, the "friend of God," said:

Numbers 11:29b (NASB): "Would that **all** the Lord's people were prophets, that the Lord would put His Spirit upon them!"

So who are God's prophets? Males only? No. As we've seen, women can be used mightily in prophetic ministry, just as men can. Read this, from one of David's psalms:

Psalm 68:11 (KJV): The Lord gave the word: great was the company of **those** that published it.

81

Note the male-dominant bias in the KJV here and some other translations, minimizing and obscuring the fact that it is the women who are carrying the word of the Lord here. Let's look at some other translations:

> AMP: The Lord gives the word [of power]; **the women who bear and publish [the news] are a great host.**
>
> GWORD: The Lord gives instructions. **The women who announce the good news are a large army.**
>
> NET: The Lord speaks; **many, many women spread the good news.**
>
> YLT: The Lord doth give the saying, **The female proclaimers [are] a numerous host.**

So here we have the Lord giving the word of power, instructions, and the good news, and an army—not just a scattered few, but an *army*—of women bear, publish, announce, spread, and proclaim the word of the Lord. (For more discussion on this passage, see the section "The Army of Women" in Book 13: *Arise, My Beloved Daughter.*)

So we can see from the passages above that, like Isaiah said, we can expect God to talk to us *every day.* And, like Amos said, God would like to tell us *everything.* And like Jesus said, He won't tell us more than we can handle. And, like David said, the *women* can proclaim the word of the Lord, just like the men. And many times, as you will discover, it will be on behalf of others. Now *that's* pretty cool.

If we actually wrap our brains around this, and every time, we are intentionally listening for God to speak to us on someone else's behalf, we will realize very quickly that God does indeed speak a lot. And *many* times He speaks to us for the benefit of others—which is the essence of prophetic ministry. If we did that consistently, we would grow in our Christian lives more quickly than we would have imagined.

Chapter 3:

How Do You *Perceive* Prophetic Words?

That is a very good question. Any person receiving a prophetic word for himself or for someone else must perceive it somehow. God has quite a bit of imagination, so unsurprisingly, there are many ways people can perceive it when God reveals something. In other words, God can use any of a large number of approaches when He is communicating with one of His children. This chapter discusses some of these, both from a Scriptural point of view, and from personal experience.

Does Prophecy Still Happen?

In Protestantism, ever since it began about 500 years ago, there has been deliberate stifling and suppression of the idea of hearing directly from God. This unbiblical doctrine that "God doesn't talk directly to people anymore" was invented as a reaction to the Roman Catholic popes claiming to have heard from God, and introducing all kinds of ideas and practices that clearly contradicted Scripture.

In an overreaction to this, the founders of Protestantism blatantly declared that God simply didn't talk directly to people anymore: the *only* way you could hear from God is by reading the Bible. This is not an exaggeration; read the paragraph below, which is the introductory paragraph of the Westminster Confession of Faith, a document that heavily influenced the doctrinal stance of most of the mainline churches:

> Although the light of nature, and the works of creation and providence do so far manifest the goodness, wisdom, and power of God, as to leave men inexcusable; yet are they not sufficient to give that knowledge of God, and of His will, which is necessary unto salvation: therefore it pleased the Lord, at sundry times, and in divers manners, to reveal Himself, and to declare that His will unto His Church; and afterwards, for the better preserving and propagating of the truth, and for the more sure establishment and comfort of the Church against the corruption of the flesh, and the malice of Satan and of the world, *to commit the same wholly unto writing; which maketh the Holy Scripture to be most necessary; those former ways of God's revealing His will unto His people being now ceased.* (Emphasis added)

The subject of this very long sentence is how God declares His will to His church. The italicized part at the end states very plainly that this has now been committed "*wholly* unto writing" and that the ways God used to use to talk to people—speaking directly to a person's spirit by His Holy Spirit—"being now ceased." Since the WCF makes this claim that communication by, and interaction with, the Holy Spirit is "now ceased," this doctrine is called "cessationism."

The particular aspect of cessationism that says the Bible is the *only* place you can get reliable instruction for faith and practice, is called "sola scriptura" (Latin for "by Scripture alone").

The ironic part of this whole idea is that the WCF and the doctrines contained therein were created to "protect" the Bible from the popes and others who overreached their spiritual authority. But in their effort to protect the Bible, they came up with a doctrine that contradicts—it flies in the face of—the main emphasis of the whole Bible: *hearing God and obeying Him.*

In other words, *sola scriptura refutes even itself!* Here's how:

1. Premise: The *only* reliable source of doctrine for faith and practice is the written Word of God.

2. Observation: In many places, the written Word of God commands people to listen to and obey the Spirit of God speaking to them, even up to the time of the Second Coming of Christ.

3. Because Item #2 is in the written Word of God, it must be true and valid.

4. Therefore, Item #1, sola scriptura, *cannot* be true and valid.

Note that the conclusion in Item #4 above is *not* "The Bible isn't a reliable source of doctrine for faith and practice;" the conclusion is "The Bible is not the *only* reliable source of doctrine for faith and practice." The other reliable source is, clearly, the Spirit of God, as shown by God's communication with countless people before the Bible was even written: Adam, Eve, Abel, Enoch, Noah, Abraham, Isaac, Jacob, Joseph, Job, and myriad others unnamed in Scripture. Hence, if you *accept* sola scriptura, its very meaning compels you to *reject* it.

In attempting to adhere to this made-up doctrine of sola scriptura and its encompassing doctrine of cessationism, we are obligated to throw out many things Jesus said.

For example:

Matthew 10:19–20 (BBE): But when you are given up into their hands, do not be troubled about what to say or how to say it: for **in that hour what you are to say will be given to you;** [20]**Because** *it is not you who say the words, but the Spirit of your Father* **in you.**

Mark 13:11 (NIV): Whenever you are arrested and brought to trial, do not worry beforehand about what to say. Just **say whatever is given you at the time, for** *it is not you speaking, but the Holy Spirit.*

Luke 12:11–12 (NIV): "When you are brought before synagogues, rulers and authorities, do not worry about how you will defend yourselves or what you will say, [12]for **the Holy Spirit will teach you** *at that time* **what you should say.**"

Now isn't *that* interesting? That was Jesus prophesying about the *end times,* and He says that the Holy Spirit will still be talking to people!

And how about these?

> John 14:26 (CEV): But the Holy Spirit will come and help you, because the Father will send the Spirit to take my place. *The Spirit will teach you everything* **and will remind you of what I said while I was with you.**

> John 15:26 (TEV): The Helper will come—*the Spirit,* **who reveals the truth about God** and who comes from the Father. I will send him to you from the Father, and he *will speak* **about me.**

> John 16:13–14 (BBE): However, when **he,** *the Spirit* **of true knowledge,** has come, he *will be your guide* **into all true knowledge:** for his words will not come from himself, but whatever has come to his hearing, that he will say: and **he** *will make clear* **to you the things to come.** [14]He will give me glory, because **he will** take of what is mine, and *make it clear* **to you.**

So here we have the Holy Spirit:

- . . .teaching us everything,
- . . .reminding us about what Jesus said,
- . . .revealing truth about God,
- . . .speaking about Jesus,
- . . .guiding us into all true knowledge,
- . . .telling us clearly about the future, and
- . . .telling us what Jesus is saying.

All of that, just from four verses! Perhaps the rumors of the Holy Spirit's "ceasing" have been greatly exaggerated. . .

Remember what God said about Jesus on the Mount of Transfiguration?

> Mark 9:7 (AMP): And a cloud threw a shadow upon them, and a voice came out of the cloud, saying, This is My Son, the [most dearworthy] Beloved One. **Be constantly listening to and obeying Him!**

Wow—"be *constantly* listening to and obeying Him!" Now wouldn't it be silly for God to tell us to "constantly" listen to Jesus if Jesus didn't talk to us anymore? And the fact that we are also supposed to be constantly "obeying" Him shows that He will be giving us commands on a regular basis.

Even though the Reformed doctrines, spearheaded primarily by John Calvin and Martin Luther, say that God doesn't speak directly by His Spirit to people anymore, because God's communication with man has been committed "wholly to Scripture," it's interesting to note what Martin Luther says about John Huss (pronounced "hoose;" it rhymes with "goose," and actually means "goose" in the Bohemian language of his day).

John Huss was burned at the stake 100 years before Luther became well known, and Huss gave a prophecy in a Bohemian prison right before his death, saying that even though he himself would be martyred by being burned at the stake, God would raise up someone else one hundred years later to carry on the ministry, and who would not be burned at the stake. In this prophecy, Huss refers to himself as a goose, apparently for two reasons. Firstly, as mentioned above, Huss meant "goose" in the Bohemian language, and secondly, a goose is not particularly known for wisdom or beauty. In contrast, Huss's successor a century later, he referred to as a swan.

Here is Huss's prophecy:

> "This day you roast a goose; but an hundred years hence you shall hear a swan sing, that you shall not roast."

One hundred years later, Luther claimed very unambiguously that John Huss's prophecy referred to Luther himself. Here's how he stated that:

> "In God's name and calling, I will tread upon the lion and adder, and trample the young lion and dragon under foot. This shall commence during my life, and be accomplished after my death. **St. John Huss prophesied of me,** writing out of prison to Bohemia: 'Now

shall they roast a goose' (for Huss means a goose), but an hundred years hence shall they hear a swan sing, that they shall be forced to endure.' So must it be, God willing." [2]

One wonders how Luther could claim that John Huss prophesied about him, since, according to Reformed doctrine, prophecy didn't happen anymore.

If you are unsure whether or not God still talks to His people today, I would encourage you to read Book 7: *Be Filled with the Spirit.* As mentioned, there are teachings present even today that claim God no longer speaks to His people. The Bible, clearly and repeatedly, says otherwise, but if this is not settled in your heart, seeking to be used in prophetic ministry will be fruitless. If there is any doubt in your heart as to whether God still speaks to people today, please read *Be Filled with the Spirit* before continuing in this book.

The Sufficiency of Scripture

Some people reject the whole idea of prophetic ministry because, allegedly, it flies in the face of "sufficiency of Scripture." In other words, the fact that the prophetic types think prophecy is useful in providing explanation, specific application, exhortation, confirmation, or instruction, shows that they consider the Bible to somehow be "lacking," and that it is not sufficient to answer all our spiritual questions. Hence, the attacks on prophecy in an effort to protect the concept of the Sufficiency of Scripture.

Is this a valid objection? If a prophetic person gives explanation, specific application, exhortation, confirmation, or instruction of some spiritual concept, is he disrespecting the Scriptures by insinuating they aren't "sufficient?"

If the Scripture is completely sufficient, in the sense that it is *never* appropriate to provide explanation, specific application, exhortation, confirmation, or instruction on spiritual topics, then the entire body of Christ should also discontinue all preaching, all Sunday school

---

[2] Doles, Jeff. *Miracles and Manifestations of the Holy Spirit in the History of the Church* (p. 128). Walking Barefoot Ministries. Kindle Edition.

classes, Bible studies, all publication of commentaries, indeed, *all* future books on Biblical topics. Indeed, we should never even *talk* about Biblical concepts because someone might receive an explanation of something, or see how it applies to his life, or be exhorted, or have something confirmed to him, or even (gasp!) *be instructed!*

We certainly can't have *that,* can we? Because, after all, the Bible is "sufficient," is it not? And all of these other activities imply that the Bible is not quite "sufficient," don't they? If the Bible were completely sufficient, we wouldn't need preaching; we wouldn't need Sunday school classes; we wouldn't need Bible studies; we wouldn't need commentaries, we wouldn't need any Bible-based books, we wouldn't even need any spiritually based conversations, correct?

The people who disallow prophetic ministry on the grounds of the "sufficiency of Scripture" are thus disingenuous (although probably unknowingly), because they allow these other ways of clarification, instruction, and exhortation, which are intended to edify the church in the same way as prophetic ministry.

And as mentioned earlier, the Bible itself shows that the Bible itself is not strictly necessary, as we see in the lives of Adam and Eve, Abel, Enoch, Noah, Job, Abraham, Isaac, Jacob, Joseph, and innumerable others who heard the Holy Spirit just fine before *any* of the Bible was written.

Now that the Bible is here, of course, it is a precious gift of God and an extremely valuable tool that we should use regularly and be intimately familiar with. The written Bible is the standard by which we judge prophetic messages (Acts 17:11, I Corinthians 14:29, I Thessalonians 5:19–21, etc.). But God is not *limited* to speaking to us through the Bible. He never was, and He never will be. It *reveals* Him but it does not limit or constrain Him in any way.

But the objection to prophetic ministry stems from the fact that prophecy is not just a *human* decision to do something: it's *God* telling us to say or do something. That is the terrifying part to those who believe God doesn't say anything anymore. But Jesus plainly said that the Holy Spirit would be speaking to us and telling us what to say, even to the end of the age, as we saw above, and as we'll see in even more detail below. This gets back to the intrinsic self-contradiction of *sola scriptura,* where the *scriptura* itself says that the Holy Spirit will still be speaking, even to the end of the age.

Listen to Jesus' heart-cry in this verse:

Matthew 23:37 (NLT): O Jerusalem, Jerusalem, the city that **kills the prophets and stones God's messengers!** How often I have wanted to gather your children together as a hen protects her chicks beneath her wings, but **you wouldn't let me.**

Note that Jesus was grieving over those who, through hardness of heart, killed the prophets that God sent to them. *And these people already had Scripture in written form: the Law of Moses.* But apparently God didn't consider it to be a violation of Sufficiency of Scripture to *also* send prophets to urge people back to living as God had commanded. A very important question that the church needs to ask herself today: Are we *still* killing God's prophets?

The Bible certainly does *not* indicate that prophecy and written Scripture cannot co-exist, nor that either one of these things obviates the need for the other, nor that God has stopped (or ever *will* stop) talking to people. Far from it, as the passages below confirm:

II Kings 17:13 (AMP): Yet the Lord warned Israel and Judah **through all the prophets and all the seers,** saying, Turn from your evil ways and **keep My commandments and My statutes, according to all the Law** which I commanded your fathers and **which I sent to you by My servants the prophets.**

Nehemiah 9:26 (NIV): But they *[the Jews]* were disobedient and rebelled against you; **they put your law behind their backs. They killed your prophets, who had admonished them in order to turn them back to you;** they committed awful blasphemies.

Lamentations 2:9 (NLT): Jerusalem's gates have sunk into the ground. He *[God]* has smashed their locks and bars *[in punishment for their unrepentant sin].* Her kings and princes have been exiled to distant lands; **her law has ceased to exist. Her prophets receive no more visions from the Lord.**

Daniel 9:2–3, 20–23 (NIV): . . .in the first year of his *[Darius']* reign, I, Daniel, **understood from the Scriptures,** according to the word of the

Lord given to Jeremiah the prophet, that the desolation of Jerusalem would last seventy years. [3]So I turned to the Lord God and pleaded with him in prayer and petition, in fasting, and in sackcloth and ashes. . . . [20]While I was speaking and praying, confessing my sin and the sin of my people Israel and making my request to the Lord my God for his holy hill— [21]while I was still in prayer, **Gabriel**, the man I had seen in the earlier vision, **came to me in swift flight about the time of the evening sacrifice.** [22]He instructed me and said to me, "Daniel, I have now come to give you insight and understanding. [23]**As soon as you began to pray, an answer was given, which I have come to tell you, for you are highly esteemed. Therefore, consider the message and understand the vision. . .**"

Matthew 5:18, John 10:27 (NIV): I tell you the truth, until heaven and earth disappear, **not the smallest letter, not the least stroke of a pen, will by any means disappear from the Law** until everything is accomplished. . . . **My sheep listen to my voice;** I know them, and they follow me.

John 2:22: When therefore he was risen from the dead, his disciples remembered that **he had said this unto them; and they believed the scripture, and the word which Jesus had said.**

John 14:26 (NASB): But the Helper, **the Holy Spirit,** whom the Father will send in My name, He **will teach you all things,** and bring to your remembrance all that I said to you.

John 16:13–14 (GWORD): **When the Spirit of Truth comes, he will guide you into the full truth.** He won't speak on his own. **He will speak what he hears and will tell you about things to come.** [14]He will give me glory, because **he will tell you what I say.**

Romans 8:16 (NET): **The Spirit himself bears witness to our spirit** that we are God's children.

I Corinthians 14:29–31 (RSV): **Let two or three prophets speak,** and let the others weigh what is said. [30]**If a revelation is made to another sitting by,** let the first be silent. [31]For **you can all prophesy** one by one, so that all may learn and all be encouraged;

Ephesians 1:17 (NIV): I keep asking that the God of our Lord Jesus Christ, the glorious Father, may give you the Spirit of wisdom and **revelation, so that you may know him better.**

I John 2:27 (NLT): But you have received the Holy Spirit, and he lives within you, so you don't need anyone to teach you what is true. For

the Spirit teaches you everything you need to know, and what he teaches is true—it is not a lie. So **just as he has taught you, remain in fellowship with Christ.**

And as usual, the list above could have been much longer.

Pertaining to what this book talks about, the purpose of prophecy is "edification, exhortation, and comfort" (I Corinthians 14:3), which the church needed then, and the church still needs today. But if prophecy was removed at the end of the first century, God would have removed one of the primary tools with which we can impart said edification, exhortation, and comfort.

In effect, He would be saying to us as carpenters, "I want you to pound those nails, but I'll take away your hammer first. I want you to cut those boards, but I'll take away your saw first. I want you to drive those screws, but I'll take away your screwdriver first." Or, even more apropos, He would be saying to us as warriors: "I want you to go fight the enemy, but I'll take away your, sword, spear, bow and arrows, and shield. Use this sharp stick instead." God is much more courteous and sensible than that; He is not a house divided against Himself.

How to Minister

In the following passage, Paul gives us instruction on how to bless each other and minister to each other in the body of Christ:

> Romans 12:4–8 (NIV): Just as each of us has one body with many members, and these members do not all have the same function, [5]so in Christ we who are many form one body, and each member belongs to all the others. [6]We have different gifts, according to the grace given us. **If a man's gift is prophesying, let him use it in proportion to his faith.** [7]If it is serving, let him serve; if it is teaching, let him teach; [8]if it is encouraging, let him encourage; if it is contributing to the needs of others, let him give generously; if it is leadership, let him govern diligently; if it is showing mercy, let him do it cheerfully.

According to the doctrine of cessationism, prophecy should be removed from this list because allegedly it doesn't happen anymore. But all the others still *are* functional. Why should prophecy be removed from the list of "valid" ministries? What actual Scriptural reason is there for arbitrarily removing a kind of ministry that actually requires God to show up?

If you'll notice, all the other kinds of ministries listed here can be done even without the empowerment of the Holy Spirit (although empowerment by the Holy Spirit would certainly make them more effective). Even heathens can be administrators, or givers, or teachers, or merciful, and so forth. But in order to prophesy, you *have* to hear the Holy Spirit speaking to you at that moment. Cessationism appears to be terrified at that prospect.

Moving On

For the purposes of this book, the above evidence is enough confirmation that the Holy Spirit is still interacting with and speaking to people today (for more in-depth study on this topic, see Book 4: *Gold Dust, Jewels, and More: Manifestations of God?* and Book 7: *Be Filled with the Spirit*), so let's get back to the topic at hand: *how* does God speak to us? It's hard to imagine a better source of prophetic examples than the prophets of the Bible, so we will look at them in some detail.

You may notice that in many of the following examples, it is not clear exactly *which* spiritual gift is being employed to communicate any given message. Specifically, sometimes it's not clear whether a particular bit of information was an example of a word of knowledge, a word of wisdom, a prophetic download, or something else that's not listed in I Corinthians 12:8–10. (It's entirely possible that God could use gifts that were not mentioned in that list; God is bigger than His book. Again, the Bible *reveals* God but it certainly does not *limit* Him.)

Also, be aware that anything that can be perceived as a vision (which can include seeing, hearing, feeling, tasting, smelling, etc.) when you're awake can also be perceived as a dream when you're asleep. For this reason, dreams won't be covered separately because, other than the fact that the perceiver is awake for visions and asleep for dreams, there seems to be no significant difference between them.

Seeing

If you have read Book 1: *Prophets vs. Seers: Is There a Difference?*, you have already seen that prophets—also called seers—often see images. For example, Isaiah opens his book with:

> Isaiah 1:1 (NLT): **These are the visions that Isaiah son of Amoz saw** concerning Judah and Jerusalem. **He saw these visions** during the years when Uzziah, Jotham, Ahaz, and Hezekiah were kings of Judah.

The word "visions" in the above verse is not a figurative or metaphorical term—Isaiah actually *saw* recognizable things that God showed him. Awe-inspiring, even terrifying things, but recognizable nonetheless. He describes some of these things as follows:

> Isaiah 6:1–2 (TEV): In the year that King Uzziah died, **I saw the Lord.** He was **sitting** on his **throne, high** and exalted, and his **robe filled** the whole **Temple.** ²**Around** him **flaming creatures** were **standing,** each of which had **six wings.** Each creature **covered its face** with two wings, and **its body** with two, and used **the other two for flying.**

There are a *lot* of visual information in these two verses. Notice all the things he saw:

- He saw the Lord.
- He saw the throne.
- He saw the location of the Lord, relative to the throne ("sitting on").
- He saw the relative position of the Lord on His throne to other objects in the scene ("high and exalted").
- He saw the Lord's robe.
- He saw the temple.
- He saw the size of the robe, relative to the temple ("filled the whole temple").

And that's just from verse 1! In verse 2, Isaiah sees even more:

- He saw the other beings (seraphim).
- He saw that they were not self-existent, but created beings ("creatures").

- He saw the glory of God emanating from them ("flaming").
- He saw their locations, relative to the Lord ("around him").
- He saw their bodily positions ("standing").
- He saw that their shapes were similar ("each of which").
- He saw *how* they were similar ("six wings," "faces," "bodies").
- He saw that the wings acted in pairs ("with two").
- He saw that each pair of wings had a different function.
- He saw their method of locomotion ("flying").
- He saw that all the creatures used their wings in the same way.
- He saw that one pair of wings covered their faces.
- He saw that another pair of wings covered their bodies.
- He saw that the third pair of wings enabled them to fly.

A moment's reflection shows clearly that these things would have been perceived visually, and not through hearing, taste, smell, or touch.

Many other prophets perceived things visually also; some are listed below, though not in nearly as great a detail as Isaiah's vision above:

I Kings 22:19ff ‖ II Chronicles 18:18 (AMP): And Micaiah said, Hear **the word of the Lord: I saw the Lord** sitting on His throne, and all the host of heaven standing by Him on His right hand and on His left. ‖ [Micaiah] said, Therefore hear **the word of the Lord: I saw the Lord** sitting on His throne, and all the host of heaven standing at His right hand and His left.

Isaiah 2:1 (NASB): **The word which Isaiah** the son of Amoz **saw** concerning Judah and Jerusalem.

Jeremiah 1:11, 13 (BBE): Again the **word of the Lord came** to me, saying, Jeremiah, **what do you see?** And I said, **I see** a branch of an almond-tree. [13]And **the word of the Lord came** to me a second time, saying, **What do you see?** And I said, **I see** a boiling pot, and its face is from the north.

Jeremiah 2:31: O generation, **see ye the word of the Lord.** Have I been a wilderness unto Israel? a land of darkness? wherefore say my people, We are lords; we will come no more unto thee?

Ezekiel 1:1, 4–28 (NASB): In the thirtieth year, in the fourth month on the fifth day, while I was among the exiles by the Kebar River, **the heavens were opened and I saw visions of God.** [4]As **I looked,** behold, a storm wind was coming from the north, a **great cloud** with **fire flashing** forth **continually** and a **bright light** around it, and **in its midst** something like **glowing metal** in the midst of the **fire.** . . . [28]As the **appearance** of the **rainbow in the clouds on a rainy day, so was the appearance of the surrounding radiance.** Such was the **appearance** of the **likeness** of the **glory** of the Lord. And when **I saw it,** I fell on my face and heard a voice speaking.

Ezekiel 2:9ff (AMP): And when **I looked,** behold, a **hand** was **stretched out to me** and behold, a **scroll** of a book was in it. . .

Ezekiel 8:2ff (NIV): **I looked, and I saw** a figure **like that of a man.** From what **appeared** to be his waist down **he was like fire,** and from there up **his appearance** was as **bright as glowing metal.** . .

Ezekiel 10:1ff (CEV): **I saw the dome** that was **above the four winged creatures,** and on it was the **sapphire throne.** . .

Daniel 7:1–2ff (GWORD): In Belshazzar's first year as king of Babylon, **Daniel had a dream. He saw a vision while he was asleep.** He wrote down the main parts of the dream. [2]**In my visions at night I, Daniel, saw** the four winds of heaven stirring up **the Mediterranean Sea.** . .

Amos 1:1 (NLT): This message was given to Amos, a shepherd from the town of Tekoa in Judah. **He received this message in visions** two years before the earthquake, when Uzziah was king of Judah and Jeroboam II, the son of Jehoash, was king of Israel.

Obadiah 1ff (NIV): **The vision** of Obadiah. This is what the Sovereign Lord says about Edom. . .

Micah 1:1 (AMP): **The word of the Lord** that came to Micah of Moresheth in the days of Jotham, Ahaz, and Hezekiah, kings of Judah, **which he *saw* [through divine revelation]** concerning Samaria and Jerusalem.

Nahum 1:1 (NIV): An oracle concerning Nineveh. **The book of the vision** of Nahum the Elkoshite.

Habakkuk 2:2–3 (NASB): Then the Lord answered me and said, "**Record the vision** and inscribe it on tablets, that the one who reads it may run. [3]For **the vision** is yet for the appointed time; it hastens toward the goal and it will not fail. Though it tarries, wait for it; for it will certainly come, it will not delay."

Zechariah 1:7–8ff, 18, 2:1, 4:2, 5:1, 9, 6:1 (RSV): On the twenty-fourth day of the eleventh month which is the month of Shebat, in the second year of Darius, **the word of the Lord** came to Zechariah the son of Berechiah, son of Iddo, the prophet; and Zechariah said, [8]**I saw in the night, and behold, a man riding upon a red horse!** He was **standing among the myrtle trees in the glen**; and **behind him** were **red, sorrel, and white horses**. . . [18]And **I lifted my eyes and saw,** and behold, **four horns!** [2:1]And **I lifted my eyes and saw,** and behold, **a man with a measuring line in his hand!** [4:2]And he said to me, **"What do you see?"** I said, "**I see, and behold, a lampstand all of gold,** with **a bowl on the top** of it, and **seven lamps** on it, with **seven lips on each of the lamps** which are on the top of it." [5:1]Again **I lifted my eyes and saw,** and behold, a **flying scroll!** [9]Then **I lifted my eyes and saw,** and behold, **two women coming forward!** The wind was in **their wings;** they had **wings like the wings of a stork,** and **they lifted up the ephah between earth and heaven.** [6:1]And again **I lifted my eyes and saw,** and behold, **four chariots** came out **from between two mountains;** and the mountains were **mountains of bronze.**

Wow. There are a lot of visions seen by these prophets! And again, many other visually imparted messages were left out. But the number of visions seen by prophets, just in the few Scriptures shown above, make it pretty clear why "seer" is another name for "prophet." Or, equivalently, why a "prophet" is also known as a "seer" (I Samuel 9:9).

Note that in Daniel's example above, he has a vision while asleep. Such a vision is usually called a dream. This is another one of the main modes of God talking to prophetic people, as the passage below shows. The context is right after Aaron and Miriam were getting a little too big for their britches, and thinking they ought to be able to talk for God too. God took a dim view of that:

Numbers 12:6–8 (NLT): And the Lord said to them, "Now listen to what I say: **If there were prophets among you,** I, the Lord, would reveal myself in visions. **I would speak to them in dreams.** [7]But not with my servant Moses. Of all my house, he is the one I trust. [8]I speak to him face to face, clearly, and not in riddles! He sees the Lord as he is. So why were you not afraid to criticize my servant Moses?"

Even though the main point here is that God talked with Moses face to face, God clearly states that He speaks to prophets in dreams.

And especially note the examples from Micaiah, Isaiah, Jeremiah, Amos, and Micah in the list above: they all "saw" the "word" of the Lord. This shows that the "word" of the Lord means simply "the communication, or message" from the Lord. The fact that they "saw" the "word of the Lord" demonstrates that the presence of the word "word" does not restrict the communication to a verbal form.

Trances

For many people in the body of Christ, the word "trance" is an evil word, and only occult and new-age people would be involved with such a thing. Respectable Christians stay away from such dangerous spiritual dabblings.

The belief described in the previous paragraph is indeed common in the body of Christ. The problem is that it's not Scriptural. So let's dig into the Word and see what it says.

Peter

Remember the story of Cornelius? He was a God-fearing Gentile who lived in Caesarea, and to whom an angel appeared. The angel told Cornelius to invite Peter, who was currently in the town of Joppa, about a day's journey away, to come and talk to him and his household. Here's what happened:

> Acts 10:9–17 (NIV): About noon the following day as they were on their journey and approaching the city, **Peter went up on the roof to pray.** [10]He became hungry and wanted something to eat, and **while the meal was being prepared, he fell into a trance.** [11]He saw heaven opened and something like a large sheet being let down to earth by its four corners. [12]It contained all kinds of four-footed animals, as well as reptiles of the earth and birds of the air. [13]Then a voice told him, "Get up, Peter. Kill and eat." [14]"Surely not, Lord!" Peter replied. "I have never eaten anything impure or unclean." [15]The voice spoke to him a second time, "Do not call anything impure that God has made clean." [16]This happened three times, and immediately the sheet was taken back to heaven. [17]While Peter was wondering about the meaning of the vision, the men sent by Cornelius found out where Simon's house was and stopped at the gate.

Notice that Peter fell into a trance. Notice also that he *recognized* that it was a trance, and didn't react negatively to it. He simply watched and listened to the message that was given in the vision he had while in the trance, and pondered what it might mean. Even though he didn't understand the meaning right away, there is no indication that he had any qualms about receiving something from God while in a trance.

If you are a Gentile who is a believer in Jesus as your Redeemer, you can be very grateful that God put Peter into this trance, because it was during this trance that Peter received the revelation that Gentiles were invited into the Kingdom of God *just like Jews.* This was paradigm-shattering for a Jew that had been hearing his whole life that the Jews were God's chosen people. And that wasn't wrong, but it was commonly misunderstood.

Many Jews believed that since *they* were God's chosen people, everybody else was not. But Peter was starting to realize from the vision he received while in the trance, that the Jews were God's chosen people *to bring the rest of the world to God.* Through Jesus, God considered Gentiles to be as "clean" as Jews. As God told Abraham:

> Genesis 12:3 (NIV): I will bless those who bless you, and whoever curses you I will curse; and **all peoples on earth will be blessed through you.**

So Peter and six other guys go to Cornelius' house and heard his story about the angel. Then, as Peter preached to Cornelius and his household, he began to realize the fuller import of that promise to Abraham:

> Acts 10:28, 34–35, 44–46a (NIV): He *[Peter]* said to them: "You are well aware that **it is against our law for a Jew to associate with a Gentile or visit him.** But God has shown me that I should not call any man impure or unclean." . . . Then Peter began to speak: "I now realize how true it is that God does not show favoritism [35]**but accepts men from every nation who fear him and do what is right."** . . . While Peter was still speaking these words, the Holy Spirit came on all who heard the message. [45]The circumcised believers who had come with Peter were astonished that **the gift of the Holy Spirit had been poured out even on the Gentiles.** [46]For they heard them speaking in tongues and praising God.

Since the Jews considered it against their law to associate with Gentiles, this caused quite a stir among the apostles and other Jews, who had not yet had that revelation. So they called Peter on the carpet, and basically demanded, "What were you *thinking?*"

> Acts 11:4–5 (NIV): Peter began and explained everything to them precisely as it had happened: [5]"I was in the city of Joppa praying, and **in a trance I saw a vision.** I saw something like a large sheet being let down from heaven by its four corners, and it came down to where I was."

Again, Peter acknowledges he fell into a trance, and the other Jews, apostles and otherwise, seemed to have no problem with the trance itself, even though the message given was astonishing to them. Peter tells them the whole story and ends with:

> Acts 11:17–18 (NIV): "So if God gave them the same gift as he gave us, who believed in the Lord Jesus Christ, who was I to think that I could oppose God?" [18]When they heard this, they had no further objections and praised God, saying, "So then, God has granted even the Gentiles repentance unto life."

Had the apostles in Jerusalem had the same mindset as so many modern American churchgoers, they would have categorically rejected anything seen in a trance as "of the devil." Again, if you are a Gentile believer in the Messiah, you can be grateful they didn't reject the message simply because it was given in a trance.

Paul

Years after Cornelius and his household got filled with the Holy Spirit, Paul had an adventure. When the Jews wanted to kill Paul for supposedly heretical teaching, some Roman soldiers rescued him from the mob that was beating him. At Paul's request, they gave him permission to address the crowd. Paul then told them his testimony about how he was blinded on the road to Damascus, Jesus spoke to him, and Ananias came and prayed for him for healing and the baptism of the Holy Spirit.

Right after that, Paul continued, he went to the temple in Jerusalem and. . .

> Acts 22:17–21 (NIV): "When I returned to Jerusalem and was praying at the temple, **I fell into a trance** [18]and saw the Lord speaking. 'Quick!' he said to me. 'Leave Jerusalem immediately, because they will not accept your testimony about me.' [19]'Lord,' I replied, 'these men know that I went from one synagogue to another to imprison and beat those who believe in you. [20]And when the blood of your martyr Stephen was shed, I stood there giving my approval and guarding the clothes of those who were killing him.' [21]Then the Lord said to me, 'Go; I will send you far away to the Gentiles.'"

Like Peter's story above, Paul freely talks about how he fell into a trance—as if it were a perfectly normal way to hear from God—and heard Jesus speak to him and give him a warning that saved his life from the mob who already wanted to kill him, even though he had just recently met the Lord. Again, we can be glad Paul heeded the warning Jesus gave him in the trance, because if he hadn't, he would likely have been killed almost before his ministry started, and he wouldn't have written the huge chunk of the New Testament that he ultimately did.

Others

The two mentioned above are certainly not the only two occurrences of trances in the Bible, but they are perhaps the most clear and obvious cases. Several other times in this book, I have mentioned that when the KJV or other translation refers to a "deep sleep," that it was not the sleep of dormancy, but a sleep of the Holy Spirit entirely arresting someone's attention. Many times, other translations of the Bible explain the phenomenon more clearly than the KJV, as we'll see below.

When the Lord overwhelmingly arrests someone's attention like this, and the person goes into a trance, the two most common visible manifestations are:

- The body going completely limp so the person collapses (also known as "falling under the power," or "being slain in the spirit"), and

- The body going rigid so the person freezes like a statue.

When a person freezes as still as a statue, it is perhaps more recognizable as a trance, but it is no less a trance when the person goes limp and simply collapses. This latter situation, of the body going limp and collapsing, is apparently more common; see the "Falling Under the Power" chapter in Book 4: *Gold Dust, Jewels, and More: Manifestations of God?* for numerous Scriptural examples.

Other occurrences of trances in the Bible are shown below; I encourage you to do your own deeper study of these passages, or others, on the topic of trances, comparing how the various translations describe the occurrence:

Numbers 24:4 (HCSB): . . .the oracle of one who hears the sayings of God, who sees a vision from the Almighty, **who falls into a trance with his eyes uncovered.** . .

Numbers 24:16 (BRG): He hath said, which heard the words of God, and knew the knowledge of the most High, which saw the vision of the Almighty, **falling into a trance, but having his eyes open.** . .

I Samuel 19:20 (VOICE): . . .so he sent officers to arrest him and bring him back. But when they came, they found **a group of prophets in a prophetic trance** with Samuel standing and leading them, and the Spirit of the True God entered Saul's officers so that they, too, were caught up and prophesied.

I Samuel 19:23 (VOICE): As Saul traveled, **the Spirit of God entered him, and he, too, fell into a constant prophetic trance.** When he reached Naoith in Ramah. . .

Jeremiah 31:26 (AMP): Thereupon I [Jeremiah] awoke and looked, and **my [trancelike] sleep was sweet** [in the assurance it gave] to me.

Daniel 8:18 (LEB): And when he spoke with me **I fell into a trance with my face to the ground,** and he touched me and made me stand on by feet.

Daniel 10:8 (WYC): But I was left alone, and I saw this great vision, and strength dwelled not in me; but also my likeness was changed in me, and **I was stark (and I was made stiff, or rigid, like in a trance), and I had not in me anything of strengths.**

Daniel 10:9 (NRSV): Then I heard the sound of his words; and **when I heard the sound of his words, I fell into a trance, face to the ground.**

Revelation 1:10 (CEB): **I was in a Spirit-inspired trance on the Lord's day,** and I heard behind me a loud voice that sounded like a trumpet.

Revelation 4:2 (CEB): **At once I was in a Spirit-inspired trance** and I saw a throne in heaven, and someone was seated on the throne.

Revelation 17:3 (CEB): **Then he brought me in a Spirit-inspired trance** to a desert. There I saw a woman seated on a scarlet beast that was covered with blasphemous names. It had seven heads and ten horns.

Revelation 21:10 (CEB): **He took me in a Spirit-inspired trance** to a great, high mountain, and he showed me the holy city, Jerusalem, coming down out of heaven from God.

It's unfortunate that so many modern-day American churchgoers know so little about the Bible that they think trances are the creation of the devil. Satan cannot *create* anything; he can only take a genuine and valuable thing and try to corrupt, distort, and counterfeit it for his own purposes. But as we can see from the Scriptures above, God invented the trance; Satan only tried to co-opt it because as a rule, the church abdicated its passion and hunger for God and has gotten so lukewarm that trances rarely happen anymore. However, there is a remnant—praise God—and His people are again starting to burn with intense desire for God, and He is again answering with more and more supernatural manifestations, including visions during trances. Hallelujah!

Ways of Expressing It

Some of the other phrases, from other translations of the Bible, that can express the idea of the trance are as follows. Not only do these other ways of expressing the idea elaborate more on the functions and attributes of trances, but will also alert you to understand the concept being described when reading a translation of the Bible that uses any of these phrases instead of the word "trance" itself:

Numbers 24:4 (CEB): The oracle of one who hears God's speech, who perceives the Almighty's visions, who **falls down** with eyes uncovered.

I Samuel 19:20 (ISV): Saul sent messengers to take David, and they saw a group of prophets caught up in **prophetic ecstasy,** with Samuel standing beside them leading them. Then the Spirit of God came on Saul's messengers, and they also were caught up in **prophetic ecstasy.**

Acts 10:10 (CEB): He [Peter] became hungry and wanted to eat. While others were preparing the meal, he had a **visionary experience**.

DARBY: And he became hungry and desired to eat. But as they were making ready **an ecstasy came upon him**. . .

ERV: He was hungry and wanted to eat. But while they were preparing the food for Peter to eat, he **had a vision**.

HCSB: Then he became hungry and wanted to eat, but while they were preparing something, he **went into a visionary state**.

JUB: and he became very hungry and would have eaten; but while they made ready, he **fell into a rapture of understanding**. . .

TPT: He was hungry and wanted to eat, but while lunch was being prepared he fell into a trance and **entered into another realm**.

WYC: And when he was hungered [And when he hungered], he would have eaten. But while they made ready, **a ravishing of the Spirit felled on him [an excess of soul, or ravishing of Spirit, fell on him]**. . .

Daniel 8:18 (EXB): While Gabriel [he] was speaking, I fell into a **deep sleep [trance]** with my face on the ground. Then he touched me [strengthening him] and lifted me to my feet [made me stand in my place].

AMPC: Now as he [Gabriel] was speaking with me, I **fell stunned and in deep unconsciousness** with my face to the ground; but he touched me and set me upright [where I had stood].

DARBY: Now, as he was speaking with me, I **was in a deep stupor**, with my face toward the ground. And he touched me, and set me up where I had stood.

GWORD: As he spoke to me, I **fainted** facedown on the ground, but he touched me and made me stand up.

GNT: While he was talking, I **fell to the ground unconscious**. But he took hold of me, raised me to my feet. . .

OJB: Now while he was speaking with me, I **swooned** upon my face toward the ground, but he touched me, and made me stand upright.

Daniel 10:8 (CSB): I was left alone, looking at this great vision. **No strength was left in me; my face grew deathly pale, and I was powerless.**

CEB: So I was left alone to see this great vision all by myself. **All my strength left me. My energy was sapped, and I couldn't stay strong.**

ICB: So I was left alone, watching this great vision. **I lost my strength. My face turned white like a dead person, and I was helpless.**

Revelation 1:10 (AMPC): I **was in the Spirit [rapt in His power]** on the Lord's Day, and I heard behind me a great voice like the calling of a war trumpet. . .

CEV: On the Lord's day **the Spirit took control of me,** and behind me I heard a loud voice that sounded like a trumpet.

EXB: On the Lord's day [probably a reference to the first day of the week, Sunday, when Christians met for worship] I was in the Spirit [or spirit; **a state of deep spiritual communion with God**], and I heard a loud voice behind me that sounded like a trumpet [trumpet blasts often precede a divine appearance or speech; Ex. 19:16, 19].

GNV: And I was **ravished in spirit** on the Lord's day, and heard behind me a great voice, as it had been of a trumpet. . .

GWORD: I **came under the Spirit's power** on the Lord's day. I heard a loud voice behind me like a trumpet. . .

PHILLIPS: On the Lord's day I **knew myself inspired by the Spirit,** and I heard from behind me a voice loud as a trumpet-call saying. . .

NABRE: I was **caught up in spirit** on the Lord's day and heard behind me a voice as loud as a trumpet. . .

NIRV: The Holy Spirit **gave me a vision** on the Lord's Day. I heard a loud voice behind me that sounded like a trumpet.

TPT: I was **in the spirit realm** on the Lord's day, and I heard behind me a loud voice sounding like a trumpet. . .

So there are *many* ways to express the concept of "trance," some more clear than others.

Translational Bias

When reading about supernatural manifestations of the Holy Spirit in certain verses in some translations of the Bible, it's interesting—and a bit distressing—to see the translators' discomfort and lack of familiarity with the miraculous. The nervousness and disapproval comes across loud and clear. Read the translations below, and note the anti-supernatural "spin" the translators put into their translations. This "spin" communicates—whether deliberately or not—the idea that pursuing the miraculous requires, or perhaps *leads to,* psychological madness or emotional instability.

Unfortunately, it's this kind of fear and suspicion that has kept the supernatural away from many churches for so long that their people don't even recognize the Holy Spirit when He shows up. In the following passages, you might notice a disturbing similarity to the verbiage the liberal media applies to the moves of God they don't understand (for examples, see the section "The Words of the World" in Book 7: *Be Filled with the Spirit*):

> I Samuel 19:20 (EXB): So he *[Saul]* sent messengers [agents; soldiers] to capture him *[David]*. But they met a group of prophets prophesying [**in a frenzy**], with Samuel standing there leading [in charge of] them. So the Spirit of God entered [came upon] Saul's men, and they also prophesied [**fell into a frenzy**].

> MSG: Saul was told, "David's at Naioth in Ramah." He immediately sent his men to capture him. They saw a band of prophets prophesying with Samuel presiding over them. Before they knew it, the Spirit of God was on them, too, and they were **ranting and raving** right along with the prophets!

> I Samuel 19:23 (MSG): As he headed out for Naioth in Ramah, the Spirit of God was on him, too. All the way to Naioth he was caught up in a **babbling** trance! He ripped off his clothes and lay there **rambling gibberish** before Samuel for a day and a night, stretched out naked. People are still talking about it: "Saul among the prophets! Who would have guessed?"

Are we really to believe that if the Holy Spirit comes on us more powerfully than we approve of, or if we prophesy, that we'll "fall into a frenzy," and start "ranting and raving," "babbling," and "rambling gibberish?" Seriously? Fortunately, such disapproving translations of God's Word are a very tiny percentage of verses, in a very tiny percentage of the translations. But such editorializing reveals the bias that even Bible translators can fall prey to if they're not careful.

Spiritual Interaction

Within a vision, there is often the ability to take some action or move around as a matter of choice; in other words, as a volitional, free-will decision, to interact with some spiritual being or object or to move from one place to another in a 3D vision that God gives. These are all commands of God, but nonetheless, the prophets had the option (foolish though it would have been) to disobey God. Fortunately, they didn't.

Here are some examples:

Jeremiah 25:15–17 (NIV): This is what the Lord, the God of Israel, said to me: "**Take from my hand this cup filled with the wine of my wrath and make all the nations to whom I send you drink it.** [16]When they drink it, they will stagger and go mad because of the sword I will send among them." [17]**So I took the cup from the Lord's hand and made all the nations to whom he sent me drink it. . .**

Ezekiel 3:1–2 (NIV): And he said to me, "Son of man, **eat what is before you, eat this scroll;** then go and speak to the house of Israel." [2]**So I opened my mouth,** and he gave me the scroll to eat.

Ezekiel 8:8–10 (GWORD): He said to me, "Son of man, **dig through the wall.**" **So I dug through the wall,** and I saw a door. [9]He said to me, "**Go in, and see** the wicked, disgusting things that the people of Israel are doing here." [10]**So I went in and looked.** I saw that the walls were covered with drawings of every kind of crawling creature, every kind of disgusting animal, and all the idols in the nation of Israel.

Ezekiel 37:4, 7, 9–10 (NASB): Again He said to me, "**Prophesy over these bones** and say to them, 'O dry bones, hear the word of the Lord.'" [7]**So I prophesied** as I was commanded; and as I prophesied, there was a noise, and behold, a rattling; and the bones came together, bone to its bone. [9]Then He said to me, "**Prophesy to the breath, prophesy, son of man,** and say to the breath, 'Thus says the Lord God, "Come from the four winds, O breath, and breathe on these slain, that they come to life."'" [10]**So I prophesied** as He commanded me, and the breath came into them, and they came to life and stood on their feet, an exceedingly great army.

[To hear this passage set to music, listen to the song *Speak to These Bones* on the album *I Have Not Forgotten You*, or scan the QR code at right.]

So even during a dream or a vision, it's not necessarily like passively watching a movie. Especially when God's communication is prophetic in nature, there is often interaction with God (or angels) in the spiritual realm.

Persistence

The writer of Hebrews says that without faith it is impossible to please God, and that God is a rewarder of those who "diligently" seek him (11:6). And we saw in the previous chapter that we are to "eagerly" desire spiritual gifts, and *especially* the gift of prophecy.

How does diligently seeking God and eagerly desiring spiritual gifts apply in the context of prophetic ministry?

> Luke 11:5–13 (AMP): And He said to them, Which of you who has a friend will go to him at midnight and will say to him, Friend, lend me three loaves [of bread], ⁶For a friend of mine who is on a journey has just come, and I have nothing to put before him; ⁷And he from within will answer, Do not disturb me; the door is now closed, and my children are with me in bed; I cannot get up and supply you [with anything]? ⁸I tell you, although he will not get up and supply him anything because he is his friend, **yet because of his shameless persistence and insistence he will get up and give him as much as he needs.**

So in this parable, Jesus is implying that persistence in asking pays off. Okay, fine, but what does that have to do with our relationship with God? Let's keep reading:

> ⁹So I say to you, Ask **and keep on asking** and it shall be given you; seek **and keep on seeking** and you shall find; knock **and keep on knocking** and the door shall be opened to you. ¹⁰For everyone who asks **and keeps on asking** receives; and he who seeks **and keeps on seeking** finds; and to him who knocks **and keeps on knocking**, the door shall be opened.

Notice in the Amplified Version (and some other translations of the Bible as well), the Greek verb tense comes across much more clearly: "ask, *and keep on asking;*" "seek, *and keep on seeking;*" "knock, *and keep on knocking.*" The verbs are not implying "Just do it once, and you're done." Jesus is definitely encouraging persistence in prayer. Then Jesus makes it more personal to those in his audience, by having them consider what their own actions would be in a certain situation:

> ¹¹What father among you, if his son asks for a loaf of bread, will give him a stone; or if he asks for a fish, will instead of a fish give him a serpent? ¹²Or if he asks for an egg, will give him a scorpion?

Using the fathers in His audience as examples, Jesus points out that, *of course,* any loving father would give his children food if they needed it. It is significant that Jesus uses foods for His examples, as we will see below. He then concludes His teaching:

> [13]If you then, evil as you are, know how to give good gifts [gifts that are to their advantage] to your children, how much more will your heavenly Father give the Holy Spirit to those who ask and continue to ask Him!

Notice that the definition of "good gifts" is "gifts that are to their advantage." Here, the Holy Spirit is compared to food—that is, something absolutely necessary for life on earth—so of course the Father will give the Holy Spirit to His beloved children when they ask. And, of course, the Holy Spirit is the One who speaks the Father's words through us prophetically, which is why Jesus made another statement equating God's words coming to us with our necessary food:

> Matthew 4:4 (NIV): Jesus answered, "It is written: 'Man does not live on bread alone, but **on every word that comes from the mouth of God.**'"

Hearing God's word, then, is essential to life. And speaking God's word to others, to minister life to them, is even better. Hence, Paul's exhortation to "seek earnestly the best gifts, *especially* that you may prophesy" (I Corinthians 14:1).

Now keeping the above in mind, let's look at an example of this kind of diligence in seeking God in the context of prophetic ministry. When God gives us a little, we need to "lean into it" and seek for more, as Daniel did. Like the Amplified Version used above, the New American Standard Bible renders the Hebrew verb tenses much better than the King James, so let's read about when Daniel had one of his prophetic visions:

> Daniel 7:2 (NASB): Daniel said, "**I was looking in my vision** by night, and behold, the four winds of heaven were stirring up the great sea."
>
> Daniel 7:4 (NASB): The first was like a lion and had the wings of an eagle. **I kept looking** until its wings were plucked, and it was lifted up from the ground and made to stand on two feet like a man; a human mind also was given to it.

Daniel 7:6 (NASB): After this I kept looking, and behold, another one, like a leopard, which had on its back four wings of a bird; the beast also had four heads, and dominion was given to it.

Daniel 7:7 (NASB): After this I kept looking in the night visions, and behold, a fourth beast, dreadful and terrifying and extremely strong; and it had large iron teeth. It devoured and crushed and trampled down the remainder with its feet; and it was different from all the beasts that were before it, and it had ten horns.

Daniel 7:9 (NASB): I kept looking until thrones were set up, and the Ancient of Days took His seat; His vesture was like white snow and the hair of His head like pure wool. His throne was ablaze with flames, its wheels were a burning fire.

Daniel 7:11 (NASB): Then I kept looking because of the sound of the boastful words which the horn was speaking; I kept looking until the beast was slain, and its body was destroyed and given to the aburning fire.

Daniel 7:13 (NASB): I kept looking in the night visions, and behold, with the clouds of heaven One like a Son of Man was coming, and He came up to the Ancient of Days and was presented before Him.

Daniel 7:21–22 (NASB): I kept looking, and that horn was waging war with the saints and overpowering them [22]until the Ancient of Days came and judgment was passed in favor of the saints of the Highest One, and the time arrived when the saints took possession of the kingdom.

Do you get the feeling that Daniel was persistent in his desire to see all that God had for him? Let us be like Daniel, who was open to hearing from God, both for his own benefit and for prophetic ministry to others. Let us be like Daniel who was gracious, honoring, and respectful to all people, even when he had a stern, corrective prophecy from God for them. Let us be like Daniel who, when God started showing him something, he diligently kept looking and kept looking and kept looking (à la Hebrews 5:14). Let us be like Daniel, and not be so dazzled by what we see in the Spirit that we get distracted, or fearful, and fail to get the message that God is trying to communicate.

The more we deliberately look for God and expect Him to speak, the more clearly He will manifest himself to us: Samuel first only *heard* the voice of God, but after Eli told him that it was God was talking to him and that He would likely do it again, God came and "stood there" before him and spoke:

> I Samuel 3:10 (NIV): **The Lord came and stood there,** calling as at the other times, "Samuel! Samuel!" Then Samuel said, "Speak, for your servant is listening."

And this certainly was not the only time the Lord visited Samuel in physical form:

> I Samuel 3:21 (AMP): And **the Lord continued to appear** in Shiloh, for the Lord revealed Himself to Samuel in Shiloh by the word of the Lord.
>
> CJB: **Adonai continued appearing in Shiloh,** for Adonai revealed himself to Sh'mu'el in Shiloh by the word of Adonai.
>
> CEV: **The Lord often appeared** to Samuel at Shiloh and told him what to say.
>
> EXB: And **the Lord continued to show himself [appear; manifest himself]** at Shiloh [1:3], and he showed [revealed] himself to Samuel through his word.
>
> NIV: **The Lord continued to appear** at Shiloh, and there he revealed himself to Samuel through his word.

Such Scriptures sure increase the longing in your heart for the manifest presence of God, don't they?

Personal Examples of Seeing

Regularly serving in the prophetic rooms of the Healing Rooms ministry, the most common way the Lord gives me "words" for people (remember, "words" are not necessarily verbal, but simply "something communicated") is by giving me pictures.

In the prophetic rooms, the people coming in for words are not allowed to speak before we hear from God and give them all that we feel God has for them at the moment—we don't want their conversation to bias us or distract us from what God is telling us. After the words have been given by everyone on the ministry team (and recorded for later re-listening), then the people can tell us things if they want; since the words have already been given, it's too late to bias or distract us from what God wanted us to say.

In most cases, but not all cases, the meaning comes along with the picture. Therefore—using the concepts mentioned in "Flip It, and Flip It Good" above—in most cases, but not all cases, God provides the revelation and the interpretation. Of course, I must provide the communication; that's my role in that ministry, and I must present it lovingly and truthfully.

Here's one example: In the fall of 2016, a man came in and sat down, and I immediately got a picture of him coming out of a cave into brilliant sunlight. The light was so bright, he had to cover his eyes and wait for them to become accustomed to the brightness. There seemed to be great emphasis on the contrast between the darkness of the cave, and the brightness of the sunlight he stepped into.

After I and everyone else finished giving our words, and we were chatting afterwards, he said, "You guys have no idea who I am, do you?" We said no, and he told us that he was a pastor, and had recently moved into a nearby town. It turns out he was a prophet as well, and was just at the end of a six-year wilderness of recovery after having been cast out of his previous fellowship because they were uncomfortable (shades of Matthew 23:37?) with prophetic ministry. He said he had been feeling, for the past six years, like Elijah in the cave when Jezebel was threatening him. He had envisioned himself in that cave almost every day. Then he excitedly added that just recently, he started to feel like his cave time was over. "One of the reasons I came here was to find out if this ministry was legit. And you guys are the real deal!"

Here's another example: For another man, I saw (this was in the
spring of 2017) an image of the road
stretched out before him, but it was
strewn with boulders and other de-
bris, making passage extremely slow
and difficult. Then I saw Jesus in a
road-maintenance truck with a V-
shaped snowplow blade on the front,

barreling down the road, effortlessly bouncing all the obstructions out
of the way, leaving the road clear, smooth, and uncluttered. The man,
who had for some time been having a difficult time in life in general,
was greatly relieved at the image because of the obvious symbolism. But
it was made all the more encouraging and personalized because he himself used to drive a road-maintenance truck with a V-shaped snowplow
blade in the front. Of course, we didn't know that until after the
prophetic session was done, so it was encouraging to the prophetic team
as well.

Another example, also in
2017: Another man who had
gotten rather discouraged at
recent events, came in for a
prophetic word. I got a picture of him standing in the
bow of a sailboat that was
being blown swiftly (but not
dangerously) through the

water. The wind was blowing through his hair, he had a big smile on
his face, and he was just enjoying the whole situation immensely. The
obvious symbolism was encouraging to him. But again, it was made
even more encouraging and personalized because of the fact that he,
until recently, had lived on the East Coast of the United States, and he
used to race sailboats quite a lot and quite successfully. As in the previous example, we didn't know his sailboat connection until after the
prophetic session was done, so it was encouraging to the prophetic team
as well.

Another example, from the summer of 2017: during prophetic-room ministry to a middle-aged woman, I saw a raven. In Biblical imagery, ravens are often associated with providing food (for a discussion of this and other bird-related symbolism in the  Bible, see the "Feathers" chapter of Book 4: *Gold Dust, Jewels, and More: Manifestations of God?*), so it felt to me like she would be involved in providing food for people. And I also had a feeling (see "Impressions," below), that the food would be for children, so I mentioned that too: that she would be involved with providing food for children. She smiled real big, but didn't say anything until we were all done, and then referred to my comment about providing food for children. She then added, "I'm a school lunch lady; I work in the cafeteria. I give food to hundreds of kids every day."

One final example, from November 2017: We were ministering to a young lady who had never been to the Healing Rooms or Prophetic Rooms before. In fact, her mother insisted that she come, even though the young lady didn't want to. Another  member of the prophetic team mentioned something about a flower, and I saw a columbine—Colorado's state flower. I got the image, but I didn't know what it meant. I had the revelation, but didn't receive the interpretation, so I told her what I saw, and that I didn't know why it was significant. We continued to give her prophetic words for the next several minutes, and when we were done, she grinned and said, "Columbines are my favorite flower—I draw them all the time. It's the only flower I ever draw, and I've been drawing them since I was a little kid. All my school notebooks have columbines doodled all over them!"

Note that in all of the personal examples above, the message was imparted as an image dropped into my spirit. These were not open-eyed visions where my perception of earthly surroundings was completely replaced by a 3D technicolor perception of heaven. As of this writing, I haven't yet had one of those, but I believe it will happen. After all, we are commanded to come boldly to the throne of grace (Hebrews 4:16), and I don't think that is merely metaphorical language—I believe it means exactly what it says. It is the birthright of every believer to talk to God face to face. Moses did (Exodus 33:11, Numbers 12:6–8, Deuteronomy 34:10), and he was under an inferior covenant (Hebrews 8:6)!

I mentioned above that in most cases, but not all cases, the meaning comes along with the picture. But that is not always the case. In one situation just last week (as of the writing of this paragraph in July 2017), I got a picture for a woman of a scene from Psalm 23. The picture was that of Jesus preparing a table for her in the presence of her enemies. Since people are not our enemies, but the devil and his cohorts are (Ephesians 6:12–18), the image was of demons surrounding Jesus and the woman, but completely powerless to do anything about the fact that she was having lunch with Jesus.

I felt there was something deeper than just the obvious symbolism, but I never received understanding on that deeper part. So I just described what I saw and recommended that she take it to the Lord. In this case, all I had was the revelation; I didn't have the interpretation, so I couldn't communicate the interpretation. But I did have the original image, so that is what I communicated, and I encouraged her to seek the Lord herself to find out the further revelation that God had for her.

Hearing

Prophetic people can also *hear* things that God wants to communicate. Sometimes it's with the physical ear, indistinguishable from a human voice, and sometimes it's clearly an internal voice that may seem alarmingly loud, but is distinctly internal only.

God's Voice: Audible

A Scriptural example of someone who heard God in an audible voice—a voice that sounded so natural the hearer thought it was a person calling him—is Samuel. When Samuel was a boy, he had been dedicated to the service of the Lord and was living in the temple, being trained by Eli the priest. One night, when he was in bed. . .

> I Samuel 3:3–11 (CEB): God's lamp hadn't gone out yet, and Samuel was lying down in the LORD's temple, where God's chest was. ⁴The LORD called to Samuel. "I'm here," he said. ⁵Samuel hurried to Eli and said, "I'm here. You called me?" "I didn't call you," Eli replied. "Go lie down." So he did. ⁶Again the LORD called Samuel, so Samuel got up, went to Eli, and said, "I'm here. You called me?" "I didn't call, my son," Eli replied. "Go and lie down." ⁷(Now Samuel didn't yet know the LORD, and the LORD's word hadn't yet been revealed to him.) ⁸A third time the LORD called Samuel. He got up, went to Eli, and said, "I'm here. You called me?" Then Eli realized that it was the LORD who was calling the boy. ⁹So Eli said to Samuel, "Go and lie down. If he calls you, say, 'Speak, LORD. Your servant is listening.'" So Samuel went and lay down where he'd been. ¹⁰Then the LORD came and stood there, calling just as before, "Samuel, Samuel!" Samuel said, "Speak. Your servant is listening." ¹¹The LORD said to Samuel, "I am about to do something in Israel that will make the ears of all who hear it tingle!"

Verse 7 in the NLT says something fascinating: "Samuel did not yet know the LORD *because* he had never had a message from the LORD before." It might be a good question to ask ourselves, "If I've never had a message from God, do I yet know Him?" Apparently God considers it to be pretty important for us to listen to Him.

But Jesus-followers everywhere can breathe a sigh of relief, because the very fact that you are saved shows that you have heard the voice of God. Check out this passage:

> John 6:44–45 (NIV): No one can come to me unless the Father who sent me draws him, and I will raise him up at the last day. ⁴⁵It is written in the Prophets: 'They will all be taught by God.' **Everyone who listens to the Father and learns from him comes to me.**

As you know, Samuel goes on to be a powerful prophet/seer/man of God in Israel. So as the example above shows, sometimes God's voice sounds just like a human voice. But in other cases, God's voice is much less attenuated, and its power is intimidating at least, and even overwhelming, as Isaiah experienced. Continuing the description of his vision started above, where he saw so much, let us continue with what he heard:

> Isaiah 6:3–8 (NLT): They *[the seraphim]* were **calling out** to each other, "Holy, holy, holy is the Lord of Heaven's Armies! The whole earth is filled with his glory!" ⁴**Their voices shook the Temple** to its foundations, and the entire building was filled with smoke. ⁵Then I said, "It's all over! I am doomed, for I am a sinful man. I have filthy lips, and I live among a people with filthy lips. Yet I have seen the King, the Lord of Heaven's Armies." ⁶Then **one of the seraphim flew** to me with a burning coal he had taken from the altar with a pair of tongs. ⁷He touched my lips with it and **said,** "See, this coal has touched your lips. Now your guilt is removed, and your sins are forgiven." ⁸**Then I heard the Lord asking, "Whom should I send as a messenger to this people? Who will go for us?"** I said, "Here I am. Send me."

Here Isaiah heard the voices of the seraphim: first, worshiping the Lord, and then, addressing himself. And then he heard God Himself speaking to him. There appears to be no question at all that this was God talking to him after the seraph cleansed his lips with the coal. And notice the power of their voices! The voices of the seraphim "shook the temple to its foundations"—that sounds downright intimidating.

So here again, information, instruction, commissioning, and more can be imparted to people through *hearing* God, in addition to seeing God. Such things are inherently prophetic in nature, and when given for the sake of someone else than the prophetic person, that impartation of wisdom, commissioning, or whatever, is a prophetic utterance.

King David also had some experience with the voice of the Lord, and it made a profound impression on him. Meditate on the descriptions David uses to communicate the power in God's voice:

> Psalm 29:3–9 (NIV): The voice of the Lord is over the waters; the God of glory **thunders,** the Lord **thunders** over the mighty waters. ⁴The voice of the Lord is **powerful;** the voice of the Lord is **majestic.** ⁵The voice of the Lord **breaks the cedars;** the Lord **breaks in pieces the**

cedars of Lebanon. ⁶He makes Lebanon skip like a calf, Sirion like a young wild ox. ⁷The voice of the Lord **strikes with flashes of lightning.** ⁸The voice of the Lord **shakes the desert;** the Lord shakes the Desert of Kadesh. ⁹The voice of the Lord **twists the oaks and strips the forests bare.** And in his temple all cry, "Glory!"

He also adds this tidbit in Psalm 46:

Psalm 46:6 (AMP): The nations raged, the kingdoms tottered and were moved; **He uttered His voice, the earth melted.**

The Lord: *not* someone to trifle with.

Other prophets also heard the voice of God speaking: sometimes God was speaking: to them, sometimes to others, and the prophets simply "overheard."

Daniel 8:16 (NASB): And I heard the voice of a man between the banks of Ulai, and he called out and said, "Gabriel, give this man an understanding of the vision."

In this case, the voice sounded like that of a man, but because Daniel was in the middle of a vision, it was clearly not a mere human speaking. This is one of the cases of deliberate "overhearing:" Daniel was not being addressed here; God was actually talking to Gabriel. Then later, in another vision, Daniel sees God and hears His voice again:

Daniel 10:6, 9 (NIV): His body was like chrysolite, his face like lightning, his eyes like flaming torches, his arms and legs like the gleam of burnished bronze, and **his voice like the sound of a multitude.** ⁹**Then I heard him speaking, and as I listened to him, I fell into a deep sleep,** my face to the ground.

Note that when Daniel fell into a "deep sleep" upon hearing God's voice, it was not the deep sleep of slumber brought on by weariness; it was the deep sleep of overwhelmed-ness brought on by an overload of God's glory, and it is also known as being slain in the spirit. For a great deal of detail on this topic, including more on this particular passage, see the "Falling Under the Power" chapter of Book 4: *Gold Dust, Jewels, and More: Manifestations of God?*.

The prophets Joel and Amos also had a healthy respect for the power of the voice of God:

Joel 3:16 (NASB): The **Lord roars from Zion and utters His voice from Jerusalem, and the heavens and the earth tremble.** But the Lord is a refuge for His people and a stronghold to the sons of Israel.

Amos 1:2 (AMP): And he *[Amos]* said, **The Lord roars out of Zion and utters His voice from Jerusalem; then the pastures of the shepherds mourn and the top of [Mount] Carmel dries up.**

From the above Scriptures, we can clearly see that God communicates with people also by speaking words that people hear, whether that hearing is external and heard with one's physical ears, or internal and heard directly in one's spirit. When that content of that communication is for someone else, an utterance imparting that content would be prophetic in nature.

God's Voice: Internal

We saw above that sometimes God talks to people in an audible voice that sounds just like a person. But at other times, God talks to us internally. That is, the person to whom God is talking hears God's voice clearly and distinctly—sometimes even almost deafeningly loud—but someone sitting right next to him doesn't hear a thing.

Given the relative rarity of hearing God's audible voice, I think it's safe to say that God speaks to people internally more often than He does audibly.

Remember what happened to Philip after he started the revival in Samaria? He receives a prophetic instructions concerning a man that was ready to be saved. Here's the story:

Acts 8:26–18 (MSG): Later **God's angel spoke to Philip:** "At noon today I want you to walk over to that desolate road that goes from Jerusalem down to Gaza." [27]He got up and went. He met an Ethiopian eunuch coming down the road. The eunuch had been on a pilgrimage to Jerusalem and was returning to Ethiopia, where he was minister in charge of all the finances of Candace, queen of the Ethiopians. [28]He was riding in a chariot and reading the prophet Isaiah.

So first, an angel of the Lord speaks to Philip. Hearing an angel speak can take any of the forms that hearing God can take: an audible voice, an internal voice that bystanders can't hear, and so forth. The text doesn't specify *how* Philip perceived the message from the angel, but he did.

So what happened next?

Acts 8:29 (MSG): **The Spirit told Philip,** "Climb into the chariot."

Now that's curious. Why did the first part of the message come through an angel, and the second part of the message come from the Holy Spirit Himself? I don't know; the answer to that question comes from the book of Psalms:

Psalm 115:3 (AMP): But our God is in heaven; **He does whatever He pleases.**

In any case, you know the rest of the story: the Ethiopian eunuch gets saved and baptized, and because he was the CFO of the queen of Ethiopia, undoubtedly had much influence for the gospel when he returned home. Again we see that God knows what He's doing.

Soon after, Peter had his vision of the sheet lowered from heaven, which we read about in the first of the New Testament trance accounts, earlier—at least, the first to use that particular word for it (for discussion and many Scriptural examples of the falling-down type of trance, ordinary falling under the power, see the chapter by that name in Book 4: *Gold Dust, Jewels, and More: Manifestations of God?*).

It was a prophetic message in symbolic form (which he saw), indicating that Gentiles were welcome in the Kingdom of God. The vision was very puzzling to him, and after it ended, as he was pondering it, the Holy Spirit spoke (which he heard):

Acts 10:19 (HCSB): While Peter was thinking about the vision, **the Spirit told him,** "Three men are here looking for you. ²⁰Get up, go downstairs, and accompany them with no doubts at all, because I have sent them."

These three men were servants of Cornelius, a godly Roman centurion to whom an angel had appeared. God was about to reveal to the

Jews that not only the Samaritans (the "half-Jews" of Acts 8), but full-blown *Gentiles* (the non-Jews of Acts 10) were welcome in the Kingdom of God, and were able to receive the baptism of the Holy Spirit! This was astonishing news indeed for any Jew of that day.

So Peter goes with them back to Cornelius' home, and starts preaching to them about Jesus. Before Peter even finishes preaching, the Holy Spirit fell on Cornelius and his household, and they began speaking in tongues, to the amazement of Peter and his friends.

Later, when recounting the whole adventure to the apostles in Jerusalem, Peter described his vision of the sheet, and then continued:

> Acts 11:11–12 (HCSB): At that very moment, three men who had been sent to me from Caesarea arrived at the house where we were. [12]Then **the Spirit told me to accompany them** with no doubts at all. These six brothers accompanied me, and we went into the man's house.

Note that casual way Peter refers to the Holy Spirit talking to him and giving him instructions. Many modern-day Christians claim such things don't happen anymore, but such a claim cannot be supported by Scripture. Especially with so many Scriptures stating the opposite!

Here is a passage that, although it doesn't explicitly state that the Holy Spirit spoke internally, it seems to me likely that He did. Read the Scripture and see if you agree:

> Acts 13:1–4 (RSV): Now in the church at Antioch **there were prophets and teachers,** Barnabas, Simeon who was called Niger, Lucius of Cyrene, Mana-en a member of the court of Herod the tetrarch, and Saul. [2]While they were worshiping the Lord and fasting, **the Holy Spirit said, "Set apart for me Barnabas and Saul for the work to which I have called them."** [3]Then after fasting and praying **they laid their hands on them and sent them off.** [4]So, **being sent out by the Holy Spirit,** they went down to Seleucia; and from there they sailed to Cyprus.

Several interesting items in the above passage. First, there were prophets and teachers in the Antioch church. From the list of names, we can't tell which ones were prophets, which ones were teachers, and which ones were both. But it probably doesn't matter, because it sounds like they all heard the Holy Spirit talking to them.

Second, the Holy Spirit gave them a command: "Set apart Barnabas and Saul." This could have been audibly, internally, or some other way; the text doesn't say. But again, given the relative rarity of God's audible voice, it seems likely that it was internally, at least for some. Having prophets in the group, it's very possible that a prophetic word was given by one or more of them, and the others heard the Lord speak to them internally. Or, they could have felt impressions from God (covered below), confirming that the idea of setting apart Barnabas and Saul was from God.

The third interesting thing in this passage is how God identifies with His people, and vice versa. Similar to the sheep-and-goats judgment Jesus describes in Matthew 25:31–46, where He says "whatever you did to the least of My brethren, you did unto Me," the Bible says a similar thing here. In v. 3, it says that "they"—the group of prophets and teachers—sent Barnabas and Saul off on their mission. Then in v. 4, *in the very next sentence,* it says that the Holy Spirit sent them out! Well, which is it? Did the group send them out? Or did the Holy Spirit send them out? *Yes.*

Hearing From Evil Spirits

From the above Scriptures, we can clearly see that God communicates with people by (among other ways, of course) speaking words that people hear, whether that hearing is external and heard with one's physical ears, or internal and heard directly in one's spirit. When the content of that communication is for someone else, an utterance imparting that content would be prophetic in nature.

The above Scriptures are cool and encouraging, but here's a question: should we also hear evil spirits? By "hear," I do not mean to "heed and obey," of course; that is obviously foolish. But should we be able to perceive and understand what evil spirits are saying?

Apparently so. The Bible casually assumes that we will be able to converse with spirits, both good and bad. As Paul tells the Thessalonians:

> II Thessalonians 2:2 (CEB): We don't want you to be easily confused in your mind or upset if you hear that the day of the Lord is already here, **whether you hear it through some spirit,** a message, or a letter supposedly from us.

> ESV: . . .not to be quickly shaken in mind or alarmed, **either by a spirit** or a spoken word, or a letter seeming to be from us, to the effect that the day of the Lord has come.

Here Paul casually mentions the idea of hearing something from a spirit. From the context, we can tell that this particular spirit is an evil spirit, because he is stating something false. But the point is that it was common knowledge that people can hear things from spirits, and the content of what they say can be used to ascertain whose side they are on.

So Paul is matter-of-factly giving instruction about hearing and understanding a message from a lying spirit, analyzing the content of that message, and taking action accordingly. As if it is a common thing for demons to talk to people. *Which it is.* Of course, the last thing demons want is for you to *realize* that the idea that just popped into your head came from them, because then you would likely take the appropriate action and "cast down" that imagination (II Corinthians 10:3–5) and start thinking about godly things instead (Philippians 4:6–8).

So hearing demons talking is not only possible, but it's common, though it often goes unrecognized as such. However, we need to recognize when spirits are talking to us, because this is required in order to test them to see if they are in accordance with God's Word and His character.

John agrees with Paul:

> I John 4:1–3: Beloved, believe not every spirit, but try the spirits whether they are of God: because many false prophets are gone out into the world. [2]Hereby know ye the Spirit of God: **Every spirit that confesseth that Jesus Christ is come in the flesh is of God:** [3]And **every spirit that**

confesseth not that Jesus Christ is come in the flesh is not of God: and this is that spirit of antichrist, whereof ye have heard that it should come; and even now already is it in the world.

Here again is a casual, blunt, clear statement that we are supposed to hear from spirits. Some will confess that Jesus has come in the flesh; others will not. And based on their answers, we will know whether to welcome their assistance or to rebuke them in the name of Jesus and cast them out.

And the fact that they are answering a question, or complying with a command to present their view, implies that we talked to them first, expecting an answer. The answer they give—whether they confess that Jesus has, or has not, come in the flesh—would indicate their allegiance. But in either case, notice they are confessing one way or the other and *we are to perceive the content of their confession* and then respond accordingly. This sounds like a real good motivation to seek God for the gift of discerning of spirits, does it not?

Dealing with Antichrist

There's another tidbit in the above passage. Notice in v. 3, which is KJV, that it refers to the "spirit of antichrist." In many modern versions, it renders the phrase "spirit of *the* antichrist," as if it refers to a single person. The definition of "antichrist" that implies a single evil human person, still to come, that will gain political power in the end of the end times actually is not Scriptural, although it's very popular in modern Western theology.

The only places that "antichrist" is mentioned are in I John and II John, and none of the occurrences imply a single person yet to come. They all imply a demonically inspired mindset or worldview that is opposed to everything Jesus stands for and does. (The book of Revelation talks about the "beast" and the "false prophet," but it never mentions "antichrist.")

There are not many references to "antichrist" in the Bible, so we can look at all of them pretty quickly. Here's the first one:

I John 2:18: Little children, it is the last time: and as ye have heard that **antichrist** shall come, **even now are there many antichrists;** whereby we know that it is the last time.

So already, the one-person-yet-to-come definition of antichrist is already debunked, because when John wrote this almost 2000 years ago, there were already "many" antichrists.

Let's look at the next one:

I John 2:22: Who is a liar but he that denieth that Jesus is the Christ? **He is antichrist,** that denieth the Father and the Son.

Interesting: Anyone who denies that Jesus is the Christ is "antichrist." It should not surprising that such a person—one who denies that Jesus is the Christ—is described as being a liar. Denying that Jesus is the Christ is a sure indication that the speaker is listening to the devil, who is a liar and the father of lies (John 8:44).

And did you notice that that Scripture above very effectively blows the one-person-yet-to-come theory out of the water? If you insist that "antichrist" implies a single evil human person at the end of the story, then all the millions of people throughout history who have denied that Jesus is the Christ (and thus also denying the Father) are "that guy"— the antichrist. Yep, every single one of 'em is the one person who has not shown up yet. Hmm. . .

Here's the next one:

I John 4:3: And every spirit that confesseth not that Jesus Christ is come in the flesh is not of God: and this is that **spirit of antichrist,** whereof ye have heard that it should come; and **even now already is it in the world.**

Here is one of the plainest Scriptures showing that antichrist is a demon spirit, or the devil, and not a single person. After all, if "the antichrist" were a single human person who would do bad things at the close of the age, how could that person's spirit have already been in the world, almost 2000 years ago? He'd be really old by now.

Here's the last one (there are only four verses in the Bible that mention antichrist):

II John 7: For many deceivers are entered into the world, who confess not that Jesus Christ is come in the flesh. This is a deceiver and **an antichrist.**

This one, too, is enlightening. Anyone who is a deceiver, including (or *especially*) anyone who denies that Jesus has come in the flesh, is "an" antichrist. In other words, there have been many antichrists running around ever since Jesus walked the earth.

By the way, did you notice that in the Scriptures above, there is great emphasis put on the fact that Jesus has come in the flesh? During that point in history, Gnosticism was already a cult that was gaining popularity after Jesus ascended, and one of the things Gnosticism claimed was that Jesus didn't "really" come in the flesh; that is, in a physical body. (To see a more detailed discussion on Gnosticism, see the "Original Sin" section of the "Total Depravity" chapter in Book 6: *Free to Choose?*)

So if "antichrist" does not mean the one exceptionally powerful and evil person at the close of the age, what *does* it mean? We got some good hints from the Scriptures above, but let's look a little deeper. In order to find out what "antichrist" means, we should first think about what "Christ" means. What is "Christ?" Is that just Jesus' last name? No. "Christ" is the New Testament equivalent of the Old Testament term "Messiah," and both words mean "Anointed One."

Anointed with what? Oil? No, except symbolically, because oil is a symbol of the Holy Spirit. Jesus was anointed with the Holy Spirit, as prophesied in Isaiah and fulfilled in Luke:

Isaiah 61:1 (NASB): **The Spirit of the Lord God is upon me, because the Lord has anointed me** to bring good news to the afflicted; He has sent me to bind up the brokenhearted, to proclaim liberty to captives and freedom to prisoners. . .

[To hear this passage set to music, listen to the song *The Spirit of the Lord* on the album *Songs of the Tribe of Judah*, or scan the QR code at right.]

This Messianic prophecy refers to Jesus, as He plainly states:

> Luke 4:17–21 (NASB): And the book of the prophet Isaiah was handed to Him *[Jesus]*. And He opened the book and found the place where it was written, [18]**"The Spirit of the Lord is upon Me, because He anointed Me** to preach the gospel to the poor. He has sent Me to proclaim release to the captives, and recovery of sight to the blind, to set free those who are oppressed, [19]to proclaim the favorable year of the Lord." [20]And He closed the book, gave it back to the attendant and sat down; and the eyes of all in the synagogue were fixed on Him. [21]And He began to say to them, "Today this Scripture has been fulfilled in your hearing."

So the spirit of antichrist isn't merely opposed to Jesus as a man, or even to Jesus as the Son of God; it is most greatly opposed to Jesus *as the Anointed One.* Not merely anti-Jesus, it is anti-*Christ;* that is, anti-*anointing.* The enemy is violently opposed to the anointing of the Holy Spirit because it is through the power of that anointing that we, like Jesus, "destroy the works of the devil" (I John 3:8).

It's no wonder that the enemy hates the anointing of the Holy Spirit; in addition to the quotes from Isaiah 61 and Luke 4 above, look what else it does:

> Isaiah 10:27: And it shall come to pass in that day, that his burden shall be taken away from off thy shoulder, and his yoke from off thy neck, and **the yoke shall be destroyed because of the anointing.**

> Acts 10:38: How **God anointed Jesus of Nazareth with the Holy Ghost** and with power: who **went about doing good, and healing all that were oppressed of the devil;** for God was with him.

> I John 2:27: But **the anointing** which ye have received of him **abideth in you,** and ye need not that any man teach you: but as **the same anointing teacheth you of all things, and is truth, and is no lie, and even as it hath taught you, ye shall abide in him.**

Even the verses above that apply specifically to Jesus do not apply *exclusively* to Jesus, because He said, "As the Father has sent me, so I send you" (John 20:21), and "He that believes on Me, the works that I do shall he do also, and greater works than these shall he do. . ." (John 14:12).

So yes, the anointing of the Holy Spirit has more power than we can imagine.

The spirit of antichrist is opposed to *anyone* who carries the anointing of the Holy Spirit, be that Jesus Himself, or you and me. But that is not a big scary thing; at worst, it's only a demon, and Jesus gave us "authority to trample on snakes and scorpions and *to overcome **all the power of the enemy; nothing will harm you***" (Luke 10:17–20).

This applies to people in prophetic ministry, because you *have* to be anointed by the Holy Spirit in order to minister God-breathed prophecy. So will you be attacked from time to time? Of course. But are you in actual danger? Absolutely not, as long as you remain in obedience to God.

Personal Examples of Hearing

Below are some examples when I heard something from God. There was no image dropped into my spirit, but there were one or more words.

In one example, as I was just minding my own business one day (probably during 2013 or so), God clearly said, "Kelsey Grammer." Not audibly, but clearly. I didn't know who Kelsey Grammer was, but I figured that since I received the name so clearly, I should pray for her. (After all, the name "Kelsey" is a woman's name, right?) When I did a little research to find out who she was, I discovered that she was a "he!" Clearly, I'm not terribly knowledgable about television personalities. But I prayed for him for a while, both in English and in tongues.

By Tenebrae (talk) (Uploads) - Own work. CC BY-SA 3.0,
https://commons.wikimedia.org/w/index.php?curid=33886644
Kelsey Grammer

I have no idea what Kelsey was going through at the moment, but for some reason, God wanted me to pray for him, so I did. If this were a case of Kelsey standing right in front of me, or he were a personal friend, the Lord probably would have given me more, since I could have given him the message as a prophecy. As it is, I am likely to not know what effects my prayers had until I get to heaven. Hopefully, Kelsey will be there too.

Update as of July 2018: I was very excited to read this article published on breitbart.com[3] on July 8, 2018. The article is entitled "Kelsey Grammer: Reproductive Rights is a 'Dishonest' Name for Abortion," and it tells about Grammer being openly pro-life, and how that fact gets "under the skin" of Hollywood liberals. Along with the article is a photo of Grammer, posted by his wife to Instagram in 2015, in which he is wearing a t-shirt that is both pro-life and pro-2nd Amendment. The t-shirt advertises Abort73.com, a pro-life organization that advocates the overturning of Roe v. Wade, the infamous ruling in 1973 that has allowed more than 60,000,000—sixty *million*—babies to be legally murdered in the United States.

Also in 2015, Grammer and his wife Kayte attended the National Right to Life Convention, and in 2016, went to Washington DC to participate in the March for Life. On Instagram, Kelsey and Kayte also posted a pro-life quote from Republican Presidential candidate Ben Carson that read: "We've distorted things to the point where people believe that anyone who opposes mothers killing their babies is waging a war on women. How can we be so foolish to believe such a thing? One must be able to recognize the depravity to which we have sunken as a society when valuing a baby's life is frowned upon."

So do I think my prayers for Kelsey Grammer contributed to his boldness to stand up for babies' right to life, in the midst of a very hostile political environment? Yes, I do. When God tells us to pray for someone, it's not just because He had nothing else to do and wanted to kill some time. When we obey God in intercession (or anything else), we and others will be blessed. I daresay that we will be flabbergasted when we get to heaven and find out how much was accomplished through our prayers, and we also might cringe a little about all the opportunities we missed because of other "more important" things that had to be done.

---

[3] https://www.breitbart.com/entertainment/2018/07/08/kelsey-grammer-reproductive-rights-is-a-dishonest-name-for-abortion

Another example of hearing the Lord came during my quiet time one morning in 2017. I was sitting there in the Lord's presence, and very distinctly heard, "Listen to the glory!" Not audibly, but internally—and again, very clearly. I was somewhat startled, but quite intrigued by the statement: I had heard about *seeing* the glory of God, and *feeling* the glory of God, but *hearing* it—*listening* to it—had never even crossed my mind. Apparently, God's glory has the capacity to impart something to our hearing—at least to our spiritual hearing. I still have no idea what it means to listen to the glory, but I am seeking God for more understanding.

This next example, which happened this morning (as of the writing of this paragraph in August 2017), was similar to the Kelsey Grammer example above. My wife Kathy and I were driving home from the Bible study that we lead twice a month on Saturdays, and I simultaneously saw and heard "Cozad, Nebraska!"—Cozad is a small town in the middle of Nebraska, about a mile north of Interstate 80. I didn't hear the words as an audible voice, but I heard them with my spirit. And I didn't see an image of the town itself; I just saw the name of the town written out. (Since I am into writing and typography, words of knowledge and prophetic messages that appear as written words are usually in 24-point bold Bookman font. I don't know why they appear like that, but I do like that font.)

I hadn't thought about Cozad for years. I've never been there, and I don't know anyone who lives there. Living in Colorado, I used to take I-80 when driving to Iowa to visit my mother, but she passed away in 1998, and I hadn't been on that part of I-80 since. I literally can't remember Cozad, Nebraska ever crossing my mind any time since 1998 when I drove to Iowa for my mother's funeral. And even then, I don't remember actually noticing the sign on I-80 saying something to the effect of "Cozad, Next Exit."

So why in the world did God bring it to my attention this morning, almost twenty years later? No idea. But my suspicion is that something or someone—maybe the whole town—needed prayer for something. So I prayed for them, several times since this morning. Since I don't know the situation or people that apparently needed prayer, my prayers in English were pretty general. For the same reason, my prayers in tongues far outnumbered my prayers in English. But God knows the situation, even if I don't, so it only makes sense to allow Him to provide the words I'm praying—He's just looking for a willing vessel to partner with Him in bringing heaven to the earth.

As another example, it is not uncommon during prophetic ministry for someone—myself or someone else on the team—to hear a snippet of a song. Typically, in such a case, the lyrics to the specified song contain something the Lord wants the person receiving ministry to understand. Sometimes, the songs are spiritual in nature, but many times, they are not. They could be golden oldies, Top 40 songs, children's songs, ballads, rock-'n'-roll, or pretty much any other genre. But whichever songs, and whichever lyrics the Lord draws our attention to, they contain some wisdom or guidance for the person we're ministering to.

Another fascinating example of hearing the Lord happened to a man named Matthew on August 1, 2007, when the I-35 bridge in Minneapolis, Minnesota, collapsed during rush hour. The synopsis of the story is that God told him very firmly, just seconds before driving onto the bridge, to *stop*. After a very short argument with God, he did stop, causing many drivers behind him to start honking angrily. That is, until the bridge gave way seconds later, and collapsed into the Mississippi River, taking many other cars down with it. You can read the exclusive interview with Matthew on the *Breaking Christian News* website[4]. Listening to God's voice can indeed be a matter of life and death.

Feeling/Touching

Can God communicate with us through the sense of touch? Can He actually cause us to feel something? I'm not talking here about Him

---

[4] www.BreakingChristianNews.com/articles/display_art.html?ID=4302

making us feel an emotional state, although He can certainly do that too (e.g., Genesis 21:6, Psalm 92:4, I Peter 1:8, etc., etc.). What I'm talking about here is this: can He make us feel something with our nerves; that is, to have tactile sensations of things that exist only in the spiritual realm? Again, let's go to the Bible to find out.

One example of a spiritual touch comes from the life of the prophet Elijah, shortly after his triumph over the 850 false prophets (I Kings 18:19) on Mount Carmel, where the Lord answered by fire:

> I Kings 19:4–8 (NLT): Then he went on alone into the wilderness, traveling all day. He sat down under a solitary broom tree and prayed that he might die. "I have had enough, Lord," he said. "Take my life, for I am no better than my ancestors who have already died." ⁵Then he lay down and slept under the broom tree. But as he was sleeping, **an angel touched him** and told him, "Get up and eat!" ⁶He looked around and there beside his head was some bread baked on hot stones and a jar of water! So he ate and drank and lay down again. ⁷Then **the angel of the Lord came again and touched him** and said, "Get up and eat some more, or the journey ahead will be too much for you." ⁸So he got up and ate and drank, and the food gave him enough strength to travel forty days and forty nights to Mount Sinai, the mountain of God.

So here is an angel touching Elijah energetically enough to wake him from deep sleep—twice. And, by the way, that must have been some pretty impressive food, for one meal to last through forty days and nights of traveling!

Here's an example from Isaiah's life:

> Isaiah 6:6–7 (GWORD): Then one of the angels flew to me. In his hand was a burning coal that he had taken from the altar with tongs. ⁷**He touched my mouth with it** and said, **"This has touched your lips. Your guilt has been taken away, and your sin has been forgiven."**

Here the angel takes a burning coal from the altar and touches Isaiah's lips and mouth. Do you think Isaiah actually felt it? I would say so, because of the importance of the message that was being imparted. And it probably was not strictly necessary that the angel say what he did, about Isaiah's unclean lips having been cleansed. It seems very unlikely that after the angel touched Isaiah's lips with the hot coal, Isaiah said, "Hmm. I wonder what *that* was all about. . ." This seems especially unlikely since Isaiah had just gotten done saying, "Woe is me! I'm doomed! I am a man of unclean lips!" I doubt if the symbolism was lost on Isaiah.

So because of the context, I think it is safe to say Isaiah felt the heat from the burning coal, and also felt it touch his lips, and probably also felt a cleansing (though perhaps momentarily painful) burning when the coal made contact.

So in this one passage, Isaiah 6:1–8, Isaiah *sees* the seraphim, *sees* the Lord, *hears* the seraphim, *hears* the Lord, *sees* the coal, *feels* the burning coal touch his lips, and perhaps even *hears* a sizzling sound as it does so.

Isaiah felt God's hand upon him later also:

Isaiah 8:11 (NIV): The Lord spoke to me **with his strong hand upon me,** warning me not to follow the way of this people. He said. . .

Other people felt the Lord's hand resting upon them as well:

Ezra 7:28 (NKJV): . . .and *[God]* has extended mercy to me before the king and his counselors, and before all the king's mighty princes. So I was encouraged, as **the hand of the Lord my God was upon me;** and I gathered leading men of Israel to go up with me.

Nehemiah 2:18 (ESV): And I told them of **the hand of my God that had been upon me** for good, and also of the words that the king had spoken to me. And they said, "Let us rise up and build." So they strengthened their hands for the good work.

I Chronicles 28:19 (NASB): "All this," said David, "the Lord made me understand in writing **by His hand upon me,** all the details of this pattern."

Psalm 139:5 (GWORD): You are all around me—in front of me and in back of me. **You lay your hand on me.**

Ezekiel 3:14 (NASB): So the Spirit lifted me up and took me away; and I went embittered in the rage of my spirit, and **the hand of the Lord was strong on me.**

Ezekiel 3:22 (NIV): **The hand of the Lord was upon me** there, and he said to me, "Get up and go out to the plain, and there I will speak to you."

Ezekiel 8:1 (NKJV): And it came to pass in the sixth year, in the sixth month, on the fifth day of the month, as I sat in my house with the elders of Judah sitting before me, that **the hand of the Lord God fell upon me there.**

Ezekiel 33:22 (ESV): Now **the hand of the Lord had been upon me** the evening before the fugitive came; and he had opened my mouth by the time the man came to me in the morning, so my mouth was opened, and I was no longer mute.

Ezekiel 37:1 (NLT): **The Lord took hold of me,** and I was carried away by the Spirit of the Lord to a valley filled with bones.

Ezekiel 40:1 (MSG): In the twenty-fifth year of our exile, at the beginning of the year on the tenth of the month—it was the fourteenth year after the city fell—**God touched me** and brought me here.

Revelation 1:17 (NIV): When I saw him, I fell at his feet as though dead. Then he placed **his right hand on me** and said: "Do not be afraid. I am the First and the Last."

Some might object to my interpretation of the Scriptures above and say, "Those are just metaphorical!" Some of them, perhaps, but *all* of them? Especially with the other passages we've seen already and others soon to follow. Seems very unlikely they are *all* metaphorical.

Then there's Jeremiah's commissioning. When God authorized and empowered him to be a prophet to the nations, Jeremiah was still too young, in his own opinion. Here's how it went down:

Jeremiah 1:4–9 (BBE): Now the word of the Lord came to me, saying, [5]Before you were formed in the body of your mother I had knowledge of you, and before your birth I made you holy; I have given you the work of being a prophet to the nations. [6]Then said I, O Lord God! see, I have no power of words, for I am a child. [7]But the Lord said to me, Do not say, I am a child: for wherever I send you, you are to go, and whatever I give you orders to say, you are to say. [8]Have no fear because of them: for I am with you, to keep you safe, says the Lord. [9]Then **the Lord put out his hand, touching my mouth;** and the Lord said to me, See, I have put my words in your mouth. . .

So here we have God touching Jeremiah specifically to impart the prophetic anointing. And then, during one of Jeremiah's prophetic announcements pronouncements against Nebuchadnezzar, Babylon, and the Chaldeans, this takes place:

> Jeremiah 25:15–17 (NASB): For thus the Lord, the God of Israel, says to me, "**Take this cup of the wine of wrath from My hand** and cause all the nations to whom I send you to drink it. ¹⁶They will drink and stagger and go mad because of the sword that I will send among them." ¹⁷**Then I took the cup from the Lord's hand** and made all the nations to whom the Lord sent me drink it. . .

This act of God offering and Jeremiah receiving the cup and then causing the nations to drink it, apparently was an action that took place in the spiritual realm. After this spiritual transaction, Jeremiah did in the physical realm what had been symbolically commanded in the spiritual realm.

And then Daniel received comfort from Gabriel's touch, right before Gabriel gave him the interpretation of a vision:

> Daniel 9:21 (AMP): Yes, while I was speaking in prayer, the man **Gabriel,** whom I had seen in the former vision, being caused to fly swiftly, **came near to me and touched me** about the time of the evening sacrifice.
>
> BBE: Even while I was still in prayer, the man Gabriel, whom I had seen in the vision at first when my weariness was great, **put his hand on me** about the time of the evening offering.

Soon after this, Daniel was so overcome by the intensity of God's glory that Gabriel had to prop him up, because Daniel had sagged into a heap:

> Daniel 10:9–10 (NIV): Then I heard him speaking, and as I listened to him, I fell into a deep sleep, my face to the ground. ¹⁰**A hand touched me and set me trembling on my hands and knees.**

Again, this "deep sleep" is not the sleep of drowsiness, because Daniel just nodded off from boredom while the angel was droning on and on. No, this was the sleep of being overwhelmed by God's manifest glory, and falling under the power (see the "Falling Under the Power" chapter of Book 4: *Gold Dust, Jewels, and More: Manifestations of God?* for details).

The glory here must have been really off the charts, because Daniel was again overwhelmed a few verses later:

> Daniel 10:15–18 (NET): While he was saying this to me, I was flat on the ground and unable to speak. [16]Then one who appeared to be a human being was **touching my lips.** I opened my mouth and started to speak, saying to the one who was standing before me, "Sir, due to the vision, anxiety has gripped me and I have no strength. [17]How, sir, am I able to speak with you? My strength is gone, and I am breathless." [18]Then the one who appeared to be a human being **touched me again and strengthened me.**

Similar to Elijah needing to be touched by an angel in order to wake him up, Peter needed the same thing, only apparently more so. Peter was one of the ringleaders of this pesky new group of Jesus-followers, and the Pharisees didn't like it, so they threw him in the slammer. Peter was evidently pretty confident in the whole concept of "If God be for us, who can be against us?" (Psalm 118:6, Romans 8:31), and he is fast asleep. Meanwhile, other believers are praying, so God sends an angel to bust him out of prison.

Here's what happened:

> Acts 12:7: And behold, **the angel of the Lord** came upon him, and a light shined in the prison; and he *smote* **Peter on the side** and raised him up, saying, "Arise up quickly." And his chains fell off from his hands.
>
> AMP: Suddenly, **an angel of the Lord** appeared [beside him] and a light shone in the cell. The angel *struck* **Peter's side** and awakened him, saying, "Get up quickly!" And the chains fell off his hands.
>
> CEV: Suddenly an angel from the Lord appeared, and light flashed around in the cell. **The angel** *poked* **Peter in the side** and woke him up. Then he said, "Quick! Get up!" The chains fell off his hands. . .
>
> GNT: Suddenly an angel of the Lord stood there, and a light shone in the cell. **The angel** *shook* **Peter by the shoulder,** woke him up, and said, "Hurry! Get up!" At once the chains fell off Peter's hands.
>
> TLB: . . .when suddenly there was a light in the cell and an angel of the Lord stood beside Peter! **The angel** *slapped* **him on the side** to

awaken him and said, "Quick! Get up!" And the chains fell off his wrists!

NLV: All at once an angel of the Lord was seen standing beside him. A light shone in the building. **The angel *hit* Peter on the side** and said, "Get up!" Then the chains fell off his hands.

YLT: and lo, **a messenger of the Lord** stood by, and a light shone in the buildings, and **having *smitten* Peter on the side,** he raised him up, saying, 'Rise in haste,' and his chains fell from off [his] hands.

This seems pretty humorous: Peter is sawing logs and is *so* deeply asleep that the angel had to give him a wallop to wake him up. Now, granted, there are some translations that indicate a gentler kind of touch ("nudge" or "tap"), but they are significantly outnumbered by the more violent forms of awakening.

So the examples above show that it is not only possible, but it is apparently not uncommon for God or one of His angels to touch someone to communicate or impart something. And of course, if that which is being communicated or imparted is intended to be given to someone else, that message would inherently be prophetic in nature, because of its source.

Movement/Transportation

As an extension of the idea of contact between spiritual beings and physical beings, where God or an angelic being merely touches a person, there are also numerous examples of God and angels moving people much more assertively. These range from picking someone up off the floor to carrying someone across the countryside. We'll look at some of these in this section, although with less commentary than above:

Ezekiel 3:24 (NIV): Then **the Spirit came into me and raised me to my feet.** He spoke to me and said: "Go, shut yourself inside your house."

Ezekiel 8:3, 7 (GWORD): It stretched out **what looked like a hand and grabbed me by the hair on my head.** In these visions from God, **the Spirit carried me between heaven and earth. He took me to Jerusalem,** to the entrance to the north gate of the inner courtyard of the temple. That was where an idol that stirs up God's anger was located. ⁷**Then he took me to the entrance of the courtyard.** As I looked, I saw a hole in the wall.

137

> Ezekiel 11:1a (NLT): Then **the Spirit lifted me and brought me** to the east gateway of the Lord's Temple. . .

> Ezekiel 11:24 (TEV): In the vision **the spirit of God lifted me up and brought me back** to the exiles in Babylonia. Then the vision faded. . .

> Daniel 8:18 (NIV): While he *[Gabriel]* was speaking to me, I was in a deep sleep, with my face to the ground. Then **he touched me and raised me to my feet.**

> Daniel 10:9–10 (NET): I listened to his voice, and as I did so I fell into a trance-like sleep with my face to the ground. [10]Then **a hand touched me and set me on my hands and knees.**

Again, these two passages from Daniel are not cases of slumbering sleep, but of slain-in-the-spirit sleep, as the NET translation indicates. If it had been slumbering sleep because Daniel had nodded off, he wouldn't have known what Gabriel was saying.

Traveling in the Spirit

Above, we discussed how God can take someone from one location to another in the spirit, and this next concept of "traveling in the spirit" is related. Traveling in the spirit is the original idea, of which the New Age's "astral projection" is a poor copy. But the devil didn't invent traveling in the spirit; he only copied and corrupted the idea. The original version is God's idea.

Depending on how much you have studied this phenomenon, you may never have heard of it, or you may be aware that many people have done it throughout history. But of course, such reports are not as reliable as the Bible. So let's get into the Word.

Enoch

Enoch was an Old Testament character who was a deeply godly man. This is not the Enoch that was Cain's son (Genesis 4:17); this is Enoch the father of Methuselah (Genesis 5:21). A curious statement is made about his departure from earth:

> Genesis 5:24: And Enoch walked with God: and **he was not; for God took him.**

> > AMP: And [in reverent fear and obedience] Enoch walked with God; and **he was not [found among men], because God took him [away to be home with Him].**

CEB: Enoch walked with God and **disappeared because God took him.**

MSG: Enoch walked steadily with God. And then **one day he was simply gone: God took him.**

VOICE: . . .but Enoch had such a close and intimate relationship with God that **one day he just vanished—God took him.**

What a way to go! No death at all; not even physical death! Just walking along with God, and basically God says, "Why don't you just stay here? You're closer to My place than yours anyway. . ."

So it's undeniable that Enoch travelled in the spirit, and since he is described as having "disappeared," or "vanished," it's clear that he took his body along with his spirit. Many people consider Enoch's "translation" to heaven to be a sovereign act of God—something that just "happened to him" out of the blue, because God just decided to. But that's actually not what the Bible says.

Let's look an another passage about Enoch:

Hebrews 11:5–6: ***By faith* Enoch was translated that he should not see death; and was not found, because God had translated him:** for before his translation he had this testimony, that he pleased God. [6]But **without faith it is impossible to please him:** for he that cometh to God must believe that he is, and that he is a rewarder of them that diligently seek him.

Isn't that interesting? Most Christians know v. 6, the one about how it's impossible to please God without faith. But how many people connect v. 6 with v. 5, which is the beginning of the thought? As you can see above, v. 5 talks about how Enoch was translated *by faith.* It wasn't just a sovereign act of God that happened unexpectedly; *Enoch was believing for it!*

Look at the sequence of statements in the previous two verses:

1. Enoch was translated by faith that he should not see death.

2. Prior to being translated, he was pleasing to God.

3. You must have faith to please God.

So often, we skip the plowing, planting, and cultivating, and attempt to jump straight to the harvest, the fruits. We want good results without considering the prerequisites. We want the blessing without having to deal with the responsibility. It's so easy to say that "without faith it's impossible to please God," and completely ignore the example God just gave of being pleasing to Him by having faith. It's like those who quote "You will know the truth, and the truth will set you free" (John 8:31–32) while completely forgetting the condition that must first be met: "You are truly my disciples *if* **you remain faithful to my teaching.** *Then* you will know the truth, and the Truth will set you free."

The fact that Enoch was translated by faith has some interesting implications. We get saved by faith (Ephesians 2:8–9), we are baptized in the Holy Spirit and operate in His miraculous gifts by faith (Galatians 3:2–5), we get healed by faith (Matthew 9:22), we have access to God by faith (Romans 5:2), and so forth. Why don't we decide to have faith to be translated? If not to heaven like Enoch yet, why not to other places on earth, like Philip (Acts 8:39–40) to do God's work? Actually, this is happening more and more often recently; keep your ears open to highly prophetic people, and you'll hear some similar stories.

In many places throughout the Bible, God is described as not being a respecter of persons; that is, He doesn't play favorites. Any blessing He offers to one person, He offers to everyone. Therefore, this blessing is open to us as well.

As I've mentioned many times in other books in the THOUGHTS ON series, the chapter- and verse numbers in the Bible were added long after the text itself was written. While they are very useful to ease navigation to individual passages, the implicit "boundaries" separating one verse from another, or one chapter from another, can imply a break in the train of thought that is actually misleading. From now on, let's think about Hebrews 11:5 and Hebrews 11:6 together; it's much more exciting!

Elijah

Elijah the prophet traveled in the spirit quite a bit. About three years into the drought and resulting famine that Elijah prophesied would come as a result of King Ahab's unrepentant sin, God told Elijah to present himself to Ahab. This was when the godly Obadiah was the chief steward of Ahab's house; Obadiah had hid a hundred prophets of God in a couple caves during Jezebel's anti-prophet rampages.

In an effort to save the horses and mules from dying of thirst and starvation, Ahab went one way, and Obadiah went the other, in search of water and fresh grass for the animals:

> I Kings 18:7–12 (NASB): Now as Obadiah was on the way, behold, Elijah met him, and he recognized him and fell on his face and said, "Is this you, Elijah my master?" [8]And he said to him, "It is I. Go, say to your master, 'Behold, Elijah is here.'" [9]And he said, "What sin have I committed, that you are giving your servant into the hand of Ahab, to put me to death? [10]As the Lord your God lives, there is no nation or kingdom where my master has not sent to search for you; and when they said, 'He is not here,' he made the kingdom or nation swear that they could not find you. [11]And now you are saying, 'Go, say to your master, "Behold, Elijah is here."' [12]**And it will come about when I leave you that the Spirit of the Lord will carry you where I do not know;** so when I come and tell Ahab and he cannot find you, he will kill me, although I your servant have feared the Lord from my youth."

Notice Obadiah's reaction to Elijah's request: "when I leave you. . . the Spirit of the Lord will carry you where I do not know." Judging from Obadiah's statement, it sure sounds like God supernaturally transported Elijah from place to place pretty often. Often enough that Obadiah's first thought was essentially, "As soon as I turn my back, God will take you somewhere else!" He sounded genuinely fearful of the prospect of Ahab, having been summoned, would arrive to find that Elijah had vanished again, and then take out his anger on Obadiah. Apparently when Elijah traveled in the spirit, he took his body as well.

And then, of course, when it was time for Elijah to retire to heaven, he traveled in the spirit then as well. Elijah and his successor, Elisha, journeyed several places before Elijah actually went up. And again, his approaching translation didn't seem to be an out-of-the-blue type of sovereign act by God; it seems like it was common knowledge how it was going to happen. All the prophets at Bethel knew about it:

141

> II Kings 2:3 (NLT): The group of prophets from Bethel came to Elisha and asked him, **"Did you know that the Lord is going to take your master away from you today?"** "Of course I know," Elisha answered. "But be quiet about it."

These prophets undoubtedly knew the story of Enoch's translation, and it's interesting that they used the same terminology about Elijah's upcoming departure: they said that the Lord was going to "take" Elijah. Then Elijah and Elisha went to Jericho, and those prophets knew about it too:

> II Kings 2:5 (NLT): Then the group of prophets from Jericho came to Elisha and asked him, **"Did you know that the Lord is going to take your master away from you today?"** "Of course I know," Elisha answered. "But be quiet about it."

A short time later, Elijah's translation actually happened. Many people think that Elijah was taken to heaven in a chariot of fire, but that's not true:

> II Kings 2:11 (NLT): As they were walking along and talking, suddenly a chariot of fire appeared, drawn by horses of fire. It drove between the two men, separating them, and **Elijah was carried by a whirlwind into heaven.**

Again: What a way to go!

Elisha

You probably remember the story of Naaman the leper (II Kings 5), whom God healed through the ministry of Elisha. Naaman was so overjoyed that his leprosy was healed that he rushed back to Elisha to give him a variety of gifts and rewards, which he refused. But Elisha's servant Gehazi thought this was a really good opportunity to get rich and, after all, Naaman *wanted* to give them stuff!

So a short time after Naaman left, Gehazi runs after him and asks for some of the rewards, supposedly for two visiting prophets who had just arrived. Gehazi lied; he wanted to keep Naaman's gifts for himself. [Author's note: Don't try to lie to a prophet; it's not likely to end well.] Naaman gladly gives Gehazi all he asked for, and more, and then Gehazi brings it home, hides it, and then nonchalantly goes in to see Elisha.

Here's the rest of the story:

> II Kings 5:25–27 (AMP): He went in and stood before his master. Elisha said, Where have you been, Gehazi? He said, Your servant went nowhere. [26]Elisha said to him, **Did not my spirit go with you when the man turned from his chariot to meet you?** Was it a time to accept money, garments, olive orchards, vineyards, sheep, oxen, menservants, and maidservants? [27]Therefore the leprosy of Naaman shall cleave to you and to your offspring forever. And Gehazi went from his presence a leper as white as snow.

Ouch! That seems rather severe punishment, doesn't it? But it's another example of "the more you know, the worse the punishment for disobedience" (Luke 12:47–48). But back to the subject: Note that *Elisha's spirit went with Gehazi,* watching him execute his deceptive get-rich-quick scheme, even though his body remained at home.

And apparently, Elisha did this regularly, as a matter of course—it was very common for him to travel in the spirit. The above story with Naaman is in II Kings 5, this next portion of the story is just a few verses later:

> II Kings 6:8–12 (CEV): **Time after time,** when the king of Syria was at war against the Israelites, he met with his officers and announced, "I've decided where we will set up camp." [9]**Each time,** Elisha would send this warning to the king of Israel: "Don't go near there. That's where the Syrian troops have set up camp." [10]So the king would warn the Israelite troops in that place to be on guard.

So "time after time" when the king of Syria made battle plans, *each time* Elisha would know it, and warn the king of Israel. Look at that! Not "rarely" or "occasionally," but *"each time!"* Fascinating. You'd think that would have been terribly exasperating to the king of Syria. And indeed, it was:

> [11]The king of Syria was furious when he found out what was happening. He called in his officers and asked, "Which one of you has been telling the king of Israel our plans?" [12]"None of us, Your Majesty," one of them answered. "It's an Israelite named **Elisha. He's a prophet, so he can tell his king everything—even what you say in your own room.**"

Apparently, this was a regular thing.

Paul

Then in the New Testament, Paul does the same thing. Remember the situation in the church at Corinth, where that one man was having sex with his stepmother? And if that weren't bad enough, the Corinthian church, instead of disciplining the guy, just glossed over it. So Paul passed judgment in the spirit.

But how did he know what to do? Do we think he made his decision based on gossip or hearsay? Not likely. If we read what Paul actually said, it sounds like he traveled in the spirit and saw for himself what was happening, and so he could impose the proper discipline:

> I Corinthians 5:1–4 (BBE): It is said, in fact, that there is among you a sin of the flesh, such as is not seen even among the Gentiles, that one of you has his father's wife. ²And in place of feeling sorrow, you are pleased with yourselves, so that he who has done this thing has not been sent away from among you. ³For **I myself, being *present in spirit though not in body*, have come to a decision** about him who has done this thing; ⁴In the name of our Lord Jesus, **when you have come together with my spirit,** with the power of our Lord Jesus. . .
>
> vv. 3–4, EHV: Even though I am absent in body, **I am present in spirit**. . . ⁴In the name of our Lord Jesus Christ, when you are gathered together, and **my spirit is there,** along with the power of our Lord Jesus. . .
>
> ESV: For though absent in body, **I am present in spirit**. . . ⁴When you are assembled in the name of the Lord Jesus and **my spirit is present,** with the power of our Lord Jesus. . .
>
> NLT: Even though **I am not with you in person, I am with you in the Spirit**. . . ⁴. . .in the name of the Lord Jesus. You must call a meeting of the church. **I will be present with you in spirit,** and so will the power of our Lord Jesus.
>
> TEV: And even though **I am far away from you in body, still I am there with you in spirit**. . . ⁴As you meet together, and **I meet with you in my spirit,** by the power of our Lord Jesus present with us. . .

Part of the confusion about this verse is that the English idiom about being with someone "in spirit" carries the watered-down meaning of "I'm thinking about you." That's what many people think Paul is expressing here, and it's especially easy to think this if you've been raised under the cessationist teaching of "God doesn't do miraculous things anymore."

But we can't retroactively impose our English idioms on the Hebrew culture described by the Biblical text. We've already seen that Elisha was doing much more than just "thinking about" Gehazi's deception or the Syrian king's battle plans; he actually saw and heard what was going on, far away from where his body was.

Let's look at another of Paul's examples. In his epistle to the church at Colosse, he writes this:

Colossians 2:5: For though **I be absent in the flesh, yet am I with you in the spirit,** joying and **beholding** your order, and the stedfastness of your faith in Christ.

AMP: For though **I am away from you in body, yet I am with you in spirit,** delighted at the **sight** of your [standing shoulder to shoulder in such] orderly array and the firmness and the solid front and stedfastness of your faith in Christ. . .

CJB: For although **I am away from you physically, I am with you in spirit,** rejoicing as I **see** the disciplined and resolute firmness of your trust in the Messiah.

PHILLIPS: For though **I am a long way away from you in body, in spirit I am by your side, watching** like a proud father the solid stedfastness of your faith in Christ.

NABRE: For even if **I am absent in the flesh, yet I am with you in spirit,** rejoicing as I **observe** your good order and the firmness of your faith in Christ.

NTE: Though **I'm away from you in person, you see, I am present with you in the spirit,** and I'm celebrating as **I keep an eye on** your good order, and the solidity of your faith in the king.

Look at those words! After he says that he is absent in body but present in spirit, Paul says he "beholds" them, he's "delighted at the sight" of them, he "sees" their resolve, he's "watching" like a proud father, he's "observing" and "keeping an eye on" their good order. That sure sounds like he's actually *seeing* them, even though he is absent in body. Especially since the PHILLIPS translation says "in spirit *I am by your side."* It's getting harder and harder to maintain the position that being with them "in spirit" simply means he's "thinking about them."

And then there's the Greek word here as well. The word translated "beholding" in the KJV (and "sight" in the AMP, and "see" in the CJB, etc.) comes from the Greek word βλέπω (*blepo*, G991). The definitions of *blepo* include "to look at," "look on," "behold," "see," and "sight," and it denotes "voluntary observation." *Much* more than just "thinking about."

And there's more. If you're familiar with eye-related medicine, you'll recognize the words *blepharism* (spasm of the eyelids), *blepharitis* (inflammation of the eyelid), *parablepsis* (abnormal vision), *ablepsia* (blindness), *monoblepsis* (vision that is better when only one eye is used), and so forth. Note that all of these words that contain "blep" pertain to vision or the visual organs, the eyes.

So the Greek word *blepo*, the English translations of *blepo*, and the English words whose etymological source was *blepo* all agree: it really means to "see" or "have sight of." So when Paul says that he "sees" the Colossians even though he was not bodily present, that's exactly what he meant.

As followers of Christ, we always need to be wary of the accuser's attacks that come in the form of "That verse couldn't mean what it actually says; it must be only metaphorical or symbolic." Kinda smacks of "Hath God said?" (Genesis 3:1), doesn't it? If we read or see or hear of some miraculous event and our tendency is to pooh-pooh it as being exaggerated or impossible, we become like those Jews that God spoke to in an audible voice, but they *still* didn't get it:

> John 12:28–30 (NLT): "Father, bring glory to your name." Then a voice spoke from heaven, saying, "I have already brought glory to my name, and I will do so again." ²⁹**When *the crowd heard the voice,* some thought it was thunder, while others declared an angel had spoken to him.** ³⁰Then Jesus told them, "The voice was for your benefit, not mine."

Note that the audible voice of God spoke to the people, *and they heard it,* and it was for their benefit that God spoke. But most of the people were so unprepared or reluctant to acknowledge the possibility of a supernatural event, that they thought it was a natural occurrence (it was thunder) or, in those who were a little more spiritually astute, they conceded that it may have been supernatural, but it certainly wasn't for them (it was only "to him"—to Jesus). But it *was* for them, as Jesus plainly said. Let us not be so hard-hearted that we refuse to hear God speaking to us!

Perhaps the most well-known example of traveling in the spirit is this one:

> II Corinthians 12:2–4 (NIV): I know a man in Christ who fourteen years ago was caught up to the third heaven. **Whether it was in the body or out of the body I do not know**—God knows. ³And I know that this man—**whether in the body or apart from the body I do not know,** but God knows— ⁴was caught up to paradise. He heard inexpressible things, things that man is not permitted to tell.

So here is a case where Paul's spirit went to heaven to receive revelation, encouragement, assignments, and whatever else God wanted to give him. There is no question that his spirit traveled to heaven; what is unknown is whether his *body* went along, or whether it stayed on earth. And the answer to that question doesn't really matter, because it is clear that Paul's spirit did travel there.

Another thing that is not clear, but doesn't really matter, is whether this event "happened to" Paul as a sovereign act of God, or whether Paul "knew how to" travel in the spirit, and went there because he chose to. And remember, the Bible does say:

> Hebrews 4:16: **Let us therefore come boldly unto the throne of grace,** that we may obtain mercy, and find grace to help in time of need.

> Hebrews 10:19–22 (NASB): Since therefore, brethren, **we have confidence to enter the holy place** by the blood of Jesus, ²⁰by a new and living way which He inaugurated for us through the veil, that is, His flesh, ²¹and since we have a great priest over the house of God, ²²**let us draw near** with a sincere heart in full assurance of faith, having our hearts sprinkled clean from an evil conscience and our bodies washed with pure water.

MSG: So, friends, **we can now—without hesitation—walk right up to God, into "the Holy Place."** Jesus has cleared the way by the blood of his sacrifice, acting as our priest before God. The "curtain" into God's presence is his body.

Like being somewhere "in spirit" meaning so much more than merely *thinking about* being there, as we saw above, it seems reasonable to assume that the phrases "come boldly to the throne of grace," "enter the holy place," "draw near," and "without hesitation—walk right up to God" likely mean exactly what they say, rather than just "thinking about it," like many modern American churchgoers assume.

We often pray, "Come, Lord Jesus," or "Come, Holy Spirit," and He does. When God comes into our presence, is it a theoretical, metaphorical, symbolic presence where He's just "thinking about us," or is He actually here? He's not merely thinking about us; *He is actually there,* in a much more profound way than simply His omnipresence. In the same way, when we come into His presence, *we should actually go there and be there.*

After all, Jesus said:

John 12:26 (NIV): Whoever serves me must follow me; and **where I am, my servant also will be.** My Father will honor the one who serves me.

John 17:24 (NIV): Father, I want those you have given me **to be with me where I am, and to see my glory,** the glory you have given me because you loved me before the creation of the world.

Do you remember the prophecies about Jesus being born as a human? These are the ones I'm talking about:

Isaiah 7:14 (HCSB): Therefore, the Lord Himself will give you a sign: The virgin will conceive, have a son, and name him **Immanuel.**

Matthew 1:22–23 (HCSB): Now all this took place to fulfill what was spoken by the Lord through the prophet: [23]See, the virgin will become pregnant and give birth to a son, and they will name Him **Immanuel,** which is translated **"God is with us."**

As you can see, Immanuel means "God is with us." When God the Son was "with" us, does that mean He was merely "thinking about" us?

No, it was much more than that. John describes Jesus—God with us—like this:

> I John 1:1: That which was from the beginning, which **we have heard,** which **we have seen with our eyes,** which we have looked upon, and **our hands have handled,** of the Word of life. . .

So when Jesus was "with" us, people could see Him, people could hear Him, people could touch Him; He was really here in the flesh.

And this is where it gets interesting: the word that Matthew uses to describe Immanuel as "God with us" uses the Greek word for "with:" μετά (*meta*, G3326). This is the *same word* that Jesus used when He said that He wanted us to be "with" Him to see His glory! He wants us to be able to see His glory, and hear His glory, and feel His glory! Not just to "think about" His glory from afar, but to actually experience it! Hallelujah!

Think about it: Jesus wants us to be *with Him!* Now because Jesus is omnipresent, no matter where we are, we are "with Him" and He is "with us," since there is no place we could possibly be where He isn't. But these Scriptures clearly mean more than that. Why couldn't being "with Him" really mean being *with* Him? Even though Ephesians 3:20 talks about Jesus being able to do "immeasurably more than all we ask or imagine," we still tend to put God in our little boxes—we tend to interpret that verse as saying Jesus will do "immeasurably more than all we ask or imagine, as long as it fits within these constraints." We *gotta* stop doing that.

Let's look at the John 17 passage in a bit more detail. It is part of Jesus' high-priestly prayer He prayed shortly before the crucifixion. Let's look at a larger portion of that prayer:

> John 17:14–24 (NLT): I have given them your word. And the world hates them because they do not belong to the world, just as I do not belong to the world. ¹⁵I'm not asking you to take them out of the world, but to keep them safe from the evil one. ¹⁶They do not belong to this world any more than I do. ¹⁷Make them holy by your truth; teach them your word, which is truth. ¹⁸Just as you sent me into the world, I am sending them into the world. ¹⁹And I give myself as a holy sacrifice for them so they can be made holy by your truth. ²⁰I am pray-

ing not only for these disciples but also for all who will ever believe in me through their message. [21]I pray that they will all be one, just as you and I are one—as you are in me, Father, and I am in you. And may they be in us so that the world will believe you sent me. [22]I have given them the glory you gave me, so they may be one as we are one. [23]I am in them and you are in me. May they experience such perfect unity that the world will know that you sent me and that you love them as much as you love me. [24]Father, I want these whom you have given me to be with me where I am. Then they can see all the glory you gave me because you loved me even before the world began!

In the passage above, there are many places where Jesus is either saying that something *is* happening, or praying for something *to* happen. For each one of those things Jesus is saying, we need to ask ourselves: Is He describing something that happens even while we're on earth, or is it only for after we get to heaven? Let's take a look.

- "I have given them your word. And **the world hates them** because they do not belong to the world" (v. 14). The world hates us believers in Christ while we're still here in the world, not only after we get to heaven.

- **"I'm not asking you to take them out of the world,** but to keep them safe from the evil one" (v. 15). Because Jesus is not asking God to take us out of the world, the timeframe is clearly while we are still in this world.

- "**Make them holy** by your truth; **teach them your word,** which is truth" (v. 17). Are we supposed to be holy and learn God's Word in this world, or wait until we get to heaven to do that? Clearly, this is meant for while we are still here on earth—we need to be holy *here* or we'll never get *there* (Hebrews 12:14).

- "Just as you sent me into the world, **I am sending them into the world**" (v. 18). Is Jesus sending us into the world while we are still in the world, or only after we get to heaven? Obviously this is while we are still in the world; Jesus clearly states that.

- "And I give myself as a holy sacrifice for them **so they can be made holy** by your truth" (v. 19). Is Jesus' sacrifice to make us holy while we are still on earth, or only after we get to heaven? Again, since we can't even see God without holiness (Hebrews

12:14), we won't even get to heaven unless we become holy here on earth.

- "I am praying not only for these disciples but also **for all who will ever believe in me through their message**" (v. 20). Is Jesus talking about people believing in Him here on earth, or only after they get to heaven? Again, obviously, here on earth.

- "I pray that **they will all be one,** just as you and I are one—as you are in me, Father, and I am in you. And may they be in us **so that the world will believe** you sent me" (v. 21). Is Jesus praying that His people will be one in unity, and that the world will believe that God has sent Him, while we are still on earth, or only after we get to heaven? Undeniably, while we are still on earth.

- "**I have given them the glory** you gave me, so they may be one as we are one" (v. 22). Us receiving glory is supernatural, so that must happen later, right? Most people, especially those brought up in churches or trained by groups that claim God doesn't do the miraculous anymore, would delay this idea until after we're in heaven. Why?

- "I am in them and you are in me. May they experience **such perfect unity that the world will know that you sent me** and that you love them as much as you love me" (v. 23). Is Jesus in us, and are we to have unity, even in this world, or only in heaven? Clearly in the here and now.

- "Father, I want these whom you have given me **to be with me where I am. Then they can see all the glory you gave me** because you loved me even before the world began" (v. 24). Are we to be "with Jesus" and see "all the glory God gave Him" even on this earth, or is this only for when we're in heaven? Again, because this is supernatural, many would delay the answer to this particular prayer until after we are in heaven. But again, why?

Did you find it *easy* to believe that Jesus' prayers having to do with salvation, holiness, unity, evangelism, and so forth would happen here and now on earth, but *hard* to believe that Jesus' prayers having to do

151

with us being actually "with" Him and seeing His glory would also be in the here and now? If so, you are not alone. Many, and perhaps most, Christians nowadays were raised to defer the miraculous to another time or another place, and trained to relegate all supernatural activity until we're in heaven.

But maybe, just *maybe*, when the writer of Hebrews said we are to "come before the throne of grace," we're supposed to actually *go there*. And maybe, just *maybe*, when Jesus said He wants us to "be with Him" and see His glory, He actually meant it.

Jesus

But, speaking of Jesus (and we are), that brings up a good question: Did Jesus ever travel in the spirit? It's *very* likely, since many of His prophetic servants do. But is there a Scripture to support that contention? Perhaps. The passage below seems to indicate that He did, on this occasion, but it is not conclusive. Let's take a look.

Right after feeding the five thousand, Jesus told the disciples to get in the boat and go to the other side of the Sea of Galilee, while He went up into the mountains to pray. After dark, a storm came up, and Jesus was still alone in the mountains, praying:

> Mark 6:47: And when even was come, **the ship was in the midst of the sea,** and he alone on the land.
>
> BBE: And by evening, **the boat was in the middle of the sea,** and he by himself on the land.
>
> NIV: When evening came, **the boat was in the middle of the lake,** and he was alone on land.
>
> NLT: Late that night, the disciples were in **their boat in the middle of the lake,** and Jesus was alone on land.

Picture the scene:

- From the site of the feeding of the five thousand, Jesus went "up into a mountain" to pray, while the disciples "went down to the sea" (John 6:16). It sounds like they went in opposite directions, so it's likely they were already a couple miles apart before the disciples even reached the boat.

- The disciples in their boat were "in the middle of the lake" or thereabouts. That was at least four miles to the nearest shore, and six and a half miles from the farthest shore. In fact, John 6:19 says they had rowed "three or four miles."

- The sun had set several hours before, and it was dark (John 6:17).

- There was a severe storm with winds high enough to cause heavy waves, large enough to break inside the boat.

- The storm clouds would have blocked any moonlight and starlight.

That's all setting the scene. Now notice what Mark says about Jesus:

Mark 6:48: And **he saw them toiling in rowing;** for the wind was contrary unto them: and about the fourth watch of the night he cometh unto them, walking upon the sea, and would have passed by them.

NASB: **Seeing them straining at the oars,** for the wind was against them, at about the fourth watch of the night He came to them, walking on the sea; and He intended to pass by them.

MSG: **He could see his men struggling with the oars,** the wind having come up against them. At about four o'clock in the morning, Jesus came toward them, walking on the sea. He intended to go right by them.

Here's the point: How could Jesus have seen the disciples toiling, straining, and struggling with the oars, from at least five miles away, at night, during a violent storm, with no moonlight? With His naked eyes, He couldn't have. But if He traveled in the spirit, as experienced prophets do, it would have been easy.

Let's put it in modern-day terms. Suppose you and a friend are standing on a flat, straight road, at night, during a severe windstorm. Your friend then gets into a car and drives five miles away. Once he is five miles away from you, he stops the car, gets out, and moves his body in a variety of positions. Would *you* be able to see his bodily positions? With your naked eyes? From five miles away? At night? With no moon? During a windstorm? Very unlikely. Unless the car's lights were on, you probably wouldn't even be able to see the *car,* much less the person.

Now granted, these Scriptures are not conclusive in their proof that Jesus traveled in the spirit to see the disciples in the middle of the lake. From several miles away. At night. During a storm. With no moonlight. But neither is there any Scriptural evidence that He didn't, or couldn't, or wouldn't have done so, since other people in the Bible clearly did.

But then there's the case of Jesus seeing Nathanael:

> John 1:45–50 (NLT): Philip went to look for Nathanael and told him, "We have found the very person Moses and the prophets wrote about! His name is Jesus, the son of Joseph from Nazareth." ⁴⁶"Nazareth!" exclaimed Nathanael. "Can anything good come from Nazareth?" "Come and see for yourself," Philip replied. ⁴⁷As they approached, Jesus said, "Now here is a genuine son of Israel—a man of complete integrity." ⁴⁸"How do you know about me?" Nathanael asked. **Jesus replied, "I could see you under the fig tree before Philip found you."** ⁴⁹Then Nathanael exclaimed, "Rabbi, you are the Son of God—the King of Israel!" ⁵⁰Jesus asked him, "Do you believe this just because I told you I had seen you under the fig tree? **You will see greater things than this."**

How could Jesus have seen Nathanael sitting under the fig tree when He wasn't physically there? Because He traveled in the spirit—Jesus' spirit went on ahead of Philip even though His body stayed behind. And although Nathanael was blown away by such a supernatural sign, Jesus' comment in v. 50 implies that it wasn't that big of a deal. Almost like traveling in the spirit is an elementary-school thing, spiritually speaking.

And we can't forget how Jesus appeared out of thin air (John 20:19, 26), vanished into thin air (Luke 24:31, John 8:59), and levitated (Acts 1:9). In these cases, not only His spirit, but His *physical body as well,* were transported from one place to another, either instantly or slowly. If He can supernaturally travel from one place to another *with* His physical body, it seems silly to assume that He couldn't supernaturally travel *without* it.

Again, we are commanded to come boldly to the throne of grace (Hebrews 4:16), and I don't think that is merely metaphorical language—I believe it means exactly what it says. It is the birthright of every believer to talk to God face to face, and going to heaven to do so, like Paul did, would entail traveling in the Spirit. Moses talked to God face to face—for *forty days at a time* (Exodus 24:18, 33:11, 34:28, Numbers 12:6–8, Deuteronomy 34:10), and he was under an inferior covenant (Hebrews 8:6)!

Think of it: If we come "before the throne of grace," where is God? On the throne before which we stand. In other words, when we come boldly before the throne of grace, the whole point is that *we're standing before God,* not merely the fancy chair He sits on.

The Courts of Heaven

But can people do that? Actually stand before God, for fellowship, instruction, assignments, or whatever? It appears that Elijah and Elisha did. Look at how they describe themselves:

I Kings 17:1 (AMP): Elijah the Tishbite, of the temporary residents of Gilead, said to Ahab, As the Lord, the God of Israel, lives, **before Whom I stand,** there shall not be dew or rain these years but according to My word.

I Kings 18:15 (NASB): Elijah said *[to Obadiah]*, "As the Lord of hosts lives, **before whom I stand,** I will surely show myself to him *[Ahab]* today."

II Kings 3:14 (ESV): And Elisha said *[to Jehoram, the evil king of Israel]*, "As the Lord of hosts lives, **before whom I stand,** were it not that I have regard for Jehoshaphat the king of Judah, I would neither look at you nor see you."

II Kings 5:16 (AMP): Elisha said *[to Naaman]*, As the Lord lives, **before Whom I stand,** I will accept none. He urged him to take it, but Elisha refused.

Could it really be that Elijah and Elisha were in the habit of actually standing before the Lord? The English idiom can imply the watered-down meaning of "whom I serve," but the Hebrew text actually contains "before whom I stand." Did Elijah and Elisha actually mean that? Is that something that prophets are called to do? To literally appear in the courts of the Lord and stand before Him?

There is a Scripture we saw in Chapter 1, which quotes God explaining the true purpose of prophetic ministry. Let's look at it again, noticing a different part of the verse this time:

> Jeremiah 23:22: But **if they had stood in my counsel,** and had caused my people to hear my words, then they should have turned them from their evil way, and from the evil of their doings.

> AMP: But **if they had stood in My council,** then they would have announced My words to My people, and would have turned them back from their evil way And from the evil of their deeds.

Now already that is interesting. The two homophones "counsel" and "council," although pronounced the same in English, mean different things. "Counsel" means "advice," "guidance," or "recommendation," while "council" means "a formally constituted legislative body that meets regularly." Which one does the Bible actually say? Which one is present in the original Hebrew text?

The Hebrew word used in this passage is סוֹד (çowd, H5475), and it is defined as "a session, i.e. company of persons (in close deliberation)" and "assembly." True, the *product* of this council would be advice, guidance, judgments, and the like, but the Hebrew word *çowd* means the assembly itself. And notice that God refers to it as *His* council. In other words, *the courts of heaven,* literally.

Let's look at some other translations to see if other translation teams picked up on this idea of "council" instead of mere "counsel" in this passage. Actually, a great many of them do, and spell the English word "council," but they clarify it even further, as shown below. Other translations use other words, but express the same idea:

> CEV: **If they had been in a meeting of my council in heaven,** they would have told you people of Judah to give up your sins and come back to me.

> CJB: **If they have been present at my council,** they should let my people hear my words and turn them from their evil way and the evil of their actions.

ERV: **If they had stood in my heavenly council,** then they would have told my messages to the people of Judah. They would have stopped the people from doing bad things. They would have stopped them from doing evil.

EXB: But **if they had stood in the meeting of angels [my assembly/council],** they would have told my message to my people. They would have turned the people from their evil ways and from doing evil.

GWORD: **If they had been in my inner circle,** they would have announced my words to my people. They would have turned back from their evil ways and the evil they have done.

MSG: **If they'd have bothered to sit down and meet with me,** they'd have preached my Message to my people. They'd have gotten them back on the right track, gotten them out of their evil ruts.

NIRV: **Suppose they had stood in my courts.** Then they would have announced my message to my people. They would have turned my people from their evil ways. They would have turned them away from their sins.

NLT: **If they had stood before me and listened to me,** they would have spoken my words, and they would have turned my people from their evil ways and deeds.

VOICE: **If only they had stood in My presence and heard My voice,** then they would have spoken My words to My people! They would have turned this nation back from its evil ways and evil deeds.

Wow! Did God really mean what He said there? That prophets can and should regularly come into His council meetings? To actually appear in the courts of God?

And actually, the passage above is even more clear when we add a few verses of context that occur before v. 22. Again, God was speaking of false prophets, both describing what they did, and contrasting that to what they *should* have done:

Jeremiah 23:16–18 (NIV): This is what the Lord Almighty says: "Do not listen to what the prophets are prophesying to you; they fill you with false hopes. They speak visions from their own minds, not from the mouth of the Lord. ¹⁷They keep saying to those who despise me, 'The Lord says: You will have peace.' And to all who follow the stubbornness of their hearts they say, 'No harm will come to you.' **¹⁸But which of them has stood in the council of the Lord to see or to hear his word? Who has listened and heard his word?"**

So it seems quite clear that prophets are allowed to—even *supposed* to—go to the courts of heaven and attend the meetings of His council. Notice these prophets are being reprimanded for *not* standing in God's presence and hearing His commands. If prophets are reprimanded for not being there, we can certainly conclude that they are authorized to go there. And remember Moses' statement about wanting *all* God's people to be prophets? This could get pretty exciting, pretty fast. And as a student of the Word, you're probably already thinking of a few more examples where prophets go to the court of God and stand in His council.[5]

Job's Accusations

The book of Job opens with a little bit of biographical background on him, including his godly character, his children, his wealth, and his family gatherings. Then, the scene abruptly changes to the courts of heaven, where we see a council of God in the court of heaven: a large legislative meeting overseen by God:

> Job 1:6–12 (NIV): One day **the angels came to present themselves before the Lord,** and Satan also came with them.

So Satan appears before God. Satan was forcibly cast out of heaven because of his rebellion against God (Isaiah 14:12–17), so he is unable to take advantage of the blessings of heaven, but that doesn't mean that he has free reign to do whatever he wants. God keeps Satan on a short leash and, as you can see from the rest of the story, Satan can't do anything without God's explicit permission. But the point of this passage is that there are times—pretty often, as we can see below—when angels (including the evil ones) are called together to give an account to God of their recent activities.

---

[5] There is a great deal more about the council of God in the Bible, both Old Testament and New, than most people realize. For a deep and detailed study on the council of God, who they are, and what they do, I highly recommend this book:

Michael S. Heiser, *The Unseen Realm: Recovering the Supernatural Worldview of the Bible*, Lexham Press, Bellingham, WA, 2015.

So already, this is interesting. The good angels would have been thrilled to come before the Lord they serve, and bask in the glory and radiance of their King; that's very understandable. But why would the *fallen* angels—Satan and his demons—present themselves before the Lord? Surely it was because the Lord had summoned them. It seems unlikely they would have voluntarily chosen to go into the Lord's presence, considering that just *thinking* about God terrifies them (James 2:19, AMP).

So what happened when the angels were assembled before God?

> ⁷The Lord said to Satan, "Where have you come from?" Satan answered the Lord, "From roaming through the earth and going back and forth in it." ⁸Then the Lord said to Satan, "Have you considered my servant Job? There is no one on earth like him; **he is blameless and upright, a man who fears God and shuns evil."**

Job was a very godly man. Look at the words that God Himself uses to describe him: "blameless and upright, a man who fears God and shuns evil." Other translations render it "blameless—a man of complete integrity. He fears God and stays away from evil" (NLT), "a perfect and an upright man, one that feareth God, and escheweth evil" (KJV), "a truly good person, who respects me and refuses to do evil" (CEV), "a man without sin and upright, fearing God and keeping himself far from evil" (BBE), and so forth. May we all aspire to have God describe us that way!

Unsurprisingly, Satan starts to accuse Job, as he does to all of us:

> ⁹"Does Job fear God for nothing?" Satan replied. ¹⁰"Have you not put a hedge around him and his household and everything he has? You have blessed the work of his hands, so that his flocks and herds are spread throughout the land. ¹¹But stretch out your hand and strike everything he has, and he will surely curse you to your face." ¹²The Lord said to Satan, "Very well, then, everything he has is in your hands, but on the man himself do not lay a finger." Then Satan went out from the presence of the Lord.

You probably know the story: trying to get Job to curse God, Satan attacks him. Satan incites the Sabeans to steal Job's oxen and donkeys and kill his servants, and then causes a supernatural fire that kills Job's sheep and shepherds. In addition, Satan incites the Chaldeans to steal Job's camels, and then causes a violent windstorm that collapses the house where Job's ten children were gathered, killing them all. Satan certainly lives up to his description of not even showing up unless he can "steal, kill, and destroy" (John 10:10).

But Job's maturity and character show forth through it all:

Job 1:22 (NASB): Through all this **Job did not sin** nor did he blame God.

Soon after, there was another summons of the angels, good and bad, to appear before God:

Job 2:1 (AMP): Again there was a day when the sons of God [the angels] came to present themselves before the Lord, and Satan (the adversary and the accuser) came also among them to present himself before the Lord.

To avoid making this description too long, suffice it to say that Satan next attacked Job's health, giving him agonizing boils all over his body. Then Job's wife "slipped" a little in her role as a helper for him:

Job 2:9 (NIV): His wife said to him, "Are you still holding on to your integrity? Curse God and die!"

Then four of Job's friends came to visit, at least three of them giving him false and very unhelpful advice (Job 42:7–9), but Job stayed faithful to God, and God blessed him with twice as much wealth as he had before, and ten *more* children (Job 42:12–16).

That was a very abbreviated synopsis of the book of Job, but the subject at hand is the courts of God. Notice that the angels—both good angels and fallen angels (demons)—appeared before God. Note that *they* came and appeared before *God;* God did not go anywhere to appear before them. So they were summoned to the court of God.

While in the court of God, there were legal proceedings. There was the plaintiff (the accuser: Satan), there was the defendant (the accused: Job), and there was the arbitrator (the Judge: God). God asked Satan questions, although not because God lacked any information. Arguments were made and judgments were pronounced. God's authority is far superior to that of the devil, since the limits God set were impassable:

try as he might, Satan could not do any more harm to Job than God allowed in His decrees.

So how often do these sessions in heaven's court happen? Apparently pretty often, as indicated by the very small amount of time between the two court sessions. Notice that Job got the bad news about his oxen and donkeys being stolen, his sheep being burned up, his camels being stolen, and his children being killed, all within a period of minutes, or hours at most. Notice that *three times* in Job 1:14–19 it says, while one bearer of bad news "was yet speaking," the next one arrived with more bad news.

As mentioned above, we can also see from the story that God keeps Satan on a short leash: Satan is not free to do anything and everything he would like to do in his efforts to steal, kill, and destroy. Even when people give authority to Satan (as Job did by inadvertently allowing fear to get a foothold in his life—Job 3:25), God puts limits on how much destruction Satan can cause.

We also realize, from reading this story, that Satan—or at least one of his demons—is likely to accuse us before God many times. But Satan is finite, God is not; Satan is a liar, and God is not; Satan has been defeated, and God has not. And we can read about how Satan is cast down, and how we overcome him:

> Revelation 12:10 And I heard a loud voice in heaven, saying, "Now the salvation and the power and the kingdom of our God and the authority of his Christ have come, for **the accuser of our brethren has been thrown down, who accuses them day and night before our God.** [11]And they have conquered him by **the blood of the Lamb and by the word of their testimony,** for they loved not their lives even unto death."

And here is another intriguing realization we can gain from reading the above story: How did the writer of the book of Job know these councils in the courts of heaven had happened? Clearly, God allowed some human being to witness it, who then wrote it down. Who was it? We don't know. But was this person a prophet? Very likely, as we'll see as we continue reading. It may have been Job himself, after the fact.

In Job's story of the court of heaven, we find God asking Satan questions, but more to show off the faithfulness of Job than to actually get information. Since no one can hide information from God, He doesn't need to "get" information from anyone else. However, in the next story of the courts of God, a similar (and perhaps the identical) group of angels is before God, and He is *asking advice* from them! If this sounds odd, keep reading.

The Fall of Ahab

Remember Ahab, king of Israel? He is most often remembered for the evil he did, and the awful wife that he had: Jezebel. But actually, Ahab did repent later in life. Shortly after Jezebel convinced Ahab to have Naboth assassinated to obtain the vineyard Naboth owned but was unwilling to sell, God sent Elijah to Ahab with a stern word of judgment for his sins.

Here's what happened next:

> I Kings 21:27–29 (NIV): When Ahab heard these words, **he tore his clothes, put on sackcloth and fasted. He lay in sackcloth and went around meekly.** [28]Then the word of the Lord came to Elijah the Tishbite: [29]"Have you noticed how **Ahab has humbled himself** before me? Because he has humbled himself, I will not bring this disaster in his day, but I will bring it on his house in the days of his son."

So in the spiritual realm, judgment against Israel would still happen, but the worst of it only after Ahab was dead. In the political realm, for the next three years, there was no war between Syria and Israel. But then, when Jehoshaphat, the godly king of Judah, came to visit Israel, Ahab told him basically, "The Syrians captured Ramoth-gilead and took it from us a long time ago, and I think we should take it back. Are you with me?" Jehoshaphat replied, "Of course! But let's get counsel from the Lord first."

Kings in the ancient Middle East were well aware of the spiritual realm, so they virtually all had prophets that they looked to for guidance on important decisions. Godly kings tended to have real prophets, and ungodly kings tended to have false prophets. So even though Ahab had personally repented, Jezebel's influence still allowed only false prophets to advise him.

Here's how it went down. Ahab gathered four hundred Jezebel-approved idol-worshipping prophets and asked them, "Should I attack Ramoth-gilead to take it back?" They all answered, "Yes! Go for it! The Lord will give you the victory!"

Jehoshaphat immediately smelled a rat, and he saw that these so-called prophets had no idea who God was:

> I Kings 22:7–8 (NLT): But Jehoshaphat asked, "Is there not **also a prophet of the Lord** here? We should ask him the same question."

So Jehoshaphat, very rightly leery of the reliability of these false prophets, asked Ahab if he had any prophets *of the Lord* they could consult (it's always a good idea to consult with that kind of prophet), since Jehoshaphat could see that the other four hundred were obviously not "of the Lord." Ahab's response is more than a little revealing:

> ⁸The king of Israel replied to Jehoshaphat, "There is one more man who could consult the Lord for us, but **I hate him. He never prophesies anything but trouble for me!** His name is Micaiah son of Imlah." Jehoshaphat replied, "That's not the way a king should talk! Let's hear what he has to say."

So Ahab sends a messenger to get Micaiah, and the messenger tells him, "All the other prophets are prophesying victory; make sure you agree with them." To which Micaiah replies (paraphrased): "Fat chance. I'll speak the word of the Lord instead."

When Micaiah stands before Ahab and Jehoshaphat, they ask him the question about whether to go attack Ramoth-gilead to take it back from the Syrians. Micaiah gives a sarcastic reply that both kings recognize as such, and they ask him what he *really* saw. Micaiah then tells his vision:

> I Kings 22:17–23 (NLT): Then Micaiah told him, "In a vision I saw all Israel scattered on the mountains, like sheep without a shepherd. And the Lord said, 'Their master has been killed. Send them home in peace.'" ¹⁸"Didn't I tell you?" the king of Israel exclaimed to Jehoshaphat. "He never prophesies anything but trouble for me." ¹⁹Then Micaiah continued, "Listen to what the Lord says! **I saw the Lord sitting on his throne with all the armies of heaven around him, on his**

163

right and on his left. [20]And **the Lord said, 'Who can entice Ahab to go into battle against Ramoth-gilead so he can be killed?' There were many suggestions,** [21]and finally a spirit approached the Lord and said, 'I can do it!' [22]'How will you do this?' the Lord asked. And **the spirit replied, 'I will go out and inspire all of Ahab's prophets to speak lies.' 'You will succeed,' said the Lord. 'Go ahead and do it.'** [23]So you see, the Lord has put a lying spirit in the mouths of all your prophets. For the Lord has pronounced your doom."

Here is a scene in the courts of heaven, in which a legislative assembly was convened. The topic is how to cause Ahab's death, following the standard reap-what-you-sow protocol, since he had been habitually rebelling against God, and he was about to reap what he had sown for almost twenty years. God is asking for input from the participants—not because He needs it, of course, but because He is interested in our thoughts—and various spirits offer suggestions.

Like the scene from Job that we saw above, evil spirits were apparently included in this council in the court of heaven. Since judgment was coming on Ahab for his years of rebellion, God asked for ideas on how to arrange for Ahab to die in battle. As we saw in the passage above, a lying spirit—with God's authorization—caused all Ahab's false prophets to latch onto the lie the spirit told them.

Long story short, Ahab disguised himself to look less like the King of Israel, and they went to battle. An enemy archer took a random shot, and the arrow hit Ahab between the joints of his armor, and he died later that day, just as Micaiah had foretold.

But let's look at Micaiah's vision again; here is another large group meeting in the Court of God—*all* the armies of heaven were around Him (v. 19). Judgment had been passed against Ahab, Jezebel, and Israel, but most of it would occur after Ahab died. And here, the Lord is apparently seeking advice from created beings—angels. This seems to be another case like God bringing all the animals to Adam "to see what he would name them" (Genesis 2:19). Of course God could have named the animals Himself, but God chooses to do things together with His creatures, be they angels, as above, or humans, as in Mark 16:20.

A job had to get done: Ahab had to fall in battle. How could they accomplish this task? Of course, God would have had innumerable ways to make it happen, flawless every one, but He wanted to hear the ideas of the angels in His armies. Notice that many suggestions were made, probably many of them were feasible, but God rejected them all until the final one, of a spirit being a "lying spirit" in the mouths of the false prophets.

It may seem a little strange for God to use agents of evil to get things done; are we interpreting that correctly? Apparently so:

> Proverbs 16:4 (NASB): The Lord has made everything for its own purpose, **even the wicked for the day of evil.**

But does that other part make sense? Is the Bible right when it refers to *God* putting a deceiving spirit in the mouths of all the false prophets? Would a God Who cannot lie do such a thing? Clearly, yes, and there are other Scriptures that support this idea:

> Isaiah 66:4 (AMP): So **I also will choose their delusions** and mockings, their calamities and afflictions, and I will bring their fears upon them— because when I called, no one answered; when I spoke, they did not listen or obey. But they did what was evil in My sight and chose that in which I did not delight.

> Ezekiel 14:4 (BBE): For this cause say to them, These are the words of the Lord: Every man of Israel who has taken his false god into his heart, and put before his face the sin which is the cause of his fall, and comes to the prophet; **I the Lord will give him an answer by myself in agreement with the number of his false gods. . .**

> II Thessalonians 2:11–12 (NIV): For this reason **God sends them a powerful delusion so that they will believe the lie** [12]and so that all will be condemned who have not believed the truth but have delighted in wickedness.

Notice that in every one of the passages shown above, the judgment of deception was directed toward people who were already actively rebelling against God and choosing wickedness. As I've mentioned in other books in the THOUGHTS ON series: If you choose to reject the Truth, it doesn't really matter which lie you believe. In Ahab's case, he was simply reaping what he had sown for almost twenty years, and in his case, this death was an act of mercy, since he had already repented. Other judgments, to fall later, were much more serious. He escaped the worst of it *because* he repented of his evil ways.

And again, how do we know that this is what happened in the courts of heaven? Obviously, Michaiah was there; he said, *"I saw the Lord sitting on His throne, and all the host of heaven standing by Him* on His right and on His left." And he definitely was a prophet. So here is a prophet, present in the courtroom of heaven.

Isaiah's Vision

Another example is when Isaiah "saw the Lord sitting upon a throne, high and lifted up, and His train filled the temple." After the angel cleansed Isaiah's lips with the coal taken from the altar, this happened:

> Isaiah 6:8 (NASB): Then I heard the voice of the Lord, saying, "Whom shall I send, and who will go for Us?" Then I said, "Here am I. Send me!"

Note that Isaiah *overheard* a conversation that was already being carried on without him. This conversation between the members of the Godhead was the council of God, in the court of God: His throne room. They were deliberating and making decisions, and when Isaiah heard the assignment under consideration, he volunteered.

[To hear this passage set to music, listen to the song *Send Me* on the album *Go Into All the World*, or scan the QR code at right.]

An interesting side note on this passage—angels or other kinds of spiritual beings can be involved in people's sins being forgiven:

> Isaiah 6:6 (NIV): Then **one of the seraphs** flew to me with a live coal in his hand, which he had taken with tongs from the altar. [7]With it he touched my mouth and said, "See, this has touched your lips; **your guilt is taken away and your sin atoned for.**"

Forgiveness of sins comes *from* God, of course, but apparently it can be *delivered* by angelic beings (or even us: John 20:23).

Daniel

Yet another example is when Daniel saw God the Father (the "Ancient of Days") and God the Son ("one like the son of man") in the throne room:

> Daniel 7:9–10, 13–14 (NASB): As I looked, **thrones were set in place, and the Ancient of Days took his seat.** His clothing was as white as snow; the hair of his head was white like wool. **His throne was flaming with fire,** and its wheels were all ablaze. [10]A river of fire was flowing, coming out from before him. Thousands upon thousands attended him; ten thousand times ten thousand stood before him. **The *court* was seated, and the books were opened.** . . . [13]In my vision at night I looked, and there before me was **one like a son of man,** coming with the clouds of heaven. **He approached the Ancient of Days** and was led into his presence. [14]He was given authority, glory and sovereign power; all peoples, nations and men of every language worshiped him. His dominion is an everlasting dominion that will not pass away, and his kingdom is one that will never be destroyed.

Note the terminology in v. 10: "The court was seated, and the books were opened." This is indeed the court of heaven, where decisions are made and judgments are pronounced.

Zechariah

Zechariah also had a vision of—or a visit *to*—the courts of heaven. Like the story of Job, Zechariah's experience in the court of heaven included both God and Satan, but this time the topic of conversation was the high priest Joshua.

In the Old Testament, the phrase "the Angel of the Lord" means Jesus Himself, unless clearly indicated otherwise in the text (where *"an* angel of the Lord" usually means an angelic messenger). Here in Zechariah's encounter, there is the Angel of the Lord, pronouncing love, acceptance, and forgiveness, and Satan, doing what he always does: accusing (Revelation 12:10–11).

Let's read the passage:

> Zechariah 3 (NIV): Then he *[an angel of the Lord]* showed me Joshua the high priest standing before the angel of the Lord, and Satan standing at his right side to accuse him. [2]The Lord said to Satan, "The Lord re-

buke you, Satan! The Lord, who has chosen Jerusalem, rebuke you! Is not this man a burning stick snatched from the fire?" [3]Now Joshua was dressed in filthy clothes as he stood before the angel. [4]The angel said to those who were standing before him, "Take off his filthy clothes." Then he said to Joshua, "See, **I have taken away your sin,** and I will put rich garments on you." [5]Then I said, "Put a clean turban on his head." So they put a clean turban on his head and clothed him, while the angel of the Lord stood by. [6]The angel of the Lord gave this charge to Joshua: [7]"This is what the Lord Almighty says: 'If you will walk in my ways and keep my requirements, then you will govern my house and have charge of my courts, and I will give you a place among these standing here. [8]"Listen, O high priest Joshua and your associates seated before you, who are men symbolic of things to come: I am going to bring my servant, the Branch. [9]See, the stone I have set in front of Joshua! There are seven eyes on that one stone, and I will engrave an inscription on it,' says the Lord Almighty, 'and **I will remove the sin of this land in a single day.** [10]In that day each of you will invite his neighbor to sit under his vine and fig tree,' declares the Lord Almighty."

Zechariah 1:8 says that Zechariah had a vision—"During the night I had a vision. . ."—but as we know for numerous other Biblical passages, a vision can be received by God "projecting" images into our spirits as we remain physically on earth (Genesis 15, *et al*)

Note that Zechariah was not simply a passive observer of this scene; he was an active participant. In v. 5, it is Zechariah himself ("then *I* said. . .") who recommended a clean turban for Joshua's head. This is even more clear in the Amplified:

> Zechariah 3:5 (AMP): And **I [Zechariah] said,** Let them put a clean turban on his head. So they put a clean turban on his head and clothed him with [rich] garments. And the Angel of the Lord stood by.

So in this story of the courts of heaven, there is a prophet (Zechariah) interceding for a person (Joshua) whom God wanted to bless, and whom Satan was accusing. This type of intercession seems to be a large part of what prophets do.

David

How about King David, the man after God's own heart: did *he*, or any other writers of the Psalms, actually go into the courts of God like we've been talking about? Let's take a look:

Psalm 65:4 (NIV): **Blessed are those you choose and bring near to live in your courts!** We are filled with the good things of your house, of your holy temple.

Psalm 84:2 (NIV): **My soul yearns, even faints, for the courts of the Lord;** my heart and my flesh cry out for the living God.

Psalm 84:10 (NIV): **Better is one day in your courts than a thousand elsewhere;** I would rather be a doorkeeper in the house of my God than dwell in the tents of the wicked.

Psalm 92:12–13 (NIV): The righteous will flourish like a palm tree, they will grow like a cedar of Lebanon; [13]planted in the house of the Lord, **they will flourish in the courts of our God.**

Psalm 96:8 (NIV): Ascribe to the Lord the glory due his name; **bring an offering and come into his courts.**

Psalm 100:4 (NIV): **Enter his gates with thanksgiving and his courts with praise;** give thanks to him and praise his name.

Psalm 116:18–19 (NIV): **I will fulfill my vows** to the Lord in the presence of all his people, [19]**in the courts of the house of the Lord**—in your midst, O Jerusalem. Praise the Lord.

Psalm 135:1–2 (NIV): Praise the Lord. Praise the name of the Lord; praise him, you servants of the Lord, [2]**you who minister** in the house of the Lord, **in the courts of the house of our God.**

But weren't the "courts" David is referring to the courts of the Temple? No, because the temple wasn't built yet; his son Solomon would build it years later. So the "courts" must have been the outer and inner courts of Moses' tabernacle, right? No, that's not the case either, because David didn't use Moses' tabernacle. He made his own—remember the tabernacle of David, where praise and worship was happening 24/7, and the Ark of the Covenant was right there for everyone to see (II Samuel 6:17–19, I Chronicles 25:1–31, Isaiah 16:5, Amos 9:11, Acts 15:16). So the Tabernacle of David didn't even *have* outer and inner courts.

So if it wasn't the Temple, nor Moses' tabernacle, nor David's tabernacle, what was David referring to when he talked about going into the "courts" of the Lord? Could he have been talking about actually going into the heavenly courtroom like Elijah, Elisha, Micaiah, Isaiah, and Daniel did? After all, David was a prophet too (Acts 2:29–30). Intriguing thought, isn't it?

So think about the people who stood in the courts of heaven, before the Lord: Elijah, Elisha, Micaiah, Isaiah, Daniel, and apparently David and other psalmists as well. What do they have in common? All prophets. Put that together with God's statement of what prophets are called to do (Jeremiah 23:22), and Moses' statement "Would to God that *all* the Lord's people were prophets" (Numbers 11:29), and Joel's prophecy that God would pour out His Spirit "on *all* mankind" and they would prophesy (Joel 2:28–30), and Paul's command to "desire spiritual gifts, *especially* that you may prophesy" (I Corinthians 14:1, 37), accompanied by his statement, "You may *all* prophesy" (I Corinthians 14:31), it gets downright exciting. So yes, I think it's safe to say that people who are called to prophetic ministry (i.e., all believers) are invited to literally "come to the throne of grace," just like it says. Glory!

So, as you get more and more experience in ministering in the prophetic arena, and study the teachings of reputable, world-class prophets (the number of which is growing constantly), you'll realize that God is still causing these things to happen on a regular basis.

Bodily Sensations

Feeling a sensation in one's body is a common way of receiving a message from God to communicate to someone else, as shown by the Scriptures above. But it can also be used both for impartation of anointing and for physical healing. In the former case, God can draw your attention to a particular body part that symbolizes a function with which that particular part is associated.

For example, if someone feels an anointing in his lips, it can mean that God is calling him into some kind of speaking ministry: teaching, preaching, prophetic, leading worship, and so forth (Psalm 40:9, 51:15, 63:3–5, 71:23, Malachi 2:7, Hebrews 13:15, etc.). An anointing on the hands often indicates a healing ministry (Mark 5:23, Luke 4:40, Acts 4:30, etc.), an anointing in the feet often indicates evangelism (Isaiah 52:7, Romans 10:15, Ephesians 6:15, etc.), and so forth.

What does such an anointing in a body-part feel like? Often it manifests as a pins-and-needles tingling, like when your arm or leg "wakes up" after having been asleep, or like a mild electric shock. Another common way is a sensation of fine "bubbles" in your bloodstream, as if your blood feels "fizzy" like ginger ale or champagne. Another typical feeling is a sensation of uncommon heat in the indicated body part, similar to what many people feel when God is healing someone through their hands.

The above sensations are some of the more common ones, but your particular sensation may be very different from these; God has infinite imagination and He interacts with His children in very different ways. As you practice putting yourself into situations where your obedience to Him results in situations where God "needs to" show up, you'll learn by experience how God communicates with you personally.

In the next case, one person can feel a pain that is not his, but is actually a message from God that someone nearby has a pain in that area of his body. If you have been involved with supernatural healing very long, it is likely that you've seen this one a lot.

For example, suppose someone who has perfectly healthy knees and legs goes to a healing meeting, and suddenly he feels a sharp pain in his right knee for no apparent reason. Such a person could think, "Oh, no! The devil's attacking me now since I started getting interested in all this supernatural stuff! I'd better lay off quick, before something even worse happens!" This, of course, is exactly what the devil wants you to think: he would much rather you go AWOL out of fear than to actually learn how to use the weapons God gives us against the kingdom of darkness.

Or, the person might think, "Oh, no! Of all the rotten luck! I can't minister healing to someone else now; I need it myself!" Thinking like this would also be fine with the devil. He's not particular about *why* you roll over and give up, as long as you do it.

Or, the person could think, "That's weird. There's nothing wrong with my knees. Lord, are you trying to tell me something?" This is the recommended response to a tactile word of knowledge such as this. Such a vicarious pain not only indicates that someone nearby is also feeling that pain, but also indicates that God is specifically calling it out for healing. Our best strategy is to cooperate with God.

Exactly *how* you cooperate with God depends on the circumstances. God may let you know who has the pain that you're feeling, or you may have to announce the sensation to those present, so that the people who have that condition can all be healed. Words of knowledge commonly occur this way.

The method of handling the situation in a way that is respectful, non-disruptive, and in submission to the people in authority over the meeting, could vary. Relevant factors include whether or not the person receiving this information from God is in a position of authority, whether or not a person in authority tells people in the congregation to pray for each other, and many other possible factors. God will show you what is appropriate for your particular situation.

If you honestly can't tell if God is pointing anyone out to you, and the people in authority don't pursue it for whatever reason, ask God to keep teaching you how to move in the Kingdom, and make you ever more sensitive to the still, small voice of His Spirit. We learn through practice and repetition (Hebrews 5:12–14).

Although God often indicates His desire to do physical healing with these types of bodily sensations, be aware that God also uses symbolism and plays on words frequently. And, as it pertains to prophetic ministry, this may be the more common mode. For example, a sensation in the right hand might refer to someone's "right-hand man," that is, his most trusted assistant. An unsteadiness in the ankles, to the point where it almost feels like the feet are coming loose, might indicate that someone is becoming "footloose," in the sense of soon being able to travel much more freely. And so forth; God is quite imaginative in His communication to us. (See also the "Impartation of Anointing" section below for more examples.)

When we do cooperate with God in such cases, these four things are likely to happen: 1) the person gets healed/blessed, 2) God gets the glory, 3) the healed/blessed person realizes afresh that God knows and loves him, and 4) the person who received the word of knowledge or the prophetic message grows in faith and in determination to cooperate with God in future situations, because it is so downright exhilarating.

For the two cases above—God communicating through a bodily sensation to indicate callings or anointing to heal—I haven't found any specific Scriptural examples. However, they don't contradict the written Word, nor do they conflict with God's character. That fact, plus the realization that the Bible itself says that God does *many* things that are not exemplified in the Bible, should put our hearts at ease. (For detailed study and Scriptural support for this last statement, see Book 3: *Extra-Biblical Truth: A Valid Concept?*.)

Personal Examples of Physical Sensation

In our local Healing Rooms, when people want prayer for healing (as opposed to a prophetic word), they fill out a form with contact information and what they want prayer for. The receptionist puts that sheet of paper into an opaque folder, and when one of the prayer teams is ready to pray for the next person, the team leader goes to the receptionist and gets the next folder. Without opening the folder, we all lay hands on it and ask the Lord to show us whatever He wants to show us, in anticipation of the person coming in. Almost always, God communicates something to us via one or more of the communication mechanisms being discussed in this chapter.

One time, while the prayer team was praying over someone's folder, I felt a sensation of warm oil being poured over my head, whence it dripped down my shoulders and body. When I mentioned it to the prayer-team leader, the meaning was obvious to her and she immediately said, "That means you are supposed to anoint the person with oil!" So when the person came in for prayer a few minutes later, I did anoint her with oil as we prayed.

Another common thing to happen is that when praying for someone for healing, the pray*er's* hands get hot and/or tingly feeling, like ginger-ale in the bloodstream or a mild electrical buzz. Especially with the hotness, it is common for the pray*er*, the pray*ee*, or both, to feel that the hands are much warmer than mere body temperature. This is so common, in fact, Bill Johnson mentions it as a matter-of-fact occurrence when praying for the sick: "We tell our people, 'hot is good.'"

When ministering in the prophetic rooms (as opposed to the healing rooms), and we are listening for what God would speak to the current guest, occasionally my hands will get hot, as if we're praying for healing, even though we're not currently doing so. I've concluded that this means God is going to dramatically increase the anointing for healing in the person we're currently prophesying over. At the conclusion of prophetic sessions in which I've felt this sensation, guests have so often confirmed that the Lord has already been speaking to them about moving more into healing, that it seems pretty clear what God is saying when I feel that sensation.

On another occasion in the healing rooms, I held a lady's hand while we were praying for her, and she looked up in amazement and said, "Your hands are vibrating!" That was cool, but it was also news to me, because I couldn't see them vibrating or feel them vibrating. But she did, both that time and during a different prayer a short time later. Why did God cause her to perceive that sensation? Probably to confirm to her that He was present and that He was answering her prayers in the affirmative.

To read about yet another experience in the healing rooms, in which someone felt a bodily sensation that was spiritually induced, read the section "Left Ankle and Back" in the "Personal Testimonies" chapter of Book 5: *If It Be Thy Will*. The lady definitely felt something as I prayed for the shredded tendons in her ankle.

Impartation of Anointing

A common way for God to indicate what He is doing with a person, or how He wants to bless a person, is to draw attention to a particular body part. Sometimes this happens in a large meeting where God is blessing everyone at the same time.

For example, my wife Kathy and I were in a meeting one time with a well known prophetic teacher, and Kathy felt a ginger-ale tingly feeling rush up the left side of her body and come to rest in her head, and I felt a strong heat and tingle in my hands. At that moment the speaker said, "Whoa! The Holy Spirit just came up through the floor and many of you are feeling the anointing resting on some part of your body."

The speaker continued, "Some of you are feeling a buzzing in your knees; you are being commissioned into an intercessory calling. Some of you are feeling a buzzing in your hands; you are being moved into a greater healing anointing. Some of you are feeling a buzzing in your eyes; you are being called into prophetic ministry." He went on and named several other body parts and the corresponding ministries, but he didn't mention the top of the head, so after the meeting, Kathy went up to ask him about it.

"Oh," he said, "that means renewing of the mind."

So the *location* of the sensation of the manifest anointing of God was meaningful, and indicated certain callings to those people who felt it. In this way, too, God can communicate to us His thoughts.

What Needs to be Healed

Another thing that Kathy has had happen to her, although I haven't, is to get a word of knowledge in the form of a bodily sensation, as mentioned above. Such a sensation is often a pain or other unusual sensation whose location indicates what needs to be prayed for, as in the "knees" illustration given earlier. In settings where there are many words of knowledge about bodily illnesses or injuries that need to be healed, this is a mode of communication that God uses quite often.

For example, in one meeting Kathy and I were attending, Kathy had an unusual pain in her right shoulder. It was unusual, because there was nothing wrong with her right shoulder. But then the Lord pointed out a young man sitting near us, and she felt like he needed healing in his right shoulder. When the main speaker finished his talk, he said, "Okay, now break up into groups of four. No, three." We immediately approached the young man Kathy had been thinking about since her shoulder had started hurting, and asked him if his shoulder was hurting.

"Yes!" he said, surprised. Once we prayed for him, his shoulder was healed and Kathy's shoulder stopped hurting.

Tasting

So we've read about people seeing, hearing, and feeling various beings or things in the spirit. Are there any examples of *tasting* things in the Spirit? Probably the first things that come to your mind are these, written by David and Peter, respectively:

> Psalm 34:8a (NLT): **Taste** and see that the Lord is good.

> I Peter 2:2–3 (NIV): Like newborn babies, crave pure spiritual milk, so that by it you may grow up in your salvation, ³now that **you have tasted that the Lord is good.**

"But that's just metaphorical language!" someone objects. Is it? People consider many things to be metaphorical or symbolic until they experience the actual things for themselves. Then they are astonished at the realization that God really meant what He said.

So can you actually *taste* things in the spiritual realm? Is there a sense of "spiritual taste?" Actually, yes:

> Ezekiel 3:1–3 (BBE): And he said to me, Son of man, take this roll for your food, and go and say my words to the children of Israel. ²And, on my opening my mouth, he made me take the roll as food. ³And he said to me, Son of man, let your stomach make a meal of it and let your inside be full of this roll which I am giving you. Then I took it, and **it was sweet as honey in my mouth.**

Here, God was communicating something to Ezekiel through the sense of taste. Later God did a similar thing with the apostle John:

> Revelation 10:9–10 (NLT): So I went to the angel and told him to give me the small scroll. "Yes, take it and eat it," he said. **"It will be sweet as honey in your mouth, but it will turn sour in your stomach!"** ¹⁰So I took the small scroll from the hand of the angel, and I ate it! **It was sweet in my mouth, but when I swallowed it, it turned sour in my stomach.**

In both of these cases, God was communicating something through the sweetness and the bitterness of the spiritual thing that was tasted and eaten. The symbolism is clear.

We can also get so close to God that we can detect, through our spiritual senses, when something is not of God. Job, the one whom God Himself described as "a man perfect and upright, fearing God, and turning aside from evil" (YLT), described his sense of discernment in terms of taste:

> Job 6:30 Is there iniquity in my tongue? **cannot my taste discern perverse things?**
>
> AMP: Is there injustice or malice on my tongue? **Can my palate not discern what is destructive?**
>
> NET: Is there any falsehood on my lips? **Can my mouth not discern evil things?**

Maybe "taste and see that the Lord is good" is more profound than we thought.

Smelling

The sense of smell is also very important to God. He invented it, and it is unlikely that it was an accident that He did so. To get a feeling for how much the sense of smell communicates something to God, go to your concordance and look up various forms of the words "smell," "odor" (or "odour" if you're using KJV), "savor" (or "savour" if you're using KJV), "stink," "aroma," "fragrance," or other synonyms, depending on which translation you're using.

God receives our prayers, thanksgiving, affection, and worship of Him, and even our loving deeds to each other, as a desirable, pleasant smell, as the following examples indicate (and of course, there are many other examples not shown):

> Genesis 8:20–21 (NIV): Then Noah built an altar to the Lord and, taking some of all the clean animals and clean birds, he sacrificed burnt offerings on it. ²¹**The Lord smelled the pleasing aroma** and said in his heart: "Never again will I curse the ground because of man, even

though every inclination of his heart is evil from childhood. And never again will I destroy all living creatures, as I have done."

Exodus 29:18 (NET): . . .and burn the whole ram on the altar. It is a burnt offering **to the Lord, a soothing aroma;** it is an offering made by fire to the Lord.

Numbers 15:7 (AMP): And for the drink offering you shall offer a third of a hin of wine, **for a sweet and pleasing odor to the Lord.**

Song of Solomon 1:12 (NASB): While the king was at his table, **my perfume gave forth its fragrance.**

Song of Solomon 4:10 (GWORD): How beautiful are your expressions of love, my bride, my sister! How much better are your expressions of love than wine and **the fragrance of your perfume** than any spice. [11]Your lips drip honey, my bride. Honey and milk are under your tongue. **The fragrance of your clothing is like the fragrance of Lebanon.**

Ezekiel 20:41 (NET): When I bring you out from the nations and gather you from the lands where you are scattered, **I will accept you along with your soothing aroma.** I will display my holiness among you in the sight of the nations.

Hosea 14:5–6 (RSV): I will be as the dew to Israel; he shall blossom as the lily, he shall strike root as the poplar; [6]his shoots shall spread out; his beauty shall be like the olive, and **his fragrance like Lebanon.**

II Corinthians 2:14–16a (NASB): But thanks be to God, who always leads us in triumph in Christ, and manifests through us **the sweet aroma of the knowledge of Him** in every place. [15]For we are **a fragrance of Christ** to God among those who are being saved and among those who are perishing; [16]to the one **an aroma from death** to death, to the other **an aroma from life** to life.

Ephesians 5:2 (BBE): And be living in love, even as Christ had love for you, and gave himself up for us, **an offering to God for a perfume of a sweet smell.**

Philippians 4:18 (RSV): I have received full payment, and more; I am filled, having received from Epaphroditus **the gifts you sent, a fragrant offering,** a sacrifice acceptable and pleasing to God.

Revelation 5:8 (TEV): As he did so, the four living creatures and the twenty-four elders fell down before the Lamb. Each had a harp and gold bowls filled with **incense, which are the prayers of God's people.**

The above examples are godly *people,* or their godly actions and attitudes, being described in terms of pleasing smells. But in the following passage, note that it is God Himself that has a pleasant fragrance:

> Psalm 45:6–8 (NIV): Your throne, O God, will last for ever and ever; a scepter of justice will be the scepter of your kingdom. [7]You love righteousness and hate wickedness; therefore God, your God, has set you above your companions by anointing you with the oil of joy. [8]**All your robes are fragrant with myrrh and aloes and cassia;** from palaces adorned with ivory the music of the strings makes you glad.

The psalm quoted above was written by the sons of Korah. Who was Korah? This is not the one who rebelled against God and Moses, and was swallowed up by the earth (Numbers 16:27–33). No, the one whose sons (descendents) wrote Psalm 45 were men that King David put in charge of the round-the-clock worship of God in David's tabernacle (I Chronicles 25). The three main ones were Heman, Asaph, and Ethan (a.k.a. Jeduthun), all descendants of the Korah who was a Levite priest.

The point is that these guys were intimately familiar with the intense manifest presence of God, and so much so, that they could apparently perceive His fragrance during worship.

On the flip side, our deeds of cruelty, selfishness, and hypocrisy, whether directed against the Lord Himself or against other people, are perceived by the Lord as an unpleasant smell—even a stink or stench:

> Psalm 5:9 > Romans 3:13 (NLT): My enemies cannot speak a truthful word. Their deepest desire is to destroy others. **Their talk is foul, like the stench from an open grave.** Their tongues are filled with flattery. > "**Their talk is foul, like the stench from an open grave.** Their tongues are filled with lies." "Snake venom drips from their lips."
>
> Isaiah 65:5 (NLT): Yet they say to each other, 'Don't come too close or you will defile me! I am holier than you!' **These people are a stench in my nostrils, an acrid smell** that never goes away.
>
> Amos 5:21–24 (AMP): I hate, I despise your feasts, and **I will not smell a savor** or take delight in your solemn assemblies. [22]Though you offer Me your burnt offerings and your cereal offerings, I will not accept them, neither will I look upon the peace or thank offerings of your fatted beasts. [23]Take away from Me the noise of your songs, for I will not

179

listen to the melody of your harps. [24]But let justice run down like waters and righteousness as a mighty and ever-flowing stream.

Because smell is used so often as an indicator of desirability or undesirability, it should not be surprising that God would use it as a communication mechanism when imparting a message to someone, whether that message is for the person who detects the odor, or someone else.

Modern Examples

I have not personally had an experience of smelling a fragrance that was supernaturally caused, but it is still happening, and is on the rise as God pours out His Spirit. The following two examples are excerpts from Book 4: *Gold Dust, Jewels, and More: Manifestations of God?*, from the "Glory Cloud" chapter and the "Oil Exuding from People's Hands" chapter, respectively. But notice that both have a component of fragrance to the message.

First, the one about the glory cloud:

> Writer Tommy Welchel interviewed Sister Lucille, an eyewitness and participant in the Azusa Street revival, and asked her to describe what the Shekinah glory cloud was like:
>
> She would get such joy in her eyes as she told me how much she loved to be in the center of the mistlike cloud. She was so little in stature, she would sit down in it and, when it was thick, the mist was about up to her neck. Like a kid, she would have fun and play in the mist. She would often lie down, breathing it in. She could feel the energy of it and described that it was like pure oxygen being breathed into her lungs. **She could smell it, too. The scent was like lilacs to her. Others said it smelled like roses. The aroma depended upon what part of the building you were in at the time.**[6]

And here, the one about the oil:

_____

[6] Tommy Welchel, *True Stories of the Miracles of Azusa Street and Beyond,* Chapter 6, "What's In a Name?", emphasis added.

A manifestation of God that has been on the rise recently is that of oil exuding from people's hands, or feet, or head. No, this is not sweat, and no, it's not a skin disease. And it is fragrant—**it might smell like Rose of Sharon, or cinnamon, or something else attractive**—not like a gym locker room. It is oil, and it's getting more common to hear reports of it happening. As I write this, the last time I heard about it happening was last Saturday night: two people being called to missions work in the Philippine Islands suddenly had oil start coming out of their hands at the same time, to the surprise of both of them.

The prophetic healing evangelist Joshua Mills[7] often experiences this phenomenon of fragrant oil exuding from him.

In 2016, when ministering in the prophetic rooms, the two ladies in my room both smelled a wonderful floral fragrance that began abruptly during the prophetic ministry. I myself didn't smell it, but they were both greatly blessed, because they (very reasonably) took it as an indication from God that He was pleased with the ministry that had just happened.

Impressions

An "impression," in the context of receiving a communication from God, is not a sensory perception, either with physical senses nor spiritual senses. Rather, it is simply an awareness that appears in your heart. It could be as weak as a hunch or a feeling, or as strong as an assurance or absolute certainty, or anything in between.

An impression is what it appears to have been when God told Nehemiah what to do to rebuild the walls of the Jerusalem.

Nehemiah 2:12 (NKJV): Then I arose in the night, I and a few men with me; I told no one what my **God had put in my heart** to do at Jerusalem; nor was there any animal with me, except the one on which I rode.

---

[7] See the website for Joshua and Janet Angela Mills at NewWineInternational.org for information on their ministry.

> Nehemiah 7:5a (NKJV): Then my **God put it into my heart** to gather the nobles, the rulers, and the people, that they might be registered by genealogy.

An impression is also apparently how Luke perceived God's instructions in this passage, as he remembers the decision to write the gospel bearing his name:

> Luke 1:3 (NIV): Therefore, since I myself have carefully investigated everything from the beginning, **it seemed good also to me** to write an orderly account for you, most excellent Theophilus. . .
>
> GWORD: I, too, have followed everything closely from the beginning. **So I thought it would be a good idea** to write an orderly account for Your Excellency, Theophilus.

So was it God's will that Luke write his gospel account? If you believe that the Bible is inspired by God, you would have to come to this conclusion. How did Luke know he was supposed write an account of the gospel? From the wording above—"*it seemed good* to me. . ." or "*I thought. . .*"—it sounds like he had an impression from the Holy Spirit. Perhaps if Luke had resisted this impression, God would have been more forceful in His command, but this is only speculation. Apparently, an impression was enough.

After Pentecost, when the apostles in Jerusalem heard of Judaizers who were preaching that people had to be circumcised to be saved, they realized someone had to teach the truth of the matter. So they sent Paul, Barnabas, Barsabbas (also known as Judas), and Silas on a mission trip to counter the wrong teaching and to strengthen the churches along the way. So was it God's will that these men go on this missionary journey to Antioch, Syria, Cilicia, and elsewhere? I think anyone would be hard-pressed to support a negative answer here; surely it's safe to say that yes, it was God's will that they go on this journey of evangelism and discipling.

But again, how did the disciples *know* it was God's will? Do we think they just stumbled upon a random course of action that coincidentally "happened" to conform to God's will? Unlikely. From reading this account in Acts, they apparently had an impression:

> Acts 15:25–26 (NASB): . . .**it seemed good to us,** having become of one mind, to select men to send to you with our beloved Barnabas and Paul, [26]men who have risked their lives for the name of our Lord Jesus Christ.

It also appears that they all had the *same* impression from the Holy Spirit: note that they all had "become of one mind" to send these men on the mission trip. If you're in a group of people who are seeking God's will on something, and *everyone* comes to the same conclusion, it is comforting and reassuring that you are hearing accurately.

The idea of the apostles receiving an impression from the Holy Spirit is even more strengthened if we read the next two verses:

> Acts 15:27–28 (NASB): Therefore we have sent Judas and Silas, who themselves will also report the same things by word of mouth. [28]For **it seemed good to the Holy Spirit and to us** to lay upon you no greater burden than these essentials. . .

Wow! "It seemed good *to the Holy Spirit?*" How did *they* know what the Holy Spirit was thinking? He apparently gave them an impression. Could the communication from God have been more rock-solid and indisputable? Of course; God can be very clear about things when He wants to. But if it had been an undeniable open-eyed vision or some such, it seems unlikely that they would have used the terminology "it *seemed*. . ." God wants us to grow sensitive enough to His leading that He doesn't always have to shout for us to get the message. An impression is a perfect example of hearing God's "still, small voice" (I Kings 19:12).

Decades after he got saved, Paul went up to Jerusalem to meet with the apostles. Here's Paul's timeline, as he describes it in Galatians:

- He got saved on the Damascus road (1:15–16),
- He went to Arabia for an unspecified amount of time (1:17),
- He went back to Damascus for three years (1:17–18),
- He visited Peter two weeks, also seeing Jesus' half-brother James (1:18–19),

- He went north into Syria and Cilicia for 14 years (1:22–2:1),
- Then he went to Jerusalem again, along with Barnabas and Titus, to see the other apostles (2:1).

So Paul goes up to Jerusalem to talk to the church leaders 17 years, plus the unspecified time spent in Arabia, after he got saved. But *why* did he go up to Jerusalem? For old times' sake? Nothing better to do? No. Apparently, he had an impression:

Galatians 2:2a: And I went up **by revelation**. . .

AMP: I went because **it was specially and divinely revealed to me** that I should go. . .

CEV: But I went there because **God had told me to go**. . .

NLT: I went there because **God revealed to me that I should go.**

PHILLIPS: My visit on this occasion was **by divine command**. . .

This revelation from God that he should go up and talk to the church leaders and Jerusalem *could* have been more intense than a mere impression, but Paul does not indicate that. So it was *at least* an impression from the Holy Spirit that he should go. With the apostle Paul, an impression probably would have been enough. After all, he was rather good at hearing God, and rather adamant about obeying Him. . .

The "Check in the Spirit"

Have you ever heard of a "check in the spirit?" It is a relatively recent phrase that means an impression that some course of action should *not* be pursued. Usually, this is the Lord warning someone of potential danger, be that merely an inconvenience, or a life-threatening peril.

What does a "check in the spirit" feel like? How does one perceive a check in the spirit? The Lord is very imaginative and creative, so there are numerous ways the Lord can communicate to His people. Let's look at an example in the Bible:

Acts 16:6–8 (GWORD): Paul and Silas went through the regions of Phrygia and Galatia because **the Holy Spirit kept them from speaking the word in the province of Asia.** [7]They went to the province of Mysia and tried to enter Bithynia, but **the Spirit of Jesus wouldn't allow this.** [8]So they passed by Mysia and went to the city of Troas.

Basically, Paul and Silas said, "Let's go preach in Asia!" But the Holy Spirit said, "No." Then they said, "Let's go preach in Bithynia!" But the Holy Spirit again said, "No."

The Bible doesn't specify exactly *how* the Holy Spirit communicated to Paul and Silas that they were not supposed to preach in Asia; it could have been any of the ways mentioned in this book, and probably any one of a large number of other ways as well. But they got the message; they didn't preach in Asia. Then they tried to go preach in Bithynia, and the Holy Spirit again prevented them from going there. So again, they received a "check in the spirit" that diverted them from their intended goals, and replaced them (good-hearted though they were) with what God's goal actually was.

If Paul and Silas had not been so experienced in hearing and recognizing the voice of the Holy Spirit, they could have misinterpreted this check in the spirit as being an attack of the devil. After all, Jesus said that we were to "go into all the world and preach the gospel" (Mark 16:15), so the Holy Spirit would never teach tell someone *not* to preach the gospel, would He?

This would have been an easy situation in which to misunderstand the Holy Spirit's instructions. God was not telling them not to preach in Asia or Bithynia; he was only telling then not to preach in Asia or Bithynia *at that time.* Why would God say that? Because God's timetable is better than ours—He sees the *whole* picture, and we do not.

So what was going on? It becomes clear when we read the next couple verses:

> Acts 16:9–10 (GWORD): During the night Paul had a vision of a man from Macedonia. The man urged Paul, **"Come to Macedonia to help us."** [10]As soon as Paul had seen the vision, we immediately looked for a way to go to Macedonia. We concluded that God had called us to tell the people of Macedonia about the Good News.

So the check in the spirit that Paul and Silas felt prevented them from losing valuable time preaching in Asia and Bithynia, because God wanted them to go to Macedonia and preach there first. God had not forgotten about Asia and Bithynia; the Gospel did reach there (Acts

19:10, 22–26, 20:4, 18, I Corinthians 16:19, II Corinthians 1:8, I Peter 1:1, Revelation 1:4). It's just that God wanted the gospel preached to Macedonia first, for an excellent reason we will probably not know until we get to heaven.

Reading

Many people receive messages from God for words of knowledge or prophetic utterances by *reading* them. For example, some people see words hanging in midair above the person who is the message's intended recipient, or written on the floor right in front of the person, or even written on the person himself.

Or, it could even be written on a wall. You may remember that Israel's unrepentant sin resulted in King Nebuchadnezzar of Babylon attacking and conquering Israel, looting and destroying its buildings (including the temple at Jerusalem), and hauling most of the Jews back to Babylon as slaves. After Nebuchadnezzar died, his son Belshazzar took the throne.

At one point, Belshazzar threw a big party for a thousand of his noblemen, and for the drinking cups for himself, his noblemen, his wives, and his concubines, he used the gold and silver goblets which had been taken from the temple in Jerusalem. And as if that weren't disrespectful enough to use the goblets this way, they were also worshiping their Babylonian idols at the same time.

Then things start getting interesting:

> Daniel 5:5–12 (NIV): Suddenly **the fingers of a human hand appeared and wrote on the plaster of the wall,** near the lampstand in the royal palace. **The king watched the hand as it wrote.** [6]His face turned pale and he was so frightened that his knees knocked together and his legs gave way. [7]The king called out for the enchanters, astrologers and diviners to be brought and said to these wise men of Babylon, "Whoever reads this writing and tells me what it means will be clothed in purple and have a gold chain placed around his neck, and he will be made the third highest ruler in the kingdom." [8]Then **all the king's wise men came in, but they could not read the writing or tell the king what it meant.** [9]So King Belshazzar became even more terrified and his face grew more pale. His nobles were baffled.

Belshazzar seemed to realize that he was messing with the wrong God. Unlike his idols of gold, silver, iron, bronze, wood, and stone, Belshazzar couldn't control this God of Israel. And apparently, Belshazzar hadn't paid much attention to the events of his father Nebuchadnezzar's reign. Intellectually, he knew of his father's ups and downs, but he hadn't taken them to heart.

The story continues:

> [10]The queen, hearing the voices of the king and his nobles, came into the banquet hall. "O king, live forever!" she said. "Don't be alarmed! Don't look so pale! [11]**There is a man in your kingdom who has the spirit of the holy gods in him. In the time of your father he was found to have insight and intelligence and wisdom like that of the gods.** King Nebuchadnezzar your father—your father the king, I say—appointed him chief of the magicians, enchanters, astrologers and diviners. [12]This man Daniel, whom the king called Belteshazzar, was found to have a keen mind and knowledge and understanding, and also the ability to interpret dreams, explain riddles and solve difficult problems. **Call for Daniel, and he will tell you what the writing means.**"

So Daniel is brought before the king to interpret the handwriting on the wall. But before he tells Belshazzar *what* the message means, Daniel boldly tells Belshazzar *why* he received the message he is asking Daniel to interpret:

> Daniel 5:18–23 (NIV): "O king, the Most High God gave your father Nebuchadnezzar sovereignty and greatness and glory and splendor. [19]Because of the high position he gave him, all the peoples and nations and men of every language dreaded and feared him. Those the king wanted to put to death, he put to death; those he wanted to spare, he spared; those he wanted to promote, he promoted; and those he wanted to humble, he humbled. [20]But **when his heart became arrogant and hardened with pride, he was deposed from his royal throne and stripped of his glory.** [21]He was driven away from people and given the mind of an animal; he lived with the wild donkeys and ate grass like cattle; and his body was drenched with the dew of heaven, until he acknowledged that the Most High God is sovereign over the kingdoms of men and sets over them anyone he wishes. [22]**But you his son, O Belshazzar, have not humbled yourself,** *though you knew all this.* [23]Instead, you have set yourself up against the Lord of heaven. You had

the goblets from his temple brought to you, and you and your nobles, your wives and your concubines drank wine from them. You praised the gods of silver and gold, of bronze, iron, wood and stone, which cannot see or hear or understand. But **you did not honor the God who holds in his hand your life and all your ways.** [24] *Therefore* he sent the hand that wrote the inscription."

I'm sure Belshazzar's face got even more pale at hearing this. Daniel continues, and the other shoe drops:

> Daniel 5:25–31 (NIV): "This is the inscription that was written: mene, mene, tekel, parsin. [26]This is what these words mean: MENE: **God has numbered the days of your reign and brought it to an end.** [27]TEKEL: You have been weighed on the scales and found wanting. [28]PERES: Your kingdom is divided and given to the Medes and Persians." [29]Then at Belshazzar's command, Daniel was clothed in purple, a gold chain was placed around his neck, and he was proclaimed the third highest ruler in the kingdom. [30]**That very night Belshazzar, king of the Babylonians, was slain,** [31]and Darius the Mede took over the kingdom, at the age of sixty-two.

So here is an example of prophetically interpreting something God had written. In Belshazzar's case, the writing was visible to everyone in the room—probably because of its national import—but more commonly, the one giving the prophecy is the only one who sees the writing.

Reading People's Thoughts

One area of receiving prophetic words that has been more often associated with New Age operation than the Holy Spirit, but which the Holy Spirit invented, is that of reading, or knowing, people's thoughts. Is such "mind reading" really Scriptural? Let's take a look.

But first, does God know our thoughts? Of course He does:

> I Kings 8:39 (NIV): . . .then hear from heaven, your dwelling place. Forgive and act; deal with each man according to all he does, since **you know his heart (for you alone know the hearts of all men)**. . .

> I Chronicles 28:9 (NET): And you, Solomon my son, obey the God of your father and serve him with a submissive attitude and a willing spirit,

for **the Lord examines all minds and understands every motive of one's thoughts.** If you seek him, he will let you find him, but if you abandon him, he will reject you permanently.

II Chronicles 6:30 (BBE): Then give ear from heaven your living-place, answering with forgiveness, and give to every man, whose **secret heart is open to you,** the reward of all his ways; (for **you, and you only, have knowledge of the hearts of the children of men;**)

Psalm 44:21 (RSV): would not God discover this? For **he knows the secrets of the heart.**

Psalm 94:11 (NIV): **The Lord knows the thoughts of man;** he knows that they are futile.

Psalm 139:2 (AMP): You know my downsitting and my uprising; **You understand my thought afar off.**

Jeremiah 20:12 (NLT): O Lord of Heaven's Armies, you test those who are righteous, and **you examine the deepest thoughts and secrets.** Let me see your vengeance against them, for I have committed my cause to you.

Acts 15:8 (CEB): **God, who knows people's deepest thoughts and desires,** confirmed this by giving them the Holy Spirit, just as he did to us.

I Corinthians 3:20 (AMP): And again, **The Lord knows the thoughts and reasonings of the [humanly] wise** and recognizes how futile they are.

So obviously, *God* knows our thoughts. But is it possible for *people* to know each other's thoughts, even occasionally? Let's look at Jesus' ministry:

Matthew 9:4 (NIV): **Knowing their thoughts,** Jesus said, "Why do you entertain evil thoughts in your hearts?"

Matthew 12:25 (ESV): **Knowing their thoughts,** he said to them, "Every kingdom divided against itself is laid waste, and no city or house divided against itself will stand."

Mark 2:8 (NIV): Immediately **Jesus knew in his spirit that this was what they were thinking in their hearts,** and he said to them, "Why are you thinking these things?"

Luke 2:34–35 (NIV): Then Simeon blessed them and said to Mary, his mother: "**This child is destined** to cause the falling and rising of many in Israel, and **to be a sign that will be spoken against,** [35]**so that the thoughts of many hearts will be revealed.** And a sword will pierce your own soul too."

Luke 5:22 (ESV): When **Jesus perceived their thoughts,** he answered them, "Why do you question in your hearts?"

Luke 6:8 (GWORD): But **Jesus knew what they were thinking.** So he told the man with the paralyzed hand, "Get up, and stand in the center of the synagogue!" The man got up and stood there.

Luke 9:47 (AMP): But Jesus, as **He perceived the thoughts of their hearts,** took a little child and put him at His side. . .

Luke 11:17 (MSG): **Jesus knew what they were thinking** and said, "Any country in civil war for very long is wasted. A constantly squabbling family falls to pieces."

John 2:25 (AMP): And He did not need anyone to bear witness concerning man [needed no evidence from anyone about men], for **He Himself knew what was in human nature.** [He could read men's hearts.]

So we can see that Jesus knew people's hearts and their thoughts. We can also see from Mark 2:8 above, that Jesus knew these things *in His spirit*—that is, by means of spiritual perception—not merely by means of an educated guess based on the Jews' usual attitudes.

And although Jesus was God, He didn't do miracles *as* God—He plainly stated that He couldn't do anything by Himself (John 5:19). On the contrary, He did all His miracles as a *man* empowered by the Holy Spirit, thus being an example for us. Because, after all, Jesus also said that the same miracles He did, we would do also (John 14:12).

Now let's look at this passage; it pertains to the subject at hand:

Hebrews 4:12 (NASB): For **the word of God is** living and active and sharper than any two-edged sword, and piercing as far as the division of soul and spirit, of both joints and marrow, and **able to judge the thoughts and intentions of the heart.**

What does "the word of God" refer to in this verse? I can think of three possibilities:

- Is "the word of God" in this verse referring to the written Bible? I don't think so; while the Bible is an amazing book in which

God says many things, salvation is not found in it. As Jesus plainly told the Pharisees in John 5:39–40, the Scriptures merely point to Jesus Himself, and *He* is the One from whom salvation and every other blessing is obtained.

- Is "the word of God" referring to Jesus? Possibly, but that doesn't tell us anything that isn't found many other places in the Bible. Nor does it really help us in *our* ministry efforts, because it would simply be saying that Jesus knows stuff. Which, of course, He does.

- Is "the word of God" referring to things that the Holy Spirit tells us? I think this is the most likely interpretation, because it is applicable to our purpose on earth. The word of God—the Holy Spirit communicating something to us through whatever avenue He chooses—enables us to know what we need to know to obey Him and do the works Jesus did.

If "the word of God" referred to in Hebrews 4:12 above is indeed a communication from the Holy Spirit to us, it could take any of several different forms, as we've already seen. So, considering the topic at hand, is it a case of one person actually reading another person's mind? Or is it simply a normal word of knowledge in which God informs one person about what another person is thinking? Technically, it could be either, but practically, it doesn't seem to matter, because it is miraculous either way, and God gets the point across regardless.

However, although such "mind reading" could be simply a word of knowledge, it does seem to be associated closely with prophetic ministry. In this passage we looked at much earlier in the book, let's read what Paul says about it, paying attention this time to *who* is prophesying, and *what* they're prophesying about:

> I Corinthians 14:24–25 (HCSB): But if **all are prophesying** and some unbeliever or uninformed person comes in, he is convicted by all and is judged by all. ²⁵**The secrets of his heart will be revealed**, and as a result he will fall facedown and worship God, proclaiming, "God is really among you."
>
> v. 25, CEV: **They will tell what is hidden in their hearts.** Then they will kneel down and say to God, "We are certain that you are with these people."

GNT: . . .their **secret thoughts will be brought into the open,** and they will bow down and worship God, confessing, "Truly God is here among you!"

NASB: . . .the **secrets of his heart are disclosed;** and so he will fall on his face and worship God, declaring that God is certainly among you.

NCV: The **secret things in their hearts will be made known.** So they will bow down and worship God saying, "Truly, God is with you."

NIV: . . .and **the secrets of his heart will be laid bare.** So he will fall down and worship God, exclaiming, "God is really among you!"

NLT: As they listen, **their secret thoughts will be exposed,** and they will fall to their knees and worship God, declaring, "God is truly here among you."

TPT: . . .for **the intimate secrets of his heart will be brought to light.** He will be mystified and fall facedown in worship and say, "God is truly among you!"

VOICE: The **very secrets of his heart would be revealed,** and right there—mystified—he would fall on his face in worship to God, proclaiming all the while that God most certainly dwells among you.

This is clearly not the person holding the secrets revealing his own secret thoughts; this is his secret thoughts being revealed to those who are prophesying, and who then prophesied about those secrets. And how many people are prophesying? Look at v. 24 above:

I Corinthians 14:24 (HCSB): But if **all** are prophesying and some unbeliever or uninformed person comes in. . .

So "all" are prophesying, and the secret thoughts of the unbeliever or uninformed person are made manifest. Fascinating. This makes it sound like people's hearts, thoughts, and motives being revealed is a pretty common thing.

And of course, such revealing of a person's secret thoughts would have to be done in love, for the purpose of redemption and restoration, not shame and humiliation. We have the ministry of reconciliation (II Corinthians 5:18–19), not the ministry of hurtful embarrassment. As Paul says in the very next verse:

II Corinthians 14:26: . . .let everything be **constructive and edifying** and for the good of all.

So if you find yourself knowing what other people are thinking, and it turns out to be spectacularly accurate, don't consider yourself to be losing your mind, or being drawn into the occult. God could be giving you prophetic vision and insight into the other person's thoughts, or He could be giving you an ordinary word of knowledge, with the same results. Remember, God is good, and He does these things for our benefit, edification, and blessing. Remember also that God invented all this stuff, and the best the devil can do is counterfeit it (poorly).

Other Ways of Perceiving God's Messages

Now that we've seen Scriptural examples of many ways that God can communicate with us—seeing, hearing, feeling, tasting, smelling, visions, dreams, impressions, and reading, at least—we realize that when we receive a prophetic word for someone, it could be perceived in any of those ways. And again, simply because we've seen those examples in the Bible, that certainly doesn't mean that He is *limited* to communicating in those ways. God is rather imaginative and creative, and there are undoubtedly more ways that he could get His point across to us. But we know that there are *at least* those ways we've seen referenced above.

Chapter 4:

How Do You *Give* Prophetic Words?

That is another very good question. Any person who has received a word from the Lord that is intended for someone else must somehow communicate that word. We already covered the attitude with which prophetic messages must be given—"the greatest of these is love"—but given that, how do you actually *communicate* them to the recipients?

Speaking

The most obvious, and perhaps the most common mode of communication, is that of simply speaking out loud. This is so common and so self-evident that little discussion will be added to the following examples:

Deuteronomy 18:18: **I** *[God]* will raise them up a Prophet *[Jesus]* from among their brethren, like unto thee, and **will put my words in his mouth; and he shall speak unto them** all that I shall command him.

II Samuel 23:2 (NIV): The Spirit of the Lord **spoke** through me; his word was **on my tongue.**

Isaiah 3:10 (NASB): **Say** to the righteous that it will go well with them, for they will eat the fruit of their actions.

Isaiah 7:3–4 (NLT): Then the Lord said to Isaiah, "Take your son Shear-jashuba and go out to meet King Ahaz. . . ⁴**Tell him** to stop worrying. **Tell him** he doesn't need to fear the fierce anger of those two burned-out embers, King Rezin of Syria and Pekah son of Remaliah."

Jeremiah 1:17 (NIV): "Get yourself ready! Stand up and **say to them** whatever I command you. Do not be terrified by them, or I will terrify you before them."

Jeremiah 23:28 (NIV): "Let the prophet who has a dream **tell** his dream, but let the one who has my word **speak it** faithfully. For what has straw to do with grain?" declares the Lord.

Ezekiel 2:3–4 (BBE): And he said to me, Son of man, I am sending you to the children of Israel, to an uncontrolled nation which has gone against me: they and their fathers have been sinners against me even to this very day. ⁴And the children are hard and stiff-hearted; I am sending you to them: and **you are to say to them,** These are the words of the Lord.

Ezekiel 21:9 (AMP): Son of man, **prophesy and say,** Thus says the Lord: **Say,** A sword, a sword is sharpened and also polished. . .

Hosea 2:1 (NIV): "**Say** of your brothers, 'My people,' and of your sisters, 'My loved one.'"

Haggai 2:1–2 (NASB): On the twenty-first of the seventh month, the word of the Lord came by Haggai the prophet saying, ²"**Speak now** to Zerubbabel. . ."

Zechariah 1:2–3 (NET): The Lord was very angry with your ancestors. ³Therefore **say to the people:** The Lord who rules over all says, "Turn to me," says the Lord who rules over all, "and I will turn to you," says the Lord who rules over all.

I Corinthians 14:29 (BBE): And let the prophets **give their words,** but not more than two or three, and let the others be judges of what they **say.**

Note how "saying," "speaking," "telling," and other synonyms are closely associated with prophetic messages. So, clearly, speaking God's words is a common way—probably the *most* common way—for prophets to communicate their messages.

Ministering Together

It's obvious from the above passages that many prophetic messages are given through speaking. But there is an additional dynamic if there are multiple people receiving prophetic messages simultaneously, whether they are ministering to a single person or a group.

One example of the proper way to do this would be to take to heart, and put into practice, a portion of Paul's teaching in his first letter to the Corinthians. (You may recognize the next few paragraphs as an excerpt from the section "Decently and In Order" in Book 7: *Be Filled with the Spirit;* see that section for an expanded discussion of this passage.) Paul says:

> I Corinthians 14:29–33 (NLT): Let two or three people prophesy, and let the others evaluate what is said. ³⁰But **if someone is prophesying and another person receives a revelation from the Lord, the one who is speaking must stop.** ³¹In this way, all who prophesy will have a turn to speak, one after the other, so that everyone will learn and be encouraged. ³²Remember that people who prophesy are in control of their spirit and can take turns.

But this brings up the question, "How am *I* supposed to know that God revealed something to the next guy?" It's not difficult; it could be as simple as a nod or meaningful glance. This is pretty common in the context of Spirit-filled ministry situations: one person is praying or prophesying over someone and *could* continue, but he glances at the other people involved in the ministry before continuing. Someone else making eye contact and/or nodding communicates to the one currently praying or prophesying, "I have something too." So the current speaker defers to the next one, who then contributes.

This can also happen where the Lord Himself tells one person about what He is telling another person. One very plausible example is this: Suppose you and your friend Joe Regularperson are ministering to Sally, and God tells you something that Sally needs to hear, but adds, "Don't bring it up yourself; I want Joe to bring it up first. You just confirm it." Sure enough, Joe speaks out that thing from the Lord, and you confirm that you had heard the same thing, and that it was indeed the Lord.

In such a situation, *Sally* gets blessed and encouraged because Joe was obedient to share something from the Lord that she needed, and the impact is doubly strong because you confirmed you heard the same thing. *Joe* gets blessed and encouraged because your confirmation affirmed to him that he had indeed heard the Lord accurately. And *you* get blessed and encouraged because as soon as Joe said his piece, that confirmed to you that you too had indeed heard the Lord accurately. God is all about relationships and encouragement in living for Him.

As Paul had just said a few verses earlier:

> I Corinthians 14:26 (NASB): What is the outcome then, brethren? When you assemble, **each one has** a psalm, has a teaching, **has a revelation,** has a tongue, has an interpretation. **Let all things be done for edification.**

Writing

Prophetic words can also be written down, of course. Any prophetic message that God gives someone that can be expressed in *spoken* words can also be expressed as *written* words. But is that Scriptural? Do we have any examples in the Bible of prophetic words being actually written, instead of merely spoken? Yes. For example: Isaiah, Jeremiah, Ezekiel, Daniel, Hosea, Joel, Amos, Obadiah, Jonah, Micah, Nahum, Habakkuk, Zephaniah, Haggai, Zechariah, and Malachi. Think about that: *whole books* composed of virtually nothing but prophetic words, plus descriptions of the relevant circumstances and people.

And the list of books above (collectively known as "The Prophets") doesn't include all the prophetic messages given through Abraham, Moses, Elijah, Elisha, David, Asaph, Jesus, Paul, Peter, John, and other lesser-known or even unnamed people in the Bible through whom God spoke. When you start thinking of all the prophetic messages given or mentioned in the Bible, you see an overarching pattern: *ever since the Garden of Eden, God has been speaking personally to, and through, people because it has always been His intention, desire, and plan, to fellowship with us.*

Okay, granted, the Bible contains many written prophecies, but should we still be doing it that way nowadays? I think so. After all, why not?

I think you'd be hard-pressed to think of a good reason why we should *not* still write prophecies down. Note that "writing" a prophecy can be done in many ways, be that longhand on stone, leather, papyrus, or paper, or recording it on a tape recorder, a smartphone's voice recorder, a video, or whatever.

Basically, "writing it down" is any way of making a more permanent version of the message, so we can refer back to it multiple times and keep gleaning understanding from it, and also so we can avoid the inaccuracies and unreliability of human memory. After all, if someone gave you a three-minute prophecy, could you recite it back word for word? Could you still do it a week, month, or year later?

So, in answer to the question asked above, yes, there are cases where something God *did,* or something He *said,* was written down so as to help us remember it better. Note that in some of the following cases, it is *God Himself* commanding people to write it down so it could be better retained in memory.

> Exodus 17:14 (BBE): And the Lord said to Moses, **Make a record of this in a book, so that it may be kept in memory,** and say it again in the ears of Joshua: that all memory of Amalek is to be completely uprooted from the earth.

> Deuteronomy 6:6, 9 (NIV): These commandments that I give you today are to be upon your hearts. ⁹**Write them** on the doorframes of your houses and on your gates.

Even before the children of Israel got into the Promised Land, God knew that they would reject Him as king (I Samuel 8:7) and want a human king. So God gave Moses a list of requirements for every new king of Israel. It included this:

> Deuteronomy 17:18 (CEV): The official copy of God's laws will be kept by the priests of the Levi tribe. So, as soon as anyone becomes king, he must go to the priests and **write out a copy of these laws** while they watch.

This way the kings would have no excuse for not following the law: not only would they have read it all, but they would have written out their own copy. *So they would remember.*

Job also knew that people remember things better when they are written down:

Job 19:23 (NASB): "Oh that my words were **written**! Oh that they were **inscribed in a book**! [24]That with an iron stylus and lead they were **engraved** in the rock forever! [25]As for me, I know that my Redeemer lives, and at the last He will take His stand on the earth."

Remember the prophetic name of Isaiah's son?

Isaiah 8:1 (BBE): And the Lord said to me, **Take a great writing-board, and on it put down in common letters,** Maher-shalal-hash-baz. . .

And of course there are many more, a few of which are below:

Isaiah 30:8 (AMP): Now, go, **write it before them on a tablet and inscribe it in a book,** that it may be as a witness for the time to come forevermore.

Jeremiah 22:30 (GWORD): This is what the Lord says: **Write this about Jehoiakin:** He will be childless. He won't prosper in his lifetime. None of his descendants will succeed him as king. They won't sit on David's throne and rule Judah again.

Jeremiah 25:13 (NIV): I will bring upon that land all the things I have spoken against it, all **that are written in this book and prophesied** by Jeremiah against all the nations.

Jeremiah 30:2 (NLT): This is what the Lord, the God of Israel, says: **Write down for the record** everything I have said to you, Jeremiah.

Jeremiah 36:2, 6 (NET): Get a scroll. **Write on it everything I have told you to say** about Israel, Judah, and all the other nations since I began to speak to you in the reign of Josiah until now. [6]So you *[Baruch]* go there the next time all the people of Judah come in from their towns to fast in the Lord's temple. **Read out loud** where all of them can hear you what I *[Jeremiah]* told you the Lord said, **which you wrote** in the scroll.

Habakkuk 2:2 (NIV): Then the Lord replied: **"Write down the revelation** and make it plain on tablets so that a herald may run with it."

Revelation 1:11 (CEV): The voice said, **"Write in a book what you see.** Then send it to the seven churches in Ephesus, Smyrna, Pergamum, Thyatira, Sardis, Philadelphia, and Laodicea."

Even God Himself writes things down—not because He has a bad memory (although we might), but also because He wants to emphasize the importance of what is written:

> Exodus 24:12 (NET): The Lord said to Moses, "Come up to me to the mountain and remain there, and I will give you the stone tablets with **the law and the commandments that I have written,** so that you may teach them."

> Psalm 139:16 (RSV): Thy eyes beheld my unformed substance; **in thy book were written, every one of them, the days that were formed for me,** when as yet there was none of them.

> Malachi 3:16 (NLT): Then those who feared the Lord spoke with each other, and the Lord listened to what they said. **In his presence, a scroll of remembrance was written** to record the names of those who feared him and always thought about the honor of his name.

> Revelation 3:5 (BBE): He who overcomes will be dressed in white, and **I will not take his name from the book of life,** and I will give witness to his name before my Father, and before his angels.

> Revelation 13:8 (GWORD): Everyone living on earth will worship it *[the beast],* **everyone whose name is not written in the Book of Life.** That book belongs to the lamb who was slaughtered before the creation of the world.

So from the above, we can clearly see that it is common for people to write down the communication God gives them, regardless of the form the communication took. Remember, the prophets wrote down descriptions of what they saw, what they heard, what they felt, and various tastes and smells. And since God Himself commanded in multiple places that the recipients of His messages write them down, He is plainly not opposed to the idea. Plus, it is simply good sense to do so, to compensate for our less-than-perfect memories.

And, as prophetic Bible teacher Mark Virkler recommends, prophetic ministry is just easier to learn that way. If you feel like you have a prophetic word for a person or a group, *write it down.* That way, you won't feel like you're "on the spot" when it comes to delivering it; you can just read it. You don't forget pieces of it, you don't forget the specific words God used, and so forth. And because there's less self-imposed "pressure" to deliver a flawless word, you're less likely to stumble because of nervousness. Makes good sense.

Prophetic Acts

Less known, but still plainly Scriptural, are "prophetic acts." What are prophetic acts? They are *situational* prophecies, rather than *verbal* prophecies. In other words, the message from God is not merely spoken; it is *acted out.*

This concept is in the Bible not only as a general principle (shown in the verse below), but in numerous examples (discussed in the following sections). Take a look at this verse, referring to the Holy of Holies in Moses' tabernacle:

> Hebrews 9:8 (GNT): The Holy Spirit clearly teaches from **all these arrangements** that the way into the Most Holy Place has not yet been opened as long as the outer tent still stands.
>
> TPT: Now **the Holy Spirit uses the symbols of this pattern of worship to reveal** that the perfect way of holiness had not yet been unveiled. For as long as the tabernacle stood. . .
>
> MSG: This was the Holy Spirit's way of showing with a **visible parable** that as long as the large tent stands, people can't just walk in on God.

Note that the entire creation of Moses' tabernacle was itself a very detailed prophetic act. Also note how The Message describes the prophetic act: a "visible parable." That is a very good definition of a prophetic act, and Hebrews mentions Moses' tabernacle being symbolic and prophetic several other times as well:

> Hebrews 8:5 (NIV): They *[human priests]* serve at a sanctuary that is a **copy and shadow of what is in heaven.** This is why Moses was warned when he was about to build the tabernacle: "**See to it that you make everything according to the patter**
> \n **shown you on the mountain.**"

So Moses' raising of his hands was a prophetic act, simultaneously expressing trust in, and dependence upon, God.

Trumpets and Shouting

After Moses had died, and Joshua was leading Israel into the Promised Land, they came upon the heavily fortified city of Jericho. This city was massively protected, in terms of current military capabilities.

But all Jericho's fortifications were to no avail, because Joshua had angelic assistance:

Joshua 5:13–15 (NET): When Joshua was near Jericho, he looked up and saw a man standing in front of him holding a drawn sword. Joshua approached him and asked him, "Are you on our side or allied with our enemies?" [14]He answered, "Truly **I am the commander of the Lord's army.** Now I have arrived!" Joshua bowed down with his face to the ground and asked, "What does my master want to say to his servant?" [15]**The commander of the Lord's army answered** Joshua, "Remove your sandals from your feet, because the place where you stand is holy." Joshua did so.

As if angelic assistance weren't enough, Joshua also had God's promise of victory:

Joshua 6:2 (GWORD): The Lord said to Joshua, "I am about to hand Jericho, its king, and its warriors over to you."

But even though there's the promise that God stated, there is also a strong implication that the victory would be contingent upon the people's obedience, because God immediately continues with:

Joshua 6:3–5 (NASB): "You shall march around the city, all the men of war circling the city once. You shall do so for six days. [4]Also seven priests shall carry seven trumpets of rams' horns before the ark; then on the seventh day you shall march around the city seven times, and the priests shall blow the trumpets. [5]It shall be that when they make a long blast with the ram's horn, and when you hear the sound of the trumpet, all the people shall shout with a great shout; and the wall of the city will fall down flat, and the people will go up every man straight ahead."

It's interesting to note that God apparently said nothing about the people remaining silent, saying not even a word, during the laps around the city. So Joshua arranges for the priests, the trumpets, and the ark, and then talks to the people:

> Joshua 6:10 (NASB): But Joshua commanded the people, saying, "You shall not shout nor let your voice be heard nor let a word proceed out of your mouth, until the day I tell you, 'Shout!' Then you shall shout!"

Fascinating. Did God actually include the part about not saying a word, but describe the conversation in an abbreviated form in the quote in vv. 3–5? Or did Joshua add that part on his own? We don't know; the Bible doesn't say. Some say that Joshua told them to be quiet so they would not speak words of doubt and unbelief (by grumbling and complaining), thereby talking themselves out of the victory.

This is plausible, because they had talked themselves out of the victory forty years earlier when ten of the twelve spies sent into the Promised Land to check it out came back with fearful reports, resulting in a forty-year delay in entering in (Number 13:1–14:11). But although this idea is plausible, if they had had a bent toward grumbling and complaining, what would have prevented the people from doing so each night when they got home from circling Jericho?

But the Israelites *did* obey God in what He said about walking around the city once a day for six days, carrying the ark and blowing the trumpets, and then seven times on the seventh day, followed by shouting. The walls indeed fell flat, as God had promised, and Jericho was conquered.

So how was this a prophetic act? A couple possibilities come to mind:

- Trumpets announced the Day of Atonement ("atonement" means reconciliation and cessation of hostilities), and God had made a covenant of atonement with Israel, on the condition of their obedience (Exodus 19:5–6). Also, the Feast of Trumpets (Numbers 29:1).

- God had commanded them to blow the trumpets when going into battle, even before this particular situation. And God promised to rescue Israel (Numbers 10:9).

So the blowing of the trumpets could have been a prophetic act that prophesied another manifestation of God's covenant of atonement, or another manifestation of God's promise of protection. In either case, it was true.

Rent

After Solomon, under the promptings of his idol-worshiping wives, turned away from God (I Kings 11:4), God rejected him as king, and He had said He would (I Chronicles 28:9), and started the process of turning the kingdom over to another: Jeroboam.

Here how it happened:

I Kings 11:28–31 (ESV): The man Jeroboam was very able, and when Solomon saw that the young man was industrious he gave him charge over all the forced labor of the house of Joseph. [29]And at that time, when Jeroboam went out of Jerusalem, the prophet Ahijah the Shilonite found him on the road. Now Ahijah had dressed himself in a new garment, and the two of them were alone in the open country. [30]Then **Ahijah laid hold of the new garment that was on him, and tore it into twelve pieces.** [31]And he said to Jeroboam, **"Take for yourself ten pieces,** for thus says the Lord, the God of Israel, 'Behold, I am about to tear the kingdom from the hand of Solomon and **will give you ten tribes. . .'"**

Note the symbolism in this prophetic act: each piece of the garment represented one tribe of Israel, and the ten pieces that Jeroboam picked up illustrated the ten tribes of Israel that God was about to put under his command.

Transferring Prophetic Authority

Elijah performed a prophetic act at the end of his ministry when, at God's command, he transferred his authority as Israel's "senior prophet" to his successor Elisha. Here's what happened:

> I Kings 19:19 (NASB): So he *[Elijah]* departed from there *[the cave where he heard God's still, small voice]* and found Elisha the son of Shaphat, while he was plowing with twelve pairs of oxen before him, and he with the twelfth. And **Elijah passed over to him and threw his mantle on him.**

Elijah throwing his mantle onto Elisha was a prophetic act; it was symbolic of the transfer of Elijah's role or responsibility. Indeed, the modern phrase of "passing the mantle" means to transfer a role, or to transfer the responsibility or authority over something to another person. This allusion, still in use today, *comes from this story.* So every time people use that phrase in the modern world, they are, whether they realize it or not, harking back to this story of Elijah and Elisha.

Arrows and Victory in Battle

One time when Joash, king of Israel, was in need of some victory over the Arameans (Syrians), whom the Lord had allowed to conquer Israel because of their sin, Elisha had a word from the Lord pertaining to the situation:

> II Kings 13:15–17 (NIV): Elisha said *[to Joash]*, "Get a bow and some arrows," and he did so. ¹⁶"Take the bow in your hands," he said to the king of Israel. When he had taken it, Elisha put his hands on the king's hands. ¹⁷"Open the east window," he said, and he opened it. "Shoot!" Elisha said, and he shot. "The Lord's arrow of victory, the arrow of victory over Aram!" Elisha declared. "You will completely destroy the Arameans at Aphek."

So in the above case, because Joash had obeyed, the word of the Lord through Elisha assured Joash of a military victory in the attempt to throw off the oppressive rule of Syria. But there's more. Because of the above, Joash could easily have seen (and *should* have seen) that arrows were being used to symbolize military victory.

Elisha's message from the Lord is not done yet, so he continues:

> II Kings 13:18–19 (NIV): Then he said, "Take the arrows," and the king took them. Elisha told him, "Strike the ground." He struck it three times and stopped. [19]The man of God was angry with him and said, "You should have struck the ground five or six times; then you would have defeated Aram and completely destroyed it. But now you will defeat it only three times."

Modern-day people often come to Joash's defense and say, "Well, how was *he* supposed to know that?" If Joash had written out his own copy of the Law as he should have (Deuteronomy 17:18, mentioned in the previous section), he would have realized that God often speaks symbolically. Also, just as a matter of the Hebrew culture, it was understood that God often speaks symbolically. So Elisha was justifiably angry at Joash for not being spiritually on the ball enough to understand what God was trying to say. And because Joash didn't get it, Israel's victories would be few, and God's people would suffer needlessly.

Jeremiah the Thespian

Jeremiah was used several times in giving prophetic messages through dramatic or theatrical methods; i.e., doing prophetic acts. As we've seen, this in no way trivializes the messages, but it simply makes them more hard-hitting and more difficult to forget.

Smashing the Pot

One time, after Israel had severely, repeatedly, and unrepentantly rebelled against God, He called upon Jeremiah to speak to Israel through a prophetic act with a clay jar, or pot.

Israel's sins included worshipping idols, even to the extent of sacrificing their children to Baal (similar to modern-day policies claiming it is a woman's "right" to sacrifice her unborn babies on the altar of convenience), and they would not repent and turn back to God, even though He sent prophets to warn them many times. Finally, to illustrate how He was going to bring discipline to Israel, God tells Jeremiah:

> Jeremiah 19:1 (NLT): This is what the Lord said to me: "**Go and buy a clay jar.** Then ask some of the leaders of the people and of the priests to follow you."

Jeremiah does so, and then God continues:

209

Jeremiah 19:10–13 (NLT): "As these men watch you, Jeremiah, **smash the jar you brought.** ¹¹Then say to them, 'This is what the Lord of Heaven's Armies says: **As this jar lies shattered, so I will shatter the people of Judah and Jerusalem beyond all hope of repair.** They will bury the bodies here in Topheth, the garbage dump, until there is no more room for them. ¹²This is what I will do to this place and its people, says the Lord. I will cause this city to become defiled like Topheth. ¹³Yes, all the houses in Jerusalem, including the palace of Judah's kings, will become like Topheth—all the houses where you burned incense on the rooftops to your star gods, and where liquid offerings were poured out to your idols.'"

So here, the prophetic act of breaking the clay pot emphasizes how Israel's culture will be broken because of their sin.

Wearing the Yoke

Later on, God tells Jeremiah to make and wear a wooden yoke, like those that are put on oxen and other beasts of burden:

Jeremiah 27:1–2 (CEB): Early in the rule of Judah's King Zedekiah, Josiah's son, this word came to Jeremiah from the Lord: ²This is what the Lord said to me: **Make a yoke of straps and bars and wear it on your neck.**

Then, along with the prophetic act of wearing the yoke of bondage and servitude, Jeremiah speaks to the kings of neighboring nations as well as to Judah's king Zedekiah, that God is giving all their nations into the hands of Nebuchadnezzar, king of Babylon. Jeremiah warned that any nation who resisted Nebuchadnezzar's conquest would be destroyed, but any nation who accepted the conquest would be delivered after "serving their time" of discipline for their sins.

Later that year, a false prophet named Hananiah gave a word that the people wanted to hear, but which was unfortunately contrary to what God had said. Hananiah spoke a verbal prophecy that within two years, the yoke of Nebuchadnezzar would be broken off of the neck of Judah and the other nations (28:1–4). Knowing the power of prophetic acts, he also took the yoke from Jeremiah's neck (which he had apparently been wearing for months), and broke it, to reinforce his message of the nations' approaching deliverance from Nebuchadnezzar's power (28:10–11).

Jeremiah basically says, "We'll see. And because you have incited the people to rebel against God, you'll die before the end of the year." And Hananiah died just a few months later (28:16–17).

Burying the Stones

Still later, right after the leaders of Judah say to Jeremiah, "Whatever the Lord says to us through you, we'll do," Jeremiah replies, "Okay. Stay in Judah. Don't go off to Egypt, thinking you'll be safe from Nebuchadnezzar there." (Jeremiah 42).

So the leaders of Judah immediately reply, "You're lying. We're gonna go to Egypt; we'll be safe from Nebuchadnezzar there." And off to Egypt they go, hauling all of Judah's remaining refugees, including Jeremiah, along with them. (43:1–7).

Once "safely" in Egypt, God tells Jeremiah to do another prophetic act: he was to take some large stones and bury them under the pavement stones at the entrance to Pharaoh's palace. Then the verbal part of the prophecy was essentially, "Nebuchadnezzar will come and conquer Egypt, and set up his throne on this very spot. Egypt will be destroyed, and so will you people from Judah, because you trusted in Pharaoh more than in God." (43:8–13).

Note that in all the Jeremiah's prophecies above, the verbal part was strengthened and reinforced by the addition of prophetic acts that spoke the same message through a different method.

Ezekiel the Thespian

Like Jeremiah, Ezekiel too was used several times in giving prophetic messages through prophetic acts. Like before, this in no way trivializes the messages, but it simply makes them more hard-hitting and more difficult to forget.

A Cartographic Prophecy

Here's a variation on the discussion above, on writing things down that God is communicating.

God told Ezekiel to write something down, but it wasn't writing in words; it was drawing and modeling—a microcosm of something that would later happen at full scale:

> Ezekiel 4:1–3 (NLT): "And now, son of man, take a large clay brick and set it down in front of you. Then **draw a map of the city of Jerusalem** on it. ²Show the city **under siege. Build a wall** around it so no one can escape. Set up the **enemy camp,** and surround the city with **siege ramps and battering rams.** ³Then **take an iron griddle and place it between you and the city.** Turn toward the city and demonstrate how harsh the siege will be against Jerusalem. This will be a warning to the people of Israel."

This prophetic act is one of the most obvious ones in the Bible. Ezekiel made a miniature 3D representation of Jerusalem and portrayed exactly how it was going to be overthrown because of their rebellion against God.

That was Phase I of this particular prophetic act; now for Phase II:

> Ezekiel 4:4–6 (NLT): "Now **lie on your left side** and place the sins of Israel on yourself. You are to bear their sins for the number of days you lie there on your side. ⁵I am requiring you to bear Israel's sins for **390 days**—one day for each year of their sin. ⁶After that, turn over and **lie on your right side for 40 days**—one day for each year of Judah's sin."

Wow! Not only is this one of the most graphical of prophetic acts, it is likely to be the longest-lasting—about *fourteen months* from beginning to end! What was Ezekiel doing all that time?

> Ezekiel 4:7 (NLT): "Meanwhile, **keep staring at the siege of Jerusalem.** Lie there with your **arm bared** and prophesy her destruction."

What's that "arm bared" thing all about? It is a prophetic act in itself: baring one's arm is an indication of getting down to business, no more messing around. We still use a variation on that phrase: when someone is getting serious about accomplishing some difficult or unpleasant task, we still describe it as "rolling up one's sleeves."

As we can see, this idea already existed in Old Testament times: Isaiah referred to it also:

> Isaiah 52:10 (NIV): The Lord will **lay bare his holy arm** in the sight of all the nations, and all the ends of the earth will see the salvation of our God.

But back to Ezekiel: I've heard it said that Ezekiel didn't *really* lie on his side for 390 days (in spite of the fact that God plainly told him to), but that he laid on his side "a few minutes each day" for 390 days. No. This is just another example of people attempting to bring the Bible down to their own level of experience, and impose upon God their own level of inabilities. Such people are usually not maliciously or deliberately deceptive, but they are inadvertently using themselves as the standard by which everything and everyone (including God) is measured.

The subconscious reasoning goes something like this: "I've never heard of that, so it couldn't be possible." But of course, they never realize that for that train of logic to be valid, they must first presume omniscience, which they would never do if they actually thought about it. If one realizes his own limitations, one is immediately driven to the conclusion "There might be real things that I don't know about, and God might do things I haven't heard of."

Actually, we *do* know that Ezekiel was actually on his side for 390 (or 430) days, because of the very next verse, which says that God *held* him there:

> Ezekiel 4:8: And, behold, **I will lay bands upon thee, and thou shalt not turn thee from one side to another,** till thou hast ended the days of thy siege.
>
> AMP: Now behold, **I will put ropes on you so that you cannot turn from one side to the other** until you have completed the days of your siege.
>
> CEV: **I will tie you up, so you can't leave** until your attack has ended.
>
> CJB: **I am tying you down with ropes, and you are not to turn from one side to the other** until you have completed the days of your siege.

213

> MSG: **I will tie you up with ropes, tie you so you can't move or turn over** until you have finished the days of the siege.

> TLB: And **I will paralyze you so that you can't turn over from one side to the other** until you have completed all the days of your siege.

God is not into cruelty, so we needn't be concerned that Ezekiel suffered agonizing bedsores, muscular cramps and atrophy, any more than Moses suffered fourth-degree burns from walking into the "volcano" at the top of Mount Sinai (Exodus 19:16–18). God was using him to speak to his people, and God rewards obedience and cooperation. It is very likely that Ezekiel experienced a breathtaking presence of God for large portions of those 430 days, while being supernaturally protected from bedsores and muscular atrophy.

A Close Shave

Israel was a stubborn and stiff-necked people (Ezekiel 2:4, 3:7, 16:50, etc.), and in another pronouncement of judgment for their continued, habitual, and unrepentant sin, God gave Ezekiel another prophetic act to perform. It involved shaving his head and beard, and then acting out symbolic things with the hair.

This is what God said to Ezekiel:

> Ezekiel 5:1–4 (CEB): You, human one, take a sharp sword. Use it like a razor and **shave your head and beard.** Then use scales to divide the hair. ²At the end of the siege, **burn one-third of it in the city. Strike another third with the sword left and right. Then scatter one-third to the wind and let loose the sword after it. ³From that third, take a few strands and hide them in your garment.** ⁴From that hair, **take yet another batch and throw it into the fire and burn it up.** From there, fire will spread to the whole house of Israel.

What were the literal meanings of the symbols in this visual parable? God explains in v. 12:

> Ezekiel 5:12 (CEB): One-third of you will die of plague and waste away by famine among you. One-third will fall by the sword all around you. And one-third I will scatter to all the winds, letting loose a sword to pursue them.

The third of the hair that was burned in the city represented the third of the people who died by sickness and starvation, the third of the hair that was struck with the sword represented the third of the people who died in battle, and the third of the hair that was scattered in the wind represented the third of the people who fled to the surrounding nations as refugees.

But what about the "few strands" that were hidden in Ezekiel's garment? Those represented the faithful remnant that God preserved through the judgment, and through which He would fulfill the promises He had given to their ancestors. Even in the midst of societal collapse because of widespread apostasy, God always preserves the faithful remnant.

Healing a Stick

Shortly after Ezekiel's vision of the dry bones coming back to life, he was instructed to tell God's people that God would reunite Israel and Judah, which had been separate since the days of Jeroboam and Rehoboam. God could have told Ezekiel to simply tell the people verbally, but, as He often does, He gave the announcement via a prophetic act.

Here's what God told Ezekiel to do:

Ezekiel 37:15–22 (NKJV): Again the word of the Lord came to me, saying, [16]"As for you, son of man, **take a stick** for yourself and write on it: 'For Judah and for the children of Israel, his companions.' **Then take another stick** and write on it, 'For Joseph, the stick of Ephraim, and for all the house of Israel, his companions.' [17]Then **join them one to another for yourself into one stick, and they will become one in your hand.** [18]And when the children of your people speak to you, saying, 'Will you not show us what you mean by these?'— [19]say to them, 'Thus says the Lord God: "Surely I will take the stick of Joseph, which is in the hand of Ephraim, and the tribes of Israel, his companions; and I will join them with it, with the stick of Judah, and make them one stick, and they will be one in My hand."' [20]And the sticks on which you write will be in your hand before their eyes. [21]Then say to them, 'Thus says the Lord God: "Surely I will take the children of Israel from among the nations, wherever they have gone, and will gather them from every side and bring them into their own land; [22]and **I will make them one nation in the land, on the mountains of Israel; and one king shall**

be king over them all; they shall no longer be two nations, nor shall they ever be divided into two kingdoms again.""""

The two sticks becoming one in Ezekiel's hand were a powerful indicator that this was not just wishful thinking on Ezekiel's part, but God confirmed His word, as He loves to do, with signs following (Mark 16:17).

Unplugging the Ears

Jesus too engaged in prophetic acts. Although He often healed people by being in contact with them, even in large crowds (Luke 4:40), Jesus was not *limited* to healing only those he could touch; for example, the centurion's servant in Matthew 8:5–13, and the the Syrophoenician woman's daughter in Mark 7:25–30.

But even though Jesus was not *restricted* to being in contact with those He was healing, He often made physical contact nonetheless. And not just in a generic hand-on-the-shoulder sort of way, as is often done nowadays. Look at how He healed this deaf man:

> Mark 7:32–35 (NKJV): Then they brought to Him one who was deaf and had an impediment in his speech, and they begged Him to put His hand on him. [33]And He took him aside from the multitude, and **put His fingers in his ears,** and He spat and touched his tongue. [34]Then, **looking up to heaven, He sighed, and said to him, "Ephphatha," that is, "Be opened."** [35]**Immediately his ears were opened,** and the impediment of his tongue was loosed, and he spoke plainly.

Do you see the prophetic act Jesus did? The deaf man's ears were metaphorically "plugged," which Jesus illustrated by putting His fingers in the man's ears. Then, when Jesus said, "Be opened," and "unplugged" his ears by removing His fingers, the man's deafness was healed.

By the way, when Jesus "sighed" in the above passage, this translation is a bit misleading because of sighing's modern connotation of annoyance at having to put up with a bothersome nuisance. Looking into the Greek word here shows us that the word translated "sighed" has an implication of "murmuring" (not the complaining kind) or "praying inaudibly." So even though He was not raising His voice, Jesus may have been rebuking the deafness as He rebuked the fever in Peter's mother-in-law (Luke 4:39), grieving in compassion for the man who had suffered for so long, as He did at Lazarus' funeral (John 11:35), or rejoicing that He was causing Satan's kingdom to crumble, as He did when the seventy returned (Luke 10:18–21), or something else. We don't know specifically what Jesus was saying here, but we can be sure that He wasn't annoyed at fulfilling the purpose for which He came to earth in the first place (I John 3:8b).

Getting Belted by the Jews

Prophetic acts are not just an Old Testament phenomenon; here is one from the New Testament:

> Acts 21:10–11 (NIV): After we had been there a number of days, a prophet named Agabus came down from Judea. ¹¹Coming over to us, **he took Paul's belt, tied his own hands and feet with it** and said, "The Holy Spirit says, 'In this way the Jews of Jerusalem will bind the owner of this belt and will hand him over to the Gentiles.'"

Agabus was correct in his prophecy and prophetic act, as shown in Acts 21:27–33, 24:1–27, but something else to note is how the other people reacted:

> Acts 21:12 (NIV): When we heard this, we and the people there **pleaded with Paul not to go** up to Jerusalem.

Why would the people do that? Part of their reasoning, of course, is that they loved Paul and didn't want to see him suffer. But another part of their reasoning was a leftover belief that suffering is always bad, and we should try to avoid it. But that is not always the case. In fact, a *great many times* it is not the case. Jesus said:

- "I am sending you out just like sheep to a pack of wolves." (Matthew 10:16, TEV)
- ". . .they will hand you over to the local councils and flog you in their synagogues." (Matthew 10:17, NIV)
- "You will be hated by all because of My name. . ." (Matthew 10:22, NASB)

217

- "...they will hand you over to suffer affliction and tribulation and put you to death, and you will be hated by all nations for My name's sake." (Matthew 24:9, AMP)

- "Even those closest to you—your parents, brothers, relatives, and friends—will betray you. They will even kill some of you." (Luke 21:16, NLT)

- "...you are no longer part of the world... so it hates you." (John 15:19, NLT)

- "If people persecuted me, they will persecute you too..." (John 15:20, TEV)

- "...an hour is coming when whoever kills you will think and claim that he has offered service to God." (John 16:2, AMP)

- "In the world ye shall have tribulation..." (John 16:33)

In the people who saw Agabus' prophetic act and heard the interpretation, there appeared to be a significant amount of good-hearted, but spiritually naïve motivation. Something on the order of "If it is unpleasant, it couldn't be God's will." That kinda brings to mind Peter's statement to Jesus, doesn't it?

> Matthew 16:21–22 (NLT): From then on Jesus began to tell his disciples plainly that **it was necessary for him to go to Jerusalem, and that he would suffer many terrible things** at the hands of the elders, the leading priests, and the teachers of religious law. He would be killed, but on the third day he would be raised from the dead. ²²But **Peter took him aside and began to reprimand him for saying such things. "Heaven forbid, Lord," he said. "This will never happen to you!"**

And we all remember Jesus' response to Peter:

> Matthew 16:23 (NLT): Jesus turned to Peter and said, **"Get away from me, Satan!** You are a dangerous trap to me. You are seeing things merely from a human point of view, not from God's."

So Peter's response to Jesus, while superficially appearing good-hearted and sincere, was actually inspired by Satan. When we obey God whole-heartedly, we do severe damage to the kingdom of darkness, so of course the enemy tries to discourage us in whatever ways he can.

218

He even uses well-meaning people who do not realize that suffering, at the hands of those still serving the enemy, comes with the territory.

But Paul knew:

> II Corinthians 4:17–18 (NLT): For **our present troubles are small and won't last very long.** Yet they produce for us a **glory that vastly out-weighs them and will last forever!** [18]So we don't look at the troubles we can see now; rather, **we fix our gaze on things that cannot be seen.** For the things we see now will soon be gone, but **the things we cannot see will last forever.**
>
> v. 17, AMP: For our **light, momentary affliction (this slight distress of the passing hour)** is ever more and more abundantly preparing and producing and achieving for us **an everlasting weight of glory [beyond all measure, excessively surpassing all comparisons and all calculations, a vast and transcendent glory and blessedness never to cease!]. . .**

The Symbolism of Prophetic Acts

As we can see from the examples above, prophetic acts can contain symbols that represent larger realities. And that is usually the case. *But not always.* Some prophetic acts seem completely disjointed and unre-lated to the miracle that fulfills them. Here are a couple examples.

One time while the children of Israel were wandering through the wilderness, their water was running out:

> Exodus 15:23–25 (NIV): When they came to Marah, they could not drink its water because it was bitter. (That is why the place is called Marah.) [24]So the people grumbled against Moses, saying, "What are we to drink?" [25]Then Moses cried out to the Lord, and **the Lord showed him a piece of wood. He threw it into the water, and the water became sweet.** There the Lord made a decree and a law for them, and there he tested them.

Here's a prophetic act where the action itself seems to be completely unrelated to the result. What does a piece of wood thrown in the water have to do with changing bitter water to fresh water? Nothing that I can see, although there may be some hidden correspondence buried in the Hebrew mindset or culture.

Here's another example: when the sons of the prophets were building a new place to live, because the old place was too small, they asked Elisha to accompany them to the construction site. They started cutting down some trees for lumber, when. . .

> II Kings 6:5–7 (NIV): As one of them was cutting down a tree, the iron axhead fell into the water. "Oh, my lord," he cried out, "it was borrowed!" ⁶The man of God asked, "Where did it fall?" When he showed him the place, **Elisha cut a stick and threw it there, and made the iron float.** ⁷"Lift it out," he said. Then the man reached out his hand and took it.

You might wonder, "What does throwing a stick in the water have to do with making an iron object float in water?" Good question; they appear to have nothing in common. Therefore, doing a prophetic act such as this entails taking more risk than doing a prophetic act which uses clearly recognized symbolism, because if the expected miracle does *not* take place, the person who did the act looks very foolish, and perhaps brings contempt on the name of God. So, make sure it is God that is telling you, if you feel like you should do a non-symbolic prophetic act.

So we can see from the Scriptural examples above—symbolic and otherwise—that prophetic acts are indeed a valid form of communication from God to us.

Music

Music, both vocal and instrumental, is also used to promote and/or communicate God's messages.

Remember when Jehoram (the evil king of Israel, and son of Ahab and Jezebel) was trying to quell an uprising of Moab, and he asked Jehoshaphat (the godly king of Judah) for assistance in the battle? Jehoshaphat agreed, and on their way to battle, they experienced seven days' march without finding water, and it was looking grim. So they decided to ask Elisha for help:

> II Kings 3:13–18 (NASB): Now Elisha said to the king of Israel, "What do I have to do with you? Go to the prophets of your father and to the prophets of your mother." And the king of Israel said to him, "No, for

the Lord has called these three kings together to give them into the hand of Moab." ¹⁴Elisha said, "As the Lord of hosts lives, before whom I stand, were it not that I regard the presence of Jehoshaphat the king of Judah, I would not look at you nor see you. ¹⁵But now **bring me a minstrel." And it came about, when the minstrel played, that the hand of the Lord came upon him.** ¹⁶He said, "Thus says the Lord, 'Make this valley full of trenches.' ¹⁷For thus says the Lord, 'You shall not see wind nor shall you see rain; yet that valley shall be filled with water, so that you shall drink, both you and your cattle and your beasts. ¹⁸This is but a slight thing in the sight of the Lord; He will also give the Moabites into your hand.'"

Isn't it interesting that it was when the musician played that the hand of the Lord came upon Elisha? And Elisha seemed to know it would happen that way: he very deliberately asked for the musician to play, and then, "the hand of the Lord came upon" Elisha. And indeed, if you're familiar with organizations like the International House of Prayer, which have 24/7 praise and worship, prophetic utterances are very common in such a setting. Why? Because people are consciously listening to God, and *God will speak if we will listen.*

But not only is music conducive to verbal prophetic utterances, but music can be the *mode* of communication—that is, you can prophesy through the music itself. This may sound a little suspect to you, so let's look at the Word:

> I Chronicles 25:1–3 (RSV): David and the chiefs of the service also set apart for the service certain of the sons of Asaph, and of Heman, and of Jeduthun, **who should prophesy with lyres, with harps, and with cymbals.** The list of those who did the work and of their duties was: ²Of the sons of Asaph: Zaccur, Joseph, Nethaniah, and Asharelah, sons of Asaph, under the direction of Asaph, who prophesied under the direction of the king. ³Of Jeduthun, the sons of Jeduthun: Gedaliah, Zeri, Jeshaiah, Shime-i, Hashabiah, and Mattithiah, six, under the direction of their father Jeduthun, **who prophesied with the lyre** in thanksgiving and praise to the Lord.

Now does this mean that the prophetic utterances were communicated *via* the sounds created by the musical instruments? Or does it mean that the prophetic utterances were in the usual verbal way, but were *accompanied* by the sounds created by the musical instruments? It could mean either, and it probably means both.

But how could a message be communicated through just the sounds of the musical instruments? Do some people "speak lyre" or "speak harp" or "speak cymbal?" God can communicate in ways we can't even imagine, so it shouldn't be too much of a stretch to think He could give a message through a musical instrument. And if people hearing the message didn't "speak harp" or whatever, the message was probably interpreted, much like modern-day messages in tongues, which are inherently unintelligible to people in most cases, and therefore need to be interpreted. Hence, the gift of interpretation of tongues. Or, the gift of "interpretation of harp," as the case may be.

And if you think about all of David's Messianic psalms, which were prophetic in nature, you realize that all the psalms were *songs;* that is, words set to music. The word "psalm" itself means "a sacred song or hymn, in particular any of those contained in the biblical Book of Psalms and used in Christian and Jewish worship."[8]

And read the intros to some of the Psalms, below:

- The intro to Psalm 4 is "To the chief Musician on **Neginoth,** A Psalm of David." So what in the world does the Hebrew word "Neginoth" mean? The ESV gives us a hint: "To the choirmaster: **with stringed instruments.** A Psalm of David." See also Psalm 54, 55, 67, 76.

- The intro to Psalm 5 says, "To the chief Musician upon **Nehiloth,** A Psalm of David." The NASB enlightens us as to the meaning of Nehiloth; it says, "For the choir director; **for flute accompaniment.** A Psalm of David."

- The intro to Psalm 6 says, "To the chief Musician on Neginoth upon **Sheminith,** A Psalm of David." We saw Neginoth in Psalm 4, but what's a Sheminith? The NKJV states: "To the Chief Musician. With stringed instruments. **On an eight-stringed harp.** A Psalm of David." See also Psalm 12.

- The intro to Psalm 7 says, "**Shiggaion** of David, which he sang unto the Lord, concerning the words of Cush the Benjamite." So what is a "Shiggaion?" The Amplified Bible tells us: "An Ode of David, [probably] in **a wild, irregular, enthusiastic strain,** which he sang to the Lord concerning the words of Cush, a Benjamite." Apparently David liked rowdy music.

- Psalm 8 starts with "To the chief Musician upon **Gittith,** A Psalm of David." The AMP shows us what Gittith means: "To the Chief Musician; **set to a Philistine lute, or [possibly] to a particular Hittite tune.** A Psalm of David." See also Psalm 81, 84.

- Psalm 9 starts "To the chief Musician upon **Muthlabben,** A Psalm of David." It's not clear what Muthlabben means; the NKJV says, "To the Chief Musician. To the tune of 'Death of the Son.' A Psalm of David." but the AMP states, "To the Chief Musician; **set for [possibly] soprano voices.** A Psalm of David."

- Psalm 16 starts, "**Michtam** of David." The ESV marginal note says that Michtam is "Probably a musical or liturgical term," but apparently the precise meaning has been lost. See also Psalm 56, 57, 58, 59, 60.

- Psalm 22 starts, "To the chief Musician upon **Aijeleth Shahar,** A Psalm of David." What is Aijeleth Shahar? The CEB says, "A psalm by David for the music leader. **To the tune 'A Deer at Dawn.'**"

- Psalm 32 starts, "A Psalm of David, **Maschil.**" What is Maschil? The AMP states it "[A Psalm of David.] **A skillful song, or a didactic or reflective poem.**" See also Psalm 42, 44, 52, 54, 55, 74, 78, 88, 89, 142.

- Psalm 45 starts, "To the chief Musician upon **Shoshannim,** for the sons of Korah, **Maschil,** A Song of loves." We saw Maschil in Psalm 32, but what is Shoshannim? The AMP says, "To the Chief Musician; **[set to the tune of] 'Lilies' [probably a popular air.** A Psalm] of the sons of Korah. A skillful song, or a didactic or reflective poem. A song of love." See also Psalm 69.

223

- Psalm 46 starts, "To the chief Musician for the sons of Korah, A Song upon **Alamoth**." The AMP give the meaning of Alamoth as "To the Chief Musician. [A Psalm] of the sons of Korah, **set to treble voices**. A song." and the NLT says, "For the choir director: A song of the descendants of Korah, **to be sung by soprano voices**." So Alamoth may mean the same thing as Muthlabben in Psalm 9.

- Psalm 53 starts, "To the chief Musician upon **Mahalath**, Maschil, A Psalm of David." Again, we've seen Maschil, but what's Mahalath? The AMP elaborates: "To the Chief Musician; **in a mournful strain**. A skillful song, or didactic or reflective poem of David."

- Psalm 56 starts, "To the chief Musician upon **Jonathelemrechokim**, Michtam of David, when the Philistines took him in Gath." That's quite a mouthful! What is Jonathelemrechokim? AMP renders it "To the Chief Musician; [**set to the tune of**] '**Silent Dove Among Those Far Away**.' Of David. A record of memorable thoughts when the Philistines seized him in Gath."

- Psalm 57 starts, "To the chief Musician, **Altaschith**, Michtam of David, when he fled from Saul in the cave." AMP introduces this Psalm with "To the Chief Musician; [**set to the tune of**] '**Do Not Destroy**.' A record of memorable thoughts of David when he fled from Saul in the cave." See also Psalm 58, 59, 75.

- Psalm 60 starts, "To the chief Musician upon **Shushaneduth**, Michtam of David, to teach; when he strove with Aramnaharaim and with Aramzobah, when Joab returned, and smote of Edom in the valley of salt twelve thousand." What is Shushaneduth? AMP says, "To the Chief Musician; [**set to the tune of**] '**The Lily of the Testimony**.' A poem of David intended to record memorable thoughts and to teach; when he had striven with the Arameans of Mesopotamia and the Arameans of Zobah, and when Joab returned and smote twelve thousand Edomites in the Valley of Salt. "

- Psalm 61 starts, "To the chief Musician upon **Neginah**, A Psalm of David." Neginah is similar, but not identical to Neginoth, which we first saw in Psalm 4. Since the NASB states it "For the choir director; **on a stringed instrument.** A Psalm of David," it's possible that Neginah is singular and Neginoth is plural.

- Psalm 80 starts, "To the chief Musician upon **Shoshannime-duth,** A Psalm of Asaph." We saw Shushaneduth in Psalm 60, and Shoshannimeduth is similar; could they have similar meanings? Apparently so; the AMP renders it, "To the Chief Musician; [**set to the tune of**] 'Lilies, a Testimony.' A Psalm of Asaph." Perhaps just a singular/plural distinction here as well.

- Psalm 88 starts, "A Song or Psalm for the sons of Korah, to the chief Musician upon **Mahalath Leannoth,** Maschil of Heman the Ezrahite." AMP clarifies, "A song. A Psalm of the sons of Korah. To the Chief Musician; **set to chant mournfully.** A didactic or reflective poem of Heman the Ezrahite."

Look at all those musical terms for these Psalms, many of which are prophetic in nature! There are instructions for wind instruments as well as stringed instruments, wild, irregular, and enthusiastic music, as well as mournful music, specific vocal ranges and tunes borrowed from already-existing music. Apparently, God is not opposed to repurposing music by adding or replacing words. And in addition to all the specific musical instructions, look at the person to whom these Psalms were delivered: they were addressed "To the Chief *Musician.*" That speaks for itself.

So many prophetic messages, delivered musically!

And David and Asaph aren't the only prophets to communicate their words in music:

Habakkuk 3:1: A prayer of Habakkuk the prophet upon **Shigionoth.**

> AMP: A prayer of Habakkuk the prophet, **set to wild, enthusiastic, and triumphal music.**

So combining the concepts of prophetic utterances with music is thousands of years old. And the fact that God would communicate with us musically should not be surprising, since *God Himself* sings:

> Zephaniah 3:17 (BBE): **The Lord your God** is among you, as a strong saviour: he will be glad over you with joy, he will make his love new again, he **will make a song of joy over you** as in the time of a holy feast.
>
> CEV: **The Lord your God** wins victory after victory and is always with you. He **celebrates and sings because of you,** and he will refresh your life with his love.
>
> NIV: **The Lord your God** is with you, he is mighty to save. He will take great delight in you, he will quiet you with his love, he **will rejoice over you with singing.**

So music and words from God are very tightly intertwined.

Chapter 5:

Where Do We Go From Here?

Now that we have seen quite a bit of teaching on prophetic ministry, and numerous Scriptural examples and commands of how to do it, what should we do now? How do we proceed?

The first thing to do is remember that very important fact that we saw in the chapter "Who Can Be Used in Prophetic Ministry?"—the fact that *all* Christians can prophesy, whether they have been called to the "office" of a prophet or not. (For a discussion of what a Biblical "office" is, see the section "Offices" in the chapter "What Is Our Part?" in Book 7: *Be Filled with the Spirit.*)

Then, when we remember that we are all *commanded* to prophesy (I Corinthians 14:1, 3–5, 31, 39), we are driven to the conclusion that hearing God's voice and speaking His words is a good thing. This is obvious by virtue of the fact that *the Lord is good* (Psalm 34:8) and all His plans for us are for our benefit (Jeremiah 29:11–14a).

Cultivating Prophetic Gifts in Others

As we've seen above, *everyone* is Scripturally authorized, enabled, and yes, *commanded* to prophesy, whether that is their greatest calling or not.

People in positions of authority in the body of Christ—pastors, leaders of parachurch organizations, and so forth—have a great deal of influence and power to encourage and nurture those called to minister primarily in prophetic ministry, or to destroy them. We must be very diligent to lead and instruct people according to loving, supportive, and Biblical standards so we can be found to be good stewards of those people whom God places into our care.

Many people who are in the occult today, or are psychics, mediums, witches or warlocks, or are into new-age spiritualism, were raised in church, and were blessed with prophetic gifts. But all too often they were told that "those things aren't real," when they knew good and well that they were—they had experienced them many times. And not seeing any power in the church, they sought it elsewhere. And of course, the enemy was more than willing to commandeer their God-given gifts for his own corrupt purposes.

Or, they were told by the church that such spiritually-perceived knowledge was "demonic" in origin because "God doesn't do that anymore." And again, not seeing any power in the church, they sought it elsewhere.

Or, when they were first learning about their gift and calling, they tried to use it, but didn't quite do it right. And instead of being encouraged and trained by those in authority how to use their gifts, they were blasted and shot down for the mistakes they made during their first few faltering steps in the new area of ministry. Finding no acceptance in the church, they found it with the psychics and witches.

The examples could go on and on, but I think I've made my point: the church is primarily responsible for the large numbers of people in the occult, because we were too Biblically untrained in prophetic matters, or were too threatened by those whose gifts were more anointed than our own, or too fearful that we'd get attacked by the devil if we dared to connect with actual spiritual power.

We, as leaders in the corporate church, need to repent of our complacency, or abdication, of learning about prophetic ministry, because we felt it was "scary." We, as leaders in the corporate church, need to repent of our insecurity in Christ that allows us to feel like "our" positions of leadership are jeopardized by others whose gifts are greater than our own. We, as leaders in the corporate church, need to repent of our fear of the devil, as if he were an actual threat to God's work and His people.

If you want to learn prophetic ministry, both Scripturally and experientially, contact any or all of the following ministries; all of them teach on prophetic ministry, and practice it as a normal part of the Christian life (which it is meant to be). The list below is certainly not exhaustive, because the Lord is constantly raising up more and more world-class prophetic voices.

- InLight Connection—Doug Addison (DougAddison.com)
- Expression 58—Shawn and Cherie Bolz (Expression58.org)
- Global Awakening—Randy and DeAnne Clark (GlobalAwakening.com)
- Eagles View Ministries—Bobby and Carolyn Conner (BobbyConner.org)
- Jamie Galloway Ministries—Jamie and Emily Galloway (JamieGalloway.com)
- Bob Hazlett Ministries—Bob and Kimberly Hazlett (BobHazlett.org)
- Streams Ministries International—John Paul Jackson (deceased, but his training materials are still available at StreamsMinistries.com)
- Bethel Church of Redding, California—Bill and Beni Johnson (Bethel.com)
- Morning Star Ministries—Rick Joyner (MorningStarMinistries.org)

- New Wine International—Joshua and Janet Angela Mills (NewWineInternational.org)
- Elisha Revolution—Jerame and Miranda Nelson (ElishaRevolution.com)
- Glory of Zion Ministries—Chuck and Pam Pierce (Glory-of-Zion.org)
- Larry Randolph Ministries—Larry and Laura Randolph (LarryRandolph.com)

As mentioned, there are others as well, including those prophetic voices sent out every day in the free email newsletter published by The Elijah List (ElijahList.com). And basically anyone who works together with, or teaches at the same conferences with, the people above; you can be pretty sure they're legit.

We, as leaders in the corporate church, have *got* to start nurturing, training, raising up, and releasing into fruitful ministry those young prophets God is calling. We no longer have the option of aborting the ministries God wants to launch into the battle. God will call us on the carpet in no uncertain terms if we continue to be lackadaisical in our attitudes toward training people up in the gifts of the Holy Spirit and His supernaturally empowered ministries, be that prophecy or anything else.

Actually Doing It

The next step is moving into a lifestyle containing prophetic utterances. This is more than having a few flash-in-the-pan experiences just so you can say you've done it; we are to actually seek God *diligently* on this. It's important, and it does take practice.

Now some will stumble over that last statement. "It takes *practice?*" they say. "If it takes *practice,* that just shows that you're prophesying out of your own flesh! If it's actually God, you will be compelled to say whatever He wants you to say!" But in point of fact, that's just not true. Let's look at this passage:

I Corinthians 14:32 (NIV): The spirits of prophets **are subject to the control of prophets.**

AMP: For the spirits of the prophets (the speakers in tongues) **are under the speaker's control [and subject to being silenced as may be necessary]**. . .

NLT: Remember that people who prophesy **are in control of their spirit and can take turns.**

This is not saying that prophets can invent their own prophecies and tack on "thus saith the Lord" at the end. That would be foolish and dangerous. What this verse is saying is that when you have a prophecy that *is* from God, you shouldn't just blurt it out, overpowering whomever else may already be speaking.

But back to the bit about practicing. Is "practicing" in the things of the Spirit actually a dirty word? No. Although we can all hear God (John 10:3–4, 16, 27), we can also hear the voice of the enemy, and we can also hear our own thoughts.

It takes practice to learn how to accurately differentiate between these varying sources, so we know what to speak out and what to silence:

Hebrews 5:12–14 (NASB): For though by this time you ought to be teachers, you have need again for someone to teach you the elementary principles of the oracles of God, and you have come to need milk and not solid food. [13]For everyone who partakes only of milk is not accustomed to the word of righteousness, for he is an infant. [14]But **solid food is for the mature, who** *because of practice* **have their senses trained** to discern good and evil.

Remember the realization (in the section "Paul's Confirmation," above) that although the Corinthians were still "infants" who were not ready for solid food, that Paul still instructed them in how to move in the gifts of the Spirit? As mentioned in an earlier chapter, this passage in Hebrews shows us the answer of how to grow up so we are no longer infants: *practice* training your spiritual senses so you can determine, more accurately every day, what things are of God (the "good") and what things are of the enemy (the "evil"). In other words, we need to start moving in the spiritual gifts even before we are perfectly, flawlessly reliable and accurate in using them.

And because we need practice at this spiritual skill we're learning, we will sometimes make honest mistakes. That is not a problem, because since God has poured out His Spirit on *all* mankind (Joel 2:28–30 > Acts 2:14–19), we *all* have the responsibility to test prophetic messages to determine whether they're really from God:

> I Corinthians 14:29 (NLT): Let two or three people prophesy, and **let the others evaluate what is said.**
>
> I Thessalonians 5:19–21 (AMP): Do not quench (suppress or subdue) the [Holy] Spirit; [20]Do not spurn the gifts and utterances of the prophets [do not depreciate prophetic revelations nor despise inspired instruction or exhortation or warning]. [21]But **test and prove all things [until you can recognize] what is good; [to that] hold fast.**

By the way, the two exhortations above, each one by itself, show that prophetic utterances are still for today—they didn't "cease" centuries ago, as some claim. How do they show that? Simply this: If all prophetic utterances really *had* ceased, there would be no need to "test" them—the very fact that they were presented as prophetic would be proof that they couldn't have been from God (since He allegedly doesn't do that anymore).

But since we *are* exhorted to test them, we can see that some prophetic messages are indeed from God. And those are the ones we should "desire" (KJV), "eagerly pursue" (AMP), "try to get" (CEV), "keep on eagerly seeking" (CJB), "be zealous for" (DOUAY), "truly want to have" (EXB), "covet" (GNV), "set your hearts on" (GNT), "strive for" (LEB), "be eager for" (NET), "want" (NLV), "long for" (NTE), and "passionately seek" (VOICE). Do you think God is trying to tell us something?

In the Old Testament, before God poured out His Spirit in a wholesale manner, most people didn't have the Holy Spirit within them to test prophetic utterances, which is why the punishment for false prophets was so severe. But now, since the Holy Spirit is available to everyone, we all have the responsibility to test prophetic messages.

As you're practicing hearing and recognizing God's voice, it helps to have other people around who are also hungry for the move of God. If someone misses it—for example, if someone prophesies something and it is pointed out that it couldn't be from God because it contradicts clear Scripture—don't scold or berate the person for making a mistake. Instead, *celebrate* the fact that the person was willing to take a risk. It can be scary to prophesy when you're just getting started.

God would much rather have you *try* to obey Him in some new area, even though you might not do it perfectly the first few times, than have you say and do nothing because you're afraid. After all, *God* has not given us a spirit of fear (II Timothy 1:7), so if we're being harassed by a spirit of fear, guess where it came from?

And how should we respond to such demonic attacks?

James 4:7 (AMP): So be subject to God. **Resist the devil [stand firm against him], and he will flee from you.**

So go ahead; get started. Just like when you were a baby learning to walk, and you fell down a few times, you will make some mistakes as you're learning to prophesy. But keep at it. After all, imagine being afraid to learn to walk because "you might fall down." And now you're twenty years old, or thirty, or sixty, or ninety, and you still haven't learned how to walk because "you might fall down." What a waste of potential!

In the same way, if you've been a Christian for any significant length of time—more than a week or two—and you've never pursued prophecy, it is high time to pursue it. In these last days, we'll need it more and more, and it is an amazing blessing to be on the giving end *or* the receiving end. But don't hang back because of fear. That would not be caution or wisdom, that would be disobedience, resulting in severely stunted growth, and an outright victory for the devil.

For you can all prophesy one by one, so that all may learn and all be encouraged. . . (I Corinthians 14:31, ESV)

Appendix A:

Bible-Study Strategies

As you have already seen, if you have read any of the books in the THOUGHTS ON series, I place a very high value on the Bible and its authority as the normative standard for Christian doctrine, teaching, and behavior. As I study the Bible, I employ quite a few different study techniques that I have found, over the decades, to be quite useful and reliable. Great wisdom can be gained from reading the Bible, and using these practices will significantly reduce misinterpretations caused by lack of awareness of Jewish culture, language, laws, and so forth.

To that end, please allow me to describe these Bible-study techniques I use when researching pretty much anything related to spiritual subjects. After that, we'll get into the main subject matter of this book. I describe these techniques below for two reasons: First, so you can see how and why I arrived at the conclusions I did, and second, so you can incorporate these practices into your own Bible study, should you choose to do so.

Multiple Translations

As you may have seen in other books in the THOUGHTS ON series, I often include relevant verses from several different translations of the Bible. This seems prudent, and more reliable, because I have seen Bible teachings that were based entirely on a single translation of the Bible, and if the "wrong" translation was used, it failed to support, and sometimes even contradicted, the whole point of the teaching.

In those cases where a passage of Scripture is quoted out of several translations, you may be tempted to read just the first one, and skip the rest. But, I encourage you to thoughtfully read each translation's rendering of the verses, and note the different shades of meaning. You will be pretty amazed at what the Bible says. . .

Multiple References

Also, you'll notice that when I make a doctrinal statement, I often support my statement with a series of Scriptures. Sometimes I use the same Scripture out of different translations as described above, but also I will often give a list of *different* Scriptures, all of which support the point I am trying to make. This also seems prudent, because it lessens the likelihood of misinterpretation. For example, if I make a statement and back it up with only a single Scripture, that's good, but someone could respond with "That's not what that says! You misinterpreted that verse!" And that is certainly possible.

But an even better approach is this: if I offer a list of *ten* different Scriptures, *all* of which support my point, it becomes more and more likely that I am understanding Scripture correctly, and less and less likely that I happened to misinterpret *all* of them in an identical manner. As a result, my assertions that are backed up with a larger number of Scriptures are probably more reliable than those backed up by only one or two.

Since my goal is to understand as accurately as possible what God is saying through His Word, and to communicate that as accurately as possible to the reader, please bear with me when I support a statement with a list of Scriptures that you may feel is excessively long. I, for one, am comforted when my doctrinal beliefs are supported by a plethora of Scriptures instead of just one or two.

The Preponderance of Scripture

This concept is similar, but not identical, to the one above, so I mention it separately.

The "preponderance of Scripture" is another good Bible-study tool. Basically, it looks at *how many* Scriptures can reasonably be interpreted one particular way, as opposed to how many can be interpreted in some alternate way. For example, if I have a verse that seems to say one thing, or at least it *could be interpreted* one particular way, but a dozen verses that say the opposite, and *couldn't* be interpreted in such a way as to support the other verse, it's not rocket science to conclude that the interpretation supported by the dozen Scriptures is more likely to be reliable than the interpretation supported by only the one.

For this reason, too, when I present a statement or doctrine that I believe to be true, I usually give quite a bit of supporting Scriptural evidence that upholds that statement or doctrine. It's all part of I Peter 3:15 (NIV): "Always be prepared to give an answer to everyone who asks you to give the reason for the hope that you have." And in doing so, I'd better have my doctrinal "ducks in a row," so to speak, because I, as a teacher, will be judged with a stricter judgment (James 3:1).

The Plain, Surface Meaning

While it is often valuable to refer back to Hebrew and Greek, the original languages in which the Bible was written, for clarification and/or subtle nuances of meaning in the text, it shouldn't be necessary to resort to the original languages for major doctrines. The Bible is for the purpose of God communicating with us, so reading it in our own language should give us plenty of understanding on the essential doctrines of Christianity.

As a result, you'll notice in this book that I refer to English translations of the Bible for most of my content, with only occasional excursions into the Hebrew or Greek, where such an excursion would be useful to clarify or reveal a nuance of meaning. In other words, I go in most cases by the *plain, surface meaning* of the text: the meaning that any unbiased, literate speaker of English would derive from the text.

If I am *required* to go to the original languages for some concept because there is insufficient evidence from plain, surface meaning at least *somewhere* in the Bible, it seems to me that that concept is either questionable or, if it is undisputable, it is relatively unimportant.

Basing major doctrines on things that can *only* be supported by a knowledge of Greek or Hebrew, sounds dangerously close to what the organized church in the Middle Ages did: keeping the Bible obscure, only in Latin, so the "common folk" were dependent upon approved religious leaders to interpret it for them. Wouldn't want them to get all confused by reading God's Word for themselves. . .

The Bible Itself Defining Its Terms

As you may have seen in other books in the Thoughts On series, one good way of finding out what the Bible means by a particular word or phrase in some verse is to see if the Bible uses, or even *defines,* that same word or phrase elsewhere. If it does, then you're more likely to have learned something that Bible actually intended, as opposed to some commentator's or theologian's opinion on what the Bible meant.

There are many verses that refer to various Scriptural concepts. Of course, that's not a problem—they are obviously Scriptural words—but the problem arises when we apply a different *meaning* to the word than that which the Biblical authors (read: "God") intended. This is very easy to do; we, as modern-day Americans, don't typically know a lot about ancient Hebrew or Greek laws, customs, feasts, traditions, vocabulary, grammar, idioms, and so forth. Usually the resulting misinterpretation is not malicious; it's just a result of insufficient study. The problem that arises here is simply: How do we know what the correct meanings of Biblical words are?

Here's an illustration: Suppose I send you a letter, and after you receive it, you redefine the words that I used in the letter. If you do that—deliberately *or* accidentally—you can "cause" me to have said any number of things I didn't intend. This is what happens all too often when people read the Bible: they use the words that appear in the Bible, but (usually unwittingly) understand different, Scripturally unsupportable meanings for those words. The result is that they can "prove" all sorts of unscriptural things. This kind of mistake can be drastically re-duced by seeing how the Bible itself uses its terms.

In some cases, we need to go back to the original languages, and that's fine when necessary, but often it's possible to learn what Biblical words mean because the Bible itself defines them. In such cases, the definition is usually in a different verse, because if it were in the *same* verse, there wouldn't have been a question in the first place.

You may have seen that this approach was used to determine the Biblical meaning of the word "repent" in the section "Jonah Preaching in Nineveh," and the word "grace" in the section "Being Under Grace," both in Book 2: *Is It Possible to Stop Sinning?*, the word "healed" in the section "Wounded For Our Transgressions" in Book 5, *If It be Thy Will*, and the word "faith" in Book 8: *Going Beyond Christianity 101*. This approach will not work in every case, because not all controversial Bib-lical words are clearly defined elsewhere in Scripture. But when it does, it is very enlightening, and *very* reliable.

Another thing that Biblical usage of words can often tell us is what a word does *not* mean. For example, I've heard it said, in an attempt to support the idea that *all* consumption of alcohol is sinful, that the "wine" back in Bible days was not actually alcoholic, but was only a kind of grape juice. But one immediately has to ask, "Why, then, does the Bible show examples of people getting drunk on it, and warn us not to do the same?" (Genesis 9:21, Isaiah 28:1, Joel 1:5, Proverbs 23:20–21, Ephesians 5:18, etc.).

It doesn't take too much deep thought to realize that the existence of Biblical stories describing people getting drunk on wine, plus the presence of Biblical warnings *not* to get drunk on wine, clearly shows that it must be possible to do it. Therefore, the wine in the Bible was not just grape juice; it must have contained alcohol. And therefore, since Jesus provided wine for others (John 2:1–11) and drank wine him-self (Matthew 11:18f ‖ Luke 7:33f) but remained sinless (Hebrews 4:15), we are forced to conclude that drinking alcohol, as long as it is not to the point of drunkenness, is not sinful.

Reading in Context

Perhaps the most neglected aspect of common-sense study of the Bible is that of reading passages in their contexts. That is, reading the passages such that they make sense in the larger environment in which they reside, so that when taken individually, the message communicated by the snippets won't contradict the message communicated by the larger passage from which they were taken.

It's astonishing how many common Christian beliefs are based on snippets of Scripture taken dramatically out of context. Some of these beliefs are admittedly minor details, but others are major doctrines. One of the largest areas in which context errors are prevalent is in studying the topic of Free Will vs. Predestination (in the TULIP sense). I was astonished when researching this topic for the book *Free to Choose?* just how common it was.

When doing the research, I read and listened to many teachings that supported Calvinistic predestination, and many short fragments of Scriptures were quoted. The messages communicated by these Scripture snippets did indeed seem to support the concept of Calvinistic predestination. But when I read those fragments in their own contexts, an entirely different message became apparent.

One of the most amazing things I realized was that so many of the messages communicated by the fragments *were completely reversed* when the entire passage was read, instead of only the strategically selected snippets that supposedly supported the doctrine. And in several cases, I found tiny passages offered where, *if one simply reads the rest of the sentence,* the tenor of the perceived message is completely reversed. For massive amounts of documentation on this topic, and numerous examples showing the critical importance of context, read Book 6: *Free to Choose?*.

Of course, the above topic is certainly not the *only* topic you could find where out-of-context Scripture fragments put forth a message that the enclosing context completely reverses. But the above topic is a textbook example, and it makes the importance of context especially obvious.

Now, Onward. . .

Hopefully, the above practices will be useful to you in your own study of the Bible. I encourage you to resolve in your heart to learn God's Word more deeply and listen to God's Spirit more intently than you ever have before. And be prepared for the Lord to absolutely astonish you with His goodness!

About the Author

David Arns was raised in church, but didn't start actually serving the Lord until his sophomore year of high school, in 1972. Being of a rather analytical turn of mind, he was delighted to see that there is a Biblical mandate for all Christians to be analytical: I Thessalonians 5:21 (NIV) says "Test everything. Hold on to the good." That, coupled with Paul's exhortation to teach what "the Holy Ghost teaches," not depending on man's wisdom (I Corinthians 2:11–14), and with the commendation of the Bereans, who "searched the Scriptures daily, whether those things were so" (Acts 17:11), pretty much define Dave's life, in the spiritual realm, as well as the natural realm. In the mid-1970s, Dave heard a sermon in which he was exhorted to "know *what* you believe and *why* you believe it," and he has been trying to put that into practice ever since. He has been known to abandon long-held beliefs when someone showed him that they were incompatible with Scripture; that attitude seems to be necessary if we want to continue to grow in the Lord.

Books in the "Thoughts On" Series

This book is a member of the "THOUGHTS ON" series of books. The phrase "Thoughts On" is deliberately ambiguous, because it is meaningful and accurate either way you interpret it. First, it indicates where the seeds of the whole series came from: they were from a large list of informal Bible studies Dave had put together for his own interest and edification as a result of his "thoughts on" various topics that occurred to him during his quiet times with the Lord. And second, it indicates one of Dave's goals as a teacher: to persuade people to turn their "thoughts on" and consider logically what God has said in His word, and how it is very much to our benefit to take heed to what He says.

When reading *The Chronicles of Narnia* to his son Matthew when he was little, Dave came across the Professor's exasperated musing: "'Logic!' said the Professor half to himself. 'Why don't they teach logic at these schools?'" Oh, did that ring true with him! Many are the times Dave has heard a preacher or Bible teacher make a statement from the pulpit, and the crowd responds with a hearty "Amen!" Dave looks around astonished, thinking, "That statement's not true! I can think of three Scriptures off the top of my head that refute it!" And he just grieves for the complacency evident in most Christians; there is *so* much God wants to bless them with, and they miss out because they don't check the Bible to verify statements they hear.

So, Dear Reader, please turn your Thoughts On. . .

To see the names and descriptions of the other books in the "THOUGHTS ON" series, see the list below. To see the sources from which they are available, or to contact the author, see the website Bible-Author.DaveArns.com. Books are available both in electronic form and in paperback. Note that the numbers of these books within the THOUGHTS ON series are merely the order in which they were written; they do not need to be read in sequential order. All of them are stand-alone books, so Book 1, for example, does not need to be read before Book 2, and so on.

BOOK 1: *Prophets vs. Seers: Is There a Difference?* This book looks at that question from a Biblical viewpoint. There are Bible teachers teaching that prophets and seers are fundamentally different, and they offer some supporting evidence, while others say they are merely variations in the manifestation of fundamentally the same gift and calling. Is there enough Scriptural evidence to conclude that they are the same kind of person, or the same kind of calling, or are they indeed different? An in-depth analysis of related Scriptures leads the author to a solid conclusion.

BOOK 2: *Is It Possible to Stop Sinning?* There are a couple common beliefs in Christianity today: one holds that Christians living on earth will inevitably continue to sin until they graduate to heaven, and the other holds that it is possible for Christians to be without sin even while living on earth. Of course, the major factor in this discussion is what the Bible says. For example, What is sin? What does God say about it? What does God tell us to do about it? What did Jesus provide in the atonement? This book delves into great detail on the subject and

includes Biblical support from many relevant Scriptures, showing God's heart on the matter, in a way that is both theologically relevant and practical in everyday life.

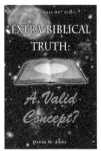

BOOK 3: *Extra-Biblical Truth: A Valid Concept?* There is a theory that says that God will not do nor say anything for which there is not a Biblical precedent, nor would He reveal a doctrine that was hitherto unheard of. Is this theory reasonable? Does the Bible itself address the question of God doing or saying things that are not already exemplified in the Bible itself? Actually, the Bible does address this question very clearly, and in several different ways. This book illustrates how to analyze and discern, from a Scriptural point of view, events and practices for which the Bible doesn't have specific examples.

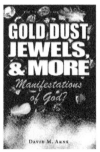

BOOK 4: *Gold Dust, Jewels, and More: Manifestations of God?* For the last couple of decades, there have been more and more reports of "unusual" occurrences taking place at meetings in which the Holy Spirit is allowed to move freely. These occurrences include gold dust appearing on people and things, jewels suddenly popping into existence, people "falling under the power" (a.k.a., being "slain in the Spirit"), glory clouds hovering or swirling, oil coming from people's hands, and more. Are these real manifestations of God, or just the result of overzealous but unethical leaders? Is there a Biblical basis for any of these? This book delves into the Scriptures and analyzes passages that are often overlooked, to give a thoughtful and Biblically sound response to these reports of unusual manifestations.

BOOK 5: *If It Be Thy Will* Many people in the Body of Christ, when they pray for physical healing, end their prayers with ". . .if it be Thy will." That brings up a very important point: *Is it* God's will to heal us? Never, sometimes, or always? How do we know? What does the Bible say? So often, Jesus said to the people He just healed, "Your faith has made you well." Where did they get that faith, and can we learn from

them? This book goes into great detail about what the Bible says—and does *not* say—about physical healing, and whether praying for it is something we are forbidden, discouraged, permitted, encouraged, or commanded to do. The Bible has much to say on this subject, and we can learn a great deal by just looking at what it says, and noting the obvious implications.

BOOK 6: *Free to Choose?* One of the most hotly debated concepts in the last 500 years or so has been that of whether or not people actually have a free will to choose their eternal destiny. People debate each other with—shall we say, *religious* fervor—and people on both sides of the debate offer Scriptures to support their viewpoints. On the one hand, we have people who believe that God offers us a choice to voluntarily repent and turn to Him. On the other hand, we have people who believe that God is sovereign, and that sovereignty necessarily means that God determines the eternal destination of everyone, with no regard to our choices. These two viewpoints can't both be correct, because they say mutually exclusive things. But fortunately, the Bible is remarkably unambiguous in its teachings: reading Scriptures in context and thinking about how various passages relate to each other make it abundantly clear which one of these viewpoints is actually the Biblical position.

BOOK 7: *Be Filled With the Spirit* In the last fifty years or so, there has been a tremendous resurgence of interest in the baptism of the Holy Spirit and the accompanying gifts of the Spirit. In some, the interest is entirely academic; in others, it is a passionate hunger to experience it firsthand. But there are people who claim that such things faded away around the end of the first century, and are therefore no longer available. Did they really fade away? We need to know because other people claim to have been baptized in the Holy Spirit and use the gifts of the Spirit every day, as a normal part of Christian life. As always, the Bible is the normative standard for living the Christian life, so what does the Bible say on this topic? Quite a lot, and if we follow what the Bible says, our

Christian lives will become much more exciting and fruitful in the things of the Kingdom.

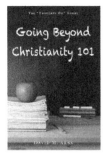

BOOK 8: *Going Beyond Christianity 101* What would be the content of a "Christianity 101" class? In other words, what is "elementary" Christianity? To avoid pet doctrines and the inevitable differences of opinion, we should see what the Bible itself describes as the "elementary doctrines" or the "foundational principles" of the faith. These are enumerated in Hebrews 6:1–2 as: repentance from sin, faith toward God, baptisms (plural), the laying on of hands, the resurrection of the dead, and eternal judgment. Listening to the amount of heated discussion in the body of Christ on these topics, we soon realize that as a whole, the body of Christ doesn't even have a good handle on the *elementary* doctrines yet. The Bible says much on these doctrines that is often overlooked by those doing only a casual study. This book looks at the Scriptures pertaining to these six topics in great detail, and then speculates on what it might mean to "go beyond" these foundational teachings, as Hebrews 6:1 encourages us to do.

BOOK 9: *Searching the Word: Bible Word-Search Puzzles on Steroids* What do you get when you cross a word-lover with a Word-lover? In other words, what do you get when you cross a person who enjoys word games with a student of the Bible? And then, for good measure, throw in a teacher and a writer. What do you get? This book. Much more than just a book of word-search puzzles, and much more than just a book of Bible lists, this book combines the fun of solving word problems with a fascinating way to study the Bible. Words or phrases from the Bible, and which fit into the same category, are used as the word lists for the puzzles. While you're looking for words, sooner or later you're bound to think, "What does *that* mean?" and when you check the info section for that puzzle, you'll learn something and realize you've discovered a delightful new way to study the Bible!

BOOK 10: *Hearing from God: A Daily Devotional*
Many daily devotionals are in very small, bite-sized in-
stallments that you can read in three minutes or less.
This may be very appropriate for people who are always on the go, and are doing so at God's leading. But
such tiny tidbits, while they may be very good and very
true, are still pretty small, and as such, have insufficient
room to get very deep. As such, they are barely spiri-
tual *hors d'oeuvres*, let alone a hearty spiritual meal of "strong meat." If
you have a bit more time, this devotional is a good alternative. It goes
into greater depth and breadth in the Scriptural support and elabora-
tion. You may notice that the list of Scripture references at the bottom
of each day's entry is longer than you have seen in other daily devotionals. This is deliberate: You'll be blessed if you read all the Scriptures for
each day's devotional, even if two or three passages seem to say the same
thing—when the Bible makes similar statements but expresses them
slightly differently, the various nuances of meaning are significant and
enlightening; they are not merely accidental. There is amazing depth
in the Scriptures. . .

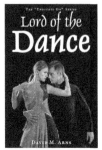

BOOK 11: *Lord of the Dance*   The Bible talks about
dancing in many places, both as an act of worship, and
as a normal expression of joy. The church, after a
lengthy period of thunder-fisted condemnation of all
dance, as if it could not possibly occur without wal-
lowing in sin, is recognizing their previous overreaction
and seeing dance in many positive aspects: as an expression of worship, an enjoyable social activity, and a
way to improve bodily fitness and mental acuity, to name but a few.
Having been a dance instructor since 1999, and a student of the Word
for even longer, the author could not help noticing that there are a great
many correlations between a man and a woman dancing, and a husband
and wife in a marriage. These correlations were vividly brought into
focus while teaching engaged couples how to dance for their upcoming
weddings—it's remarkable how often dance lessons included, almost
unavoidably, significant premarital counseling. And those same correlations apply with even more eternal import in our relationship with
Christ our Redeemer. This book explores many of those correlations

and similarities in a way that presents concepts of dance almost as parables whose meanings, for those who have ears to hear, are nothing less than profound in the marital and spiritual realms.

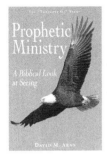

BOOK 12: *Prophetic Ministry: A Biblical Look at Seeing* Scripture tells us to "eagerly desire spiritual gifts, especially the gift of prophecy" (I Corinthians 14:1, NIV). Why "especially" the gift of prophecy? The Bible seems to emphasize prophecy as the highest gift, so there must be a good reason. And indeed, there is; in fact, there are many. This book examines Scriptures that tell us about how prophecy works: Who is authorized to pursue this gift, how people can perceive messages from God, what forms they can take, how to deliver them to the intended recipients, the necessary attitude and demeanor when doing so, common pitfalls, and more. If you have been hungering to hear the voice of God, rest assured that you can, because Jesus said, "My sheep hear my voice" (John 10:27). You *do* hear His voice. That is wonderful in itself. But when you have the privilege of speaking into someone else's life God's own words *for that specific person and moment and situation,* that is even more wonderful. Yes, eagerly desire spiritual gifts, *especially* the gift of prophecy. You'll be glad you did.

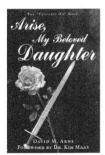

BOOK 13: *Arise, My Beloved Daughter* Recently, an increasing number of prophetic words from established, world-class prophets—of both genders—are calling for women to arise and fulfill the callings and destinies that God ordained for them before the world began. And women are rising to the call: thoughtful, godly, competent women, with compassion for the lost, deep intimacy with God, and a passion to see the mercy and blessings of Jesus poured out onto a seriously damaged world. Also, there is a dawning awareness on the part of males in church leadership that they have been missing out on much of what God wants to pour out because highly gifted women have been disregarded, ignored, passed over, and even actively suppressed in their attempts at ministry. God is opening up revelation about things that have been in the Word all along, but about which we have

long had a flawed understanding. Why is God revealing it now? Because with the glory that God is intending to pour out in the Third Great Awakening, the Church no longer has the "luxury" of limping along with half of its soldiers in the brig because the other half thinks they're incapable.

BOOK 14: *Oh, Evolve! (Good Luck With That. . .)* When the question of Creation vs. Evolution comes up, many people immediately assume it is a question of science vs. religion. But is it really? There are many scientists with impressive credentials in a variety of fields—many of them clearly *not* creationists—who are becoming more vocal all the time about the problems with the whole Darwinian idea of how everything came to be. And it's true: there are more discoveries every year that militate against the ideas of the Big Bang, deep time, the Nebular Hypothesis of how the solar system was formed, uniformitarianism, life "arising" by random and undirected processes, and more. This book examines the problems with a variety of evolutionary assumptions, many of which are expressed by evolutionists themselves, and shows, in laymen's terms, why the theory of evolution is collapsing under the weight of its own presuppositions. Evidence from cosmology, geology, chemistry, genetics, biology, and more, is becoming increasingly hostile to evolutionary notions. Because of this, more and more "rescue devices" (supplementary theories intended to explain why observations don't match evolutionary predictions) are needed each year, to prop up the teetering theory. Not only will you see that evolution is no less a religion than Christianity, but you'll see that the Creation vs. Evolution debate is science vs. science. Check out the evidence, and see which model is more supported by real-world observations!

BOOK 15: *One Nation Under God . . .Again!* One of the recent discussions that has been generating more heat than light lately pertains to the spiritual underpinnings of the Founding Fathers of these United States: whether or not they intended to include Biblical/Christian principles in the founding documents, and therefore the entire fabric of our American society. There are

some modern scholars who say the Founders were godless and secular, and other modern scholars who say they were solid Biblical Christians. Who is right? Rather than simply quoting recent writings concerning what the Founders "must have" meant, it is much more reliable to look at the writings of the Founders themselves, in context, compare their content to the Bible, and see how well they match. Unlike some modern scholars who "omit the scholarly practice" of including citations, expecting their readers to simply trust their conclusions, this book includes hundreds of footnotes containing citations, so you can go to the original documents themselves and verify the statements herein. When you do, you will see that our Declaration of Independence, Constitution, and Bill of Rights are not at all "godless" documents written from a secular mindset, but are filled with Biblical references, concepts, and wisdom. Armed with that knowledge and understanding, you will be able to confidently promote, as did the Founders, the strength of character and solid societal foundations that originally formed the basis of this country. If the Body of Christ rises to the challenge, we will indeed be one nation under God . . .*again!*

Music in the "Worship On" Series

Dave's current music project is the "Worship On" series of albums. The phrase "Worship On" not only parallels Dave's "Thoughts On" series of books, but it also points out a very significant truth about the destiny of those who choose to make Jesus Christ the Lord of their lives: Though many other aspects of normal Christian life on earth—evangelism, healing the sick, casting out demons, raising the dead, suffering persecution, and so forth—will go away once we're in heaven, worship will not. Throughout all eternity, we will worship Jesus, the King of Kings. Far from being an arduous chore we will be required to do, we will spontaneously burst out into joyous praise and worship every time we see another aspect of God's goodness and love and holiness. As we discover more of God's marvelousness moment by moment, it will be more clear than ever that He is the only One worthy of our worship—no one and nothing else even comes close. Indeed, the word "worship" comes from the Old English phrase "worth-ship," and He is certainly worth all of our worship.

So, Dear Listener, when listening to this music, feel free to Worship On. And on and on. . . :)

The music below is available both in downloadable electronic form and as CDs, and is available from the sources mentioned on the website Music.DaveArns.com.

CD 1: *Songs of the Tribe of Judah*

In the early 1980s, Dave was a member of the worship team at the church he attended. In addition to that, a subset of that worship team formed a band that sang on other occasions and in other, more public venues. This smaller group called themselves the Tribe of Judah, after the name referring to Jesus in Revelation 5:5. Dave and one other member of the group wrote most of the songs they performed, and in this album are the songs that Dave wrote, along with improved orchestration. The reason for the name of this album is twofold: first, these songs were written when Dave was writing songs to be performed by the band called the Tribe of Judah, and second, because Judah means "praise and worship," which is what Dave prays this music will inspire in you.

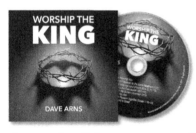

CD 2: *Worship the King*

The second album in the "Worship On" series, *Worship the King* is intended to draw the listener from a passive "listening" mode and into a more active "worshiping" mode. As you listen to the words of these songs, you'll notice than many of them are taken straight from the Bible, and as such, are excellent tools with which to learn Scripture. Even the ones that are not taken directly from the Bible are laden with Scriptural concepts, whether their context is worshiping Him in the beauty of holiness, the story of an Appalachian moonshiner who encounters the living God, a description of every believer's job on earth, a joyous proclamation of God's glorious traits, or a simple acknowledgement of the most basic understanding of every believer: that the Lord is good.

CD 3: *Go Into All the World*

This album, the third in the "Worship On" series, acknowledges the importance of Jesus' exhortation to "Go into all the world" and preach the gospel to everyone (Mark 16:15–20). The wheat field image recalls Jesus' commands to pray that laborers will go into the fields, because the harvest is plentiful (Matthew 9:37–38). Because of that emphasis, this album contains songs echoing Isaiah's cry "Send me!", marveling at God's mercy, showing how a Caribbean man sees Jesus gloriously working among his people, expressing the hunger that God's children feel to get into His presence, recalling a portion of one of David's psalms that he gave to Asaph and the other worshippers to sing, and more. My hope is that your heart will be touched with compassion for those who don't yet know the inexpressible joy of being a child of God.

CD 4: *I Have Not Forgotten You*

This album, the fourth in the "Worship On" series, endeavors to respond to those in the body of Christ who have heard God's promises, both those in the Bible and those He has spoken to them personally, who remember His prophetic words, and who feel like it is taking for*ever* for those promises to come to pass. To such people, as well as to those who have experienced great hardship in their lives, God's unchanging faithfulness comes through in *I Have Not Forgotten You*, and His love in a conversation between the heavenly Father and one of His beloved children in *That Will I Seek After*. In *Hear and Do*, a believer discovers the simple but profound secret to living in God's presence, and in *Truckin'*, a truck driver has a divine appointment with a couple of the Lord's servants. Other songs include the word of the Lord coming to a cattle driver crossing Death Valley, a believer echoing Moses' heartfelt cry to see God's glory, and an expression of intense spiritual hunger when such a large outpouring of that glory—a "glory storm"—is seen building on the horizon.

CD 5: *Dry Bones to Living Stones*

This album, the fifth in the "Worship On" series, describes several different aspects of God's process of building His people—His "living stones—into a holy and glorious temple He can inhabit. One song tells of the Father's desire to give us the Kingdom; another tells about a surfer hearing the voice of God promising a wave of the Holy Spirit; another portrays the hunger to drink deeply of God's Spirit—a hunger we should all have. Yet another describes the realization that the long-awaited revival of societal transformation into wholeness and health has finally arrived; another tells the story of a bored and lukewarm Christian discovering that there is more! Another relates the little-known key to Jesus' success in ministry, and another tells in a new way the story of Shadrach, Meshach, and Abednego being thrown into the fiery furnace. And finally, a song that expresses the passion of a believer who doesn't want to miss out on what God is doing in these days.

Books: BibleAuthor.DaveArns.com

Music: Music.DaveArns.com

Made in the USA
Middletown, DE
30 October 2023